COPING WITH TOURISTS

New Directions in Anthropology
General Editor: Jacqueline Waldren

COPING WITH TOURISTS

European Reactions to Mass Tourism

Edited by
Jeremy Boissevain

Berghahn Books
Providence • Oxford

First published in 1996 by

Berghahn Books

Editorial offices:
165 Taber Avenue, Providence, RI 02906, USA
Bush House, Merewood Avenue, Oxford, OX3 8EF, UK

Library of Congress Cataloging-in-Publication Data

```
Coping with tourists : European reactions to mass tourism / edited by
Jeremy Boissevain.
      p.   cm. -- (New directions in anthropology ; v. 1)
   Includes bibliographical references and index.
   ISBN 1-57181-878-2 (alk. paper). -- ISBN 1-57181-900-2 (pbk. :
alk. paper)
   1. Tourist trade--Europe.   I. Boissevain, Jeremy.   II. Series.
G155.E8C64  1996
338.4'79140455--dc20                                          95-37305
                                                                  CIP
```

British Library Cataloguing in Publication Data

A catalogue record for this book is available from
the British Library.

Printed in the United States on acid-free paper.

CONTENTS

PREFACE

*T*he idea for this book grew out of the experience of having watched tourism in Malta grow during the past thirty-five years. When my wife and I first moved to Malta in 1956, the only tourists were relatives visiting British Service personnel stationed there. By 1990 Malta had become a mass tourist destination, accommodating close to one million visitors annually. The Maltese Islands had developed from a poor, insular backwater to a thriving, modern tourist destination whose inhabitants were themselves increasingly becoming tourists. If in the 1960s tourists were welcomed with pride and native hospitality, by the beginning of the 1990s the welcome seemed less enthusiastic. Tourists were no longer placed on quite such a high pedestal. They had become a commodity on which Malta's economy depended. They were present throughout the year. Increasingly there were reports in the press of rudeness to tourists, of their indecent dress, of confrontations with local hunters, even of occasional fights between hosts and guests. Were the Maltese beginning to have second thoughts about hosting ever more tourists?

I began to wonder how other areas in Europe that had become mass tourist destinations were coping with their visitors. Unfortunately, the published accounts on tourism dealt mostly with the Third World. There was surprisingly little information on Europe. I decided to do something about it and organized a workshop on 'European reactions to the tourist gaze' at the meeting of the European Association of Social Anthropologists in Prague in the summer of 1992. Although Simone Abram and Annabel Black were unable to participate in the workshop, they later contributed excellent papers. This volume is the result.

I would like to thank all the contributors for their cheerful patience in discussing and rewriting their papers over the past two years. Tom Selwyn, who also attended the workshop, based his postlude on the final draft of the manuscript. This book is thus very much a collective effort. The universities of Amsterdam and Malta and the Med-Campus Programme on Sustainable Cultural and Ecological Tourism kindly provided the logistical support which made my work as editor so much easier and more pleasant.

Jeremy Boissevain
Amsterdam 1996

INTRODUCTION

Jeremy Boissevain

*T*he cultural centres and peripheral regions of Europe have for decades been the object of mass tourism. Initially these tourist masses were welcomed as guests and providers of wealth. Their numbers though, have increased. The inhabitants of tourist destinations are now more self-confident, affluent and often tourists themselves. There is growing awareness of the way tourism is affecting their physical environment and culture. How then do individuals and communities dependent on the presence of tourists cope with the commoditisation of their culture and the constant attention of outsiders? This is the central question that this collection addresses. Its focus is clearly on one pole of the host-guest tourist continuum. We are interested in the so-called hosts, the people who both service tourists' needs and are the object of their attention. The inhabitants of tourist destinations have to date received less attention than they deserve from academics and writers.

The eight case studies that follow provide some answers to our questions. Mary Crain explores the confrontation between inhabitants of the Almonte and neighbouring municipalities in Andalusia and religious, commercial, and political elites bent on the touristic development of their territory. Antonio Miguel Nogués Pedregal analyses the growing self-awareness that the expansion of tourism generates among the inhabitants of the small coastal village of Zahara de los Atunes, Andalusia. Peter Odermatt traces the conflict between the villagers of Abbasanta, Sardinia, and outside authorities over the representation and presenta-

Notes for this section begin on page 21.

tion for touristic ends of their prehistoric past. Annabel Black examines some of the responses of the Maltese to the ever-encroaching presence of tourism over the past twenty years. Cornélia Zarkia describes economic and social developments on Skyros, a Greek island that has recently entered the tourist market, and notes how these affect the attitude of the islanders to outsiders. Simone Abram deals with the development of reflexivity, which the changing nature of tourism has encouraged, among the inhabitants of the Cantal, central France. Roel Puijk sets out how the inhabitants of the fishing village of Henningsvær in the Lofoten islands in northern Norway have adapted to the arrival of tourists. Finally, Heidi Dahles explores the way the discourses developing between guides and tourists in Amsterdam have constructed parts of the inner city as a tourist attraction.

The studies reflect the continuum of the various types of tourist destinations in Western Europe. This continuum is in part geographical and in part developmental, for it also reflects the degree of modernisation and cosmopolitanism. It runs from the more marginal rural communities in Southern Europe, which are more dependent on (and thus more affected by) tourism through more modern rural municipalities in France and Norway, to cosmopolitan Amsterdam. Together, these studies provide a multifaceted perspective on how Europeans of the 1990s are dealing with mass tourism.

Tourism's Changing Face

Virtually all tourists in Europe are fellow Europeans exploring each other's countries. Every year their numbers increase. They are neighbours who hold definite views of each other built up during centuries of interaction. In this they differ from travellers who seek out exotic peoples far away.

The motives that impel tourists to undertake costly and sometimes gruelling journeys have been hotly debated. Some see the tourist as a contemporary pilgrim fleeing the superficiality, instability, and inauthenticity of modern society in quest of 'authenticity' (MacCannell 1976). Others view tourists as persons engaged in a sacred journey to a world free from the constraints of work, time, and conformity, a ludic interlude that revitalises the traveller, enabling him to cope again with the strictures and structures of everyday life (Graburn 1989). Yet others see current tourists as 'post-tourists' who accept 'that there is *no* authentic tourist experience' (Urry 1990: 11; see also Cohen 1979, 1988). They seek experience that contrasts with the ordinary.

It is obvious, I think, that it is not possible to attribute a single motive to these millions of tourists. Some seek authentic native cultures in Asia or challenging mountain peaks to conquer. Others are interested in seeing what their neighbours are up to. Some find pleasure in kitsch and Disneyfied surroundings. Yet others merely wish to opt out alongside a swimming pool or a beach for a lazy fortnight. However, it is clear that all tourists, whatever their individual motives, seek some form of contrast with their everyday existence, a break, however short, with their familiar surroundings and routines. In short, as Valene Smith wrote years ago, 'a tourist is a temporarily leisured person who voluntarily visits a place away from home for the purpose of experiencing a change' (1989a: 1).

Globally speaking, tourist tastes are also changing. Consumers generally have become increasingly dissatisfied with standard, mass-produced goods, and are demanding more varied and customised products that meet their individual needs for self-improvement and relief from the pressure and pollution of an over regimented urbanised environment (Sabel 1982; Urry 1990: 11-14; Featherstone 1991: 18-19). Similarly, many of today's tourists are rejecting standard mass package tours. More and more are seeking holidays that cater to their desire for learning, nostalgia, heritage, make-believe, action, and a closer look at the Other. Not sun, sand, and sea, but culture, nature, and 'traditional' rural life have become the objects of the postmodern tourist (cf. Urry 1990; Weiler and Hall 1992).

The destination countries along the Mediterranean littoral have been quick to capitalise on these changing trends. They are expanding the promotion of their historical and natural assets, often located far from traditional seaside tourist territories. They are developing new promotional brochures for inland itineraries, rural retreats, winter tourism, and nature parks and are building heritage parks and golf courses. By offering more varied destinations and activities, national tourist organisations all hope to attract more 'quality tourists'. These mythical visitors, whom planners think of as more affluent and cultured persons (characteristics which by no means need coincide), are being hotly pursued by National Tourist Organisations all over the globe. They are widely viewed as the key to liberating destination communities from enervating dependence on hordes of low-spending package tourists.

Cultural tourism is not limited to the summer months and the seaside. It thus also alleviates the industry's endemic seasonal unemployment and benefits areas away from favoured coastal zones. This trend is clearly illustrated by the way Spain, which in 1992 replaced its long-established national tourist slogan, 'Spain: Everything Under the Sun', with a new logo, 'Spain: Passion for Life'. The increase in cultural tourism, and in tourist motives and tastes, affects the interaction between visitors and inhabitants.

Some Characteristics of Tourism

There are some general features of tourism that affect all destination communities in one way or another. These include the transient nature of tourism and the unequal relations between tourists and locals. As they can afford to buy the services upon which the local economy depends and often come from more technologically advanced societies, tourists at times think they can denigrate and abuse locals. The locals, on the other hand, because they monopolise local knowledge and services, can cheat and exploit the tourists. As the chapter by Odermatt makes very clear, there is another general characteristic of tourism: the unequal relations between the 'host community' at the local level and more powerful agencies at higher integration levels, such as the tourist industry, the state and/or the European Union. The tourist-host relation is thus potentially fraught with ambivalence and tension (see van den Berghe and Keyes 1984: 347; MacCannell 1984: 387).

A major factor affecting relations between locals and tourists, however, is the desire of the latter for a temporary change in their life situation. They seek escape from established routines, from the constraints of time and place, and the behavioural codes that rule their daily lives. They believe this change will recharge their mental and physical batteries so that they will be better able to cope with the pressures of their daily commitments.

Thus becoming a tourist, however briefly, means shedding part of one's old identity and normal behaviour. This involves adopting a new, temporary identity that necessarily incorporates some elements that are the opposite of the habitual personality and behaviour (see Graburn 1983; Lett 1983; Boissevain 1989). As Victor Turner observed, 'cognitively, nothing underlines irregularity so well as absurdity or paradox. Emotionally, nothing satisfies as much as extravagant or temporarily permitted illicit behaviour' (1969: 176). This process is facilitated by the masking function that anonymity provides. After all, the people visited do not know the normal persona of the tourist. Tourists can consequently shed their everyday status and, temporarily, become other persons and engage in 'extravagant' if not 'illicit' behaviour. This change of status is usually signalled by donning 'leisure' clothes. These strange, often garish, occasionally inexplicably scanty costumes unambiguously mark out the wearer as a tourist (see Leach 1964). This emblematic garb often amuses but occasionally offends locals going about their daily activities, in banks, shops, or churches. Strange dress and weakening inhibitions are not infrequently accompanied by behaviour that would be quite unacceptable at home. It can be loud, lecherous, drunken, and rude. In short, many tourists, for various reasons, are occasionally most unpleasant guests. Yet those whose livelihoods depend upon their presence must somehow come to terms with their difficult behaviour and cater to their strange needs.

There are other regular features of tourism with which host communities must deal. Among these the crowding of thoroughfares, public transport, shops, and recreational facilities feature prominently. Furthermore, along the Mediterranean, mass tourist demand and overcharging during the tourist season drive up the prices of fresh vegetables, fruit, and fish. The region's scarce fresh-water resources also come under pressure. Many local inhabitants are annoyed by this. On the other hand, others accept inconveniences and overcrowding philosophically as part of the cost of the new economy. Some even welcome crowds. Puijk, for example, observes that the inhabitants of Henningsvær, which is crowded with fishermen in winter, enjoyed the summer tourists. Locals said the many holidaying visitors livened up the community during the quiet season. This gave their community an ambience that they very much appreciated, even though they sometimes were frustrated by the numbers of tourists and the inconvenience they caused.

Obviously scale is an important factor. Discomfort caused by crowding is usually more keenly felt where the tourist mass is disproportionate to the local population. This occurs during the Andalusian pilgrimage to Our Lady of the Dew. Mary Crain describes how hordes of urbanites, media men, and yuppies crowd out local residents. But circumstances differ. Annabel Black shows that despite severe crowding, the inhabitants of Mellieha do not clash with the tourists over seaside space. In part this is because locals use space differently. Where visitors choose the limited, excessively crowded sandy beaches, Maltese prefer the (cleaner) rocky areas along the coast; moreover many use their boats to travel to remote swimming areas. Summer crowding has become part of local culture and the Maltese enjoy the lively seaside cafés, pizzerias and discos established for tourists.

In fact, it is notable that in the Mediterranean area there is remarkably little friction between tourists and natives in summer. This is because both are celebrating their leisure. Summer, for both visitors and local inhabitants (except those working directly in the tourism industry), is a time for relaxing, partying, sporting, celebrating, and romancing, if possible, near the sea. The pursuits of both natives and visitors by and large harmonise in summer (Boissevain 1989). After the summer, the situation is often quite different. By then, local inhabitants have had to return to work, to their winter mode. The presence of boisterous holidaying strangers becomes dissonant; inconveniences are no longer overlooked and tension mounts (see Boissevain 1996).

Puijk, with ethnographic data from Northern Europe, makes much the same point. The inhabitants of Henningsvaer find winter tourists more difficult to deal with than summer visitors. Summer is the light season when relatives and friends on holiday come to visit the village. As along the Mediterranean, this is the festive season. In winter the days are dark. The town is crowded with working fishermen. Then well-dressed, demanding visitors on holiday circulating among men working on boats and spattered with fish blood and guts brings out class tensions. These disrupt the egalitarian ethos so characteristic of Northern Norway.

Cultural Tourists

Cultural tourism has a number of particular, sometimes contradictory, characteristics.[1] For instance, compared to recreational tourists, cultural tourists encounter a much wider section of the native population as they visit villages and towns remote from coastal tourist zones. There natives have often not (yet) developed the skills required to cope with mass tourism. While this may mean that initially they are more hospitable, they are also more vulnerable and easily exploited. As the local population becomes more familiar with tourism and gains expertise, it becomes more active in protecting its interests (see Cohen 1979: 24; Pi Sunyer 1989).

One of the most striking characteristics of tourism is the way it promotes self-awareness, pride, self-confidence and solidarity among those being visited (see Boissevain 1992b; Sofield 1991). This is especially pronounced if the host community is remote or in other ways peripheral, as are so many tourist destinations. All the contributions to this volume demonstrate this. This self-awareness is brought about by the regular presence of outsiders, which automatically creates categories of 'we' and 'they', insiders and outsiders, hosts and guests. By being looked at, examined and questioned by strangers, locals become aware of how they differ from the visitors. It is a source of pride that affluent strangers choose to come to their community to admire – for why else would they come rather than go elsewhere? – the surroundings and customs that they had always taken for granted. The heightened self-confidence in part compensates for some of the negative aspects of tourism. Later they may discover – as the Kotzebue Eskimo did when they observed tourists' horrified reactions to their fish-drying and butchering practices – that some tourists come to sneer and confirm their own superiority (Smith 1989b). These communities have discovered themselves through the interest of tourists. This has encouraged reflection about their own traditions and culture and stimulated the preservation of moribund crafts and rituals. This in turn has fed the more general revitalisation of celebrations taking place throughout Europe (Boissevain 1992a). Moreover, the importance of tourist attention and revenue has given marginal host communities the confidence and leverage to bargain for more rights from superior authorities. Nogués Pedregal observed that Zahareños used the municipality's failure to share the tourism-generated tax revenue to buttress their claim for greater independence. Self-awareness due to the presence of tourists can thus be actively used by local residents as a new resource (see Crystal 1989: 151; van den Berghe 1994: 145f.; Crain forthcoming).

National and regional tourist authorities usually commoditise and market local culture without consulting the inhabitants (see Greenwood 1989: 180). This can lead to tension between the tourists, who not surprisingly demand access to the sites and events they have been promised and have paid for, and the inhabitants whose culture, often unbeknownst to them, has been sold to visitors. Crain describes the resentment of inhabitants of many municipalities surrounding Almonte at the way tourist agencies, together with the local religious and commercial elite, converted both solemn rituals and local forests into tourist assets for their own benefit. Peter Odermatt's account of the clash between the inhabitants of Abbasanta and regional authorities in Sardinia over the representation of and tourist access to their local monument illustrates this same issue.

Curiosity, stimulated by skilful marketing, can lead to yet another characteristic of cultural tourism: the loss of privacy. As tourists search for the culture they have paid to see, they cross thresholds and boundaries (sometimes, but not always, hidden) to penetrate authentic back-stage areas. The sociologist MacCannell, following Goffman (1959), has discussed 'back' and 'front' regions in the context of tourism: 'The front is the meeting place of hosts and guests or customers and service persons, and the back is the place where members of the home team retire between performances to relax and to prepare' (MacCannell 1976: 92f.). MacCannell's back regions are normally closed to outsiders. Their mere existence implies their possible violation. The back region is somehow more 'intimate and real' as against the front region's 'show'. It is consequently viewed as more 'truthful', more authentic. The back region is where the tourist can experience true authenticity and achieve a oneness with his host (1976: 94-99). The desire to penetrate back regions is inherent in the structure of tourism. Tourists thus have a family resemblance (Blok 1976) to anthropologists, who also seek access to back regions to understand the hidden dimensions of the cultures they study.

Many cases have been reported of tourists looking around in domestic back regions or participating in private events to the discomfort of their unwilling 'hosts'. Puijk describes how curious tourists wandering into private back yards annoy Lofoten islanders. In the Austrian village of Stuhlfelden, German tourists slipped uninvited into a private party where they were observed peering into closed rooms and cupboards (Droog 1991). The indignant hosts, keenly aware of the community's dependence on German visitors, were afraid to say anything. Similarly, in September 1992, Maltese friends celebrating the annual festa of St Leonard in the village of Kirkop, discovered two tourists peering about inside their house. The curious couple had come to the village with a festa tour, had simply opened the glass inner door and walked into the brightly lit front room. Our friends politely showed them out. Then, to protect their privacy, they were obliged to close the wooden outer door that is always left open during the festa to display festive furnishings and decorations to passers-by. Such blatant infringements of privacy in Malta are increasing (see Boissevain 1996). I think they will continue to occur everywhere as cultural tourism is marketed to the masses.

Another characteristic of cultural tourism is the way massive tourist attention often destroys the very culture that visitors come to examine. Tourist complexes along much of the Mediterranean have demolished tranquillity and the environment. It forces up the cost of real estate, thus driving away the local population. This can transform a living town, an attraction in its own right, into a museum occupied only by the tourist and heritage industries. This is already occurring, among other places, in the centre of Prague and in Mdina, Malta's minuscule walled city (Boissevain 1994 and 1996). On the other hand, mass tourist attention does not always destroy local customs. The celebrations surrounding the Day of the Dead in the Mexican town of Tzintzuntzan grew spectacularly after the government began to promote it as a tourist spectacle. Brandes, the anthropologist who observed this, encountered no complaints 'about noise, impoliteness, or sacrilege as a result of tourism' (1988: 108).

The inhabitants of the more marginal and less-developed tourist destinations are faced with a particular dilemma. Tourists are attracted by their simple, rural way of life and their unspoiled, tranquil environment. These are the characteristics that cause their more affluent and powerful neighbours to regard them as backward. By developing tourism they hope to modernise and escape from the stigma of backwardness. This, in time, will destroy the very features which attract tourists and on which this new industry depends. This has happened in Torremolinos (Pollard and Rodriquez 1993). Some perceive this dilemma and are disturbed by it, for they too appreciate – often as a consequence of tourist interest – their traditional life style. Several chapters herein explore this problem. Abram describes the predicament of stall holders participating in tourist-oriented country markets. They wish to represent themselves as old-fashioned and wholesome, not as backward and ignorant (thus confirming the French stereotype of Auvergnats). She sees this quandary as one of the central issues facing officials seeking to develop tourism in the region. Zahareños face the same paradox. Tourists originally came to the village because it was backward and tranquil. In time, the inhabitants began to see their village through the tourists' eyes as underdeveloped. They now wish to pave and illuminate the streets, as Nogués Pedregal notes, 'while retaining the idea of the traditional villages shown ... and marketed in tourist brochures.'

Cultural tourism, unlike seaside tourism, is not necessarily seasonal. Those who live and work in popular seaside destinations must work extremely hard during the summer months. Once the season is over, they are able to recover from the summer onslaught and resume the more tranquil rhythm of their ordinary lives until the following high season. In contrast, inhabitants of popular cultural destinations, such as historic city centres, are exposed to tourist attention throughout the year. This exposure is increasing as cultural tourism becomes more popular and the number of annual holiday trips grow. Without some respite from the constant demands of tourists, hosts become enervated and their behaviour towards tourists hostile. For example, a negative attitude to tourists is developing among the four hundred residents of Mdina. Whereas just a few years ago, visitors came mainly in summer, they now are present throughout the year. In 1993 the town attracted more than three-quarters of a million visitors (Boissevain 1994; Boissevain and Sammut 1994). The residents now have little opportunity to recover.

Adaptation and Commercialisation

Adjustment to tourism has generally been rapid and creative. Having said that, it is important to note that by no means do all inhabitants of tourist destinations profit equally from the new industry (see Brougham and Butler 1981: 569; Dogan 1989: 226). Generally residents of seaside communities and historic centres gain more from the presence of tourists than do the inhabitants of inland villages and industrial towns. Outsiders are often the first to seize the initiative and reap the greatest profit, as did the international hotel consortium in Zahara de los Atunes. More often, local magnates and returned emigrants take the lead and the major share of the profits, as the studies of Black, Crain, and Puijk demonstrate. Occasionally, the less fortunate also profit. Zarkia describes how the poorest class on Skyros were among the first to seize the opportunities tourism offered. Hard up for cash, they were first to let rooms to tourists, thus acquiring expertise and an early stake in the tourist industry. Moreover, the poor owned the worst land, located along the shore. As tourism developed, this became extremely valuable and provided them with capital that enabled them to expand their activities. The advent of tourism thus enabled the poorest class to prosper and to rise socially (see Hermans 1981; Tsartas 1992).

Differential access to the profits of tourism changes power relations. Not surprisingly, it also influences the attitude of inhabitants to tourism. Those who have a vested financial interest in the tourism industry favour further tourist development. Those who do not profit from it often oppose developments that affect their style of life and environment. Tourist development consequently often forms the basis of structural conflict. Many destination communities are divided by pro- and anti-tourist factionalism. Several of the contributions deal with such conflicts. Crain, for example, describes a series of factional conflicts that erupted in Almonte over plans to develop a new luxury beach resort, to expand a local pilgrimage and to increase tourist access to the unique nature park located in the municipality.[2]

Generally, communities have been quick to seize the commercial opportunities that tourism presents. Sometimes, though, commercial adaptation to tourism take seemingly bizarre forms. Many humble Skyros families, for example, are quite prepared to huddle in one room for two months in order to be able to rent out their other room. Zarkia notes that 'For the time being, income is more important than tranquillity and privacy.' However, this trade-off of comfort for money is certainly not limited to poor Mediterranean peasants. Some years ago my wife and I and our four daughters spent the summer in Bergen aan Zee in Holland. We were surprised to discover that the owner of the flat we rented, a baker and his family, had moved downstairs into their bakery, where they spent the summer in one room. This practice still takes place in Dutch seaside resorts. It is evident that tourist money can buy private domestic space in developing as well as developed communities.

Just as domestic arrangements are adapted to accommodate tourist demands, so too is the annual cycle of leisure and work. The seasonal nature of the tourist trade, whether in Holland, Malta, or Greece, moulds the daily and annual sequence of work and leisure. As many must earn their annual income in a few months, working days during the high season extend into nights. Those directly involved in the Mediterranean tourist industry have little time to pursue traditional summer activities – family visits, swimming, partying, and community feasts. As one of Zarkia's informants expressed it, 'We have to work full-time in summer. When our friends and relatives come we don't have time to have a drink with them, to go to the local fiestas, to go to the beach ... we have to do the work for two and three; we run for the money.' Many who work in the tourist industry are thus obliged to carry out such social and leisure activities in winter, thus inverting the traditional annual cycle of work and play (see Hermans 1981). Many who work in the Skyros tourist industry become involuntary leisure nomads in winter, moving to Athens or Western Europe in search of amusement on which to spend their summer earnings. Similarly, Amsterdam pizzeria proprietors and Maltese restaurant owners close for a month or more in winter take to an annual vacation.

Inventing Culture and Staging Authenticity

Culture has become a major commodity in the tourist industry. Besides domestic space and leisure, many other aspects of culture are sold to tourists. Every tourist brochure demonstrates this. History is marketed via calls to visit ancient monuments and heritage parks; colourful photographs advertise carnival and religious ceremonies; illustrations of smiling natives and colourful street scenes promote the character and way of life of host communities. Besides these more or less authentic cultural features, our case studies show that culture is also invented, modified, and revitalised for tourists. The inhabitants of St. Mary in Cantal, for example, have introduced a stylised threshing performance; the Maltese now perform 'traditional' dances that are at most a few years old; and the inhabitants of the Lofoten village of Henningsvær have organised a new Stockfish Festival during the tourist high season.[3] Abram describes the development of a museum that presents a sanitised version of history and Dahles analyses new tours in Amsterdam that guide tourists into back regions of the city and purport to provide insights into the authentic life of the inhabitants.

With authentic culture readily available, why do new products have to be developed and elaborately staged for tourists? One reason is that tourists have to be entertained and kept busy. Traditional local events are sometimes not frequent or colourful enough. Nor are they able to satisfy tourist tastes. Hence new events are thought up. The canal cruises that Dahles describes are extraordinarily popular because they provide an original and pleasant way of touring Amsterdam. Moreover, as Black demonstrates, tourist promotion generates specific expectations. Local entrepreneurs must satisfy these to remain competitive with other resorts. Restaurants, 'traditional' dancing and outdoor café life, though alien to Malta, were introduced to meet tourist expectations of the Mediterranean scene. After twenty-five years they have become part of Maltese culture. Musicians stroll through restaurants singing 'La Paloma' and 'Que Sera, Sera'. Tourists realise that these are not authentic Maltese melodies. They do not care. Skyrian developers have constructed buildings with the arches and vaults indigenous to the Cyclades. In the tourist imagery which Greece has successfully developed, arches and vaults symbolise the Greek islands. Yet the new arches clash with the flat roofs and severe cubic forms of Skyrian vernacular architecture. Skyrians are quick and inventive in other ways. For example, they tell tourists that an area of warm water in the sea near the beach comes from a warm spring, when in fact it is the water used to cool the island's electric generator. Staged authenticity takes many forms. By and large, tourists are unconcerned that authenticity has been staged, providing that the fake is a good fake and they are able to enjoy themselves (see Cohen 1979).

Commoditisation

It is clear that dealing with tourists involves large-scale commoditisation of culture. Many have argued that selling 'culture by the pound' debases it and 'robs people of the very meanings by which they organise their lives' (Greenwood 1989: 179). Crain's study shows how the commercialisation of the annual pilgrimage to the Virgin of the Dew has indeed robbed some Almonteños as well as many residents of neighbouring municipalities of an important religious and social experience. Similarly, regional authorities expropriated the symbolic value of a neolithic monument from Abassanta's inhabitants. Greenwood's condemnation is sometimes echoed by local intellectuals (see Boissevain 1984). However, it is far too sweeping a generalisation. While not denying that commoditisation has destroyed nature and culture, studies show that by marketing their culture people (re)discover their own history and traditions and begin to realise their own worth (see Cohen 1988). Museums established to entertain tourists become popular with the natives, who learn about their own traditions. The same occurs with heritage parks, festivals, and food and handicraft markets. Black's study shows that in spite of dire predictions and the massive influx of tourists, the inhabitants of Mellieha have retained their integrity. Abram sums up the case for thinking with greater care about the effects of cultural commoditisation: 'commoditisation is part of a very positive process by which people are beginning to re-evaluate their history and shake off the shame of peasantry'.

Commoditisation and staged authenticity can protect the back regions and privacy of local inhabitants by keeping tourists focused on the commercialised front region. Annabel Black notes that the spatial separation of tourist accommodation, souvenir shops and restaurants in Mellieha have kept tourists away from the local residential areas. Testa (1992) describes how a *cordon sanitaire* of more than six hundred tourist attractions – ranging from shops, museums, bus tours and pretzel factories to artificial homesteads – keep the fifteen thousand Amish inhabitants in Lancaster County, Pennsylvania from being overrun by some five million annual visitors intent on photographing their archaic clothing and horse-drawn carriages and visiting their farms (see also Cohen 1989; McKean 1989).

Cultural commoditisation has also benefited peripheral communities with declining populations. Zarkia, Puijk and Nogués Pedregal all show that the development of tourism has reduced if not halted the depopulation of Skyros, Henningsvær and Zahara. The marketing of local culture has in no small measure contributed to this. Consequently it has helped to support the viability of these communities and safeguard local traditions.

Commoditisation of culture has complex consequences. It is unwise to generalise. Most communities are able to confront and cope with tourism (see Cohen 1988; Bendix 1989; McKean 1989; Boissevain forthcoming a).

Protecting Back Regions

The inhabitants of communities visited by tourists have been swift to adapt to tourism. Tourists have unquestionably also affected their way of life and customs. It would though be a serious mistake to think of natives passively submitting to tourist influences. Residents in tourist destinations have developed strategies to protect themselves from tourists bent on penetrating their back regions to stare, undergo authentic experiences, and photograph. The means they use include covert resistance, hiding, fencing, ritual, organised protest and aggression.

Covert Resistance

Values, rights, and customs threatened by tourism are often, and initially, defended by unspectacular means. These include the strategies and covert forms of resistance, the mundane, daily struggle of the weak against the powerful who seek to use them. These actions take many forms. All, however, avoid direct defiance. 'They require little or no coordination or planning; they often represent a form of individual self-help; and they typically avoid any direct symbolic confrontation with authority or with elite norms' (Scott 1985:29). Examples of this covert, low-key resistance are the sulking, grumbling, obstruction, gossip, ridicule, and surreptitious insults directed by the weak at the more powerful.

Those who work in the tourist industry depend on the goodwill of foreign visitors. Hence they are reluctant to confront them directly. The behaviour of persons who have to deal repeatedly with tourists exhibits forms of this everyday resistance: sullen waiters, rude bus drivers, and haughty shop keepers. Denigrating stereotypes are also spread about difficult tourists. Stories about arrogant Germans, complaining Dutch, and stingy Swedes circulate freely in Malta. Puijk recounts how the wife of the local doctor in Henningsvær complained to him that tourists did not respect people's leisure time. They expected prompt service just because they had money. She had therefore referred a wealthy tourist to the municipal health centre in a nearby village, rather than to her husband. In the same vein, Zarkia cites a harried restaurant owner who abruptly closes his business for three hours every afternoon: 'I don't see why I should open all day long. They can wait until after the siesta.'

Grumbling and gossiping are also a form of passive resistance. For example, the four-hundred inhabitants of the historic walled city of Mdina, Malta are becoming impatient with the way tourist authorities open their town to some three-quarters of a million tourists annually. There is an increasing feeling that they sacrifice a great deal, but receive only discomfort in return. One young woman summed the attitude up in an emotional outburst:

> We are used as carpets! … The residents have a right to live. We want to live. When we air our views, outsiders tell us that Mdina is not ours but it belongs to the Maltese population. But we live here! We have a right to our city, *pajjiezna* (Boissevain 1996:228).

Parody and ridicule are effective ways of expressing discomfort, opposition, and hostility. Nogués Pedregal gives examples of satirical Carnival songs that Zahareños direct against tourists. Deirdre Evans-Pritchard (1989:95f.) gives a striking example of the way parody is used by a Native American silversmith.

> A lady was examining the silver balls on a squash blossom necklace. She turned to Cippy Crazyhorse and in a slow, over emphasised fashion intended for someone who does not really understand English she asked 'Are these hollow?' Cippy promptly replied 'Hello' and warmly shook her hand. Again the lady asked, 'Are they hollow?' pronouncing the words even more theatrically this time. Cippy cheerily responded with another 'Hello.' This went on a few more times, by which time everyone around was laughing, until eventually the lady herself saw the joke.

Through self-parody Cippy was able to liberate himself from the dumb Indian ethnic stereotype and cajole the woman into seeing him as just as human as she (1989: 96).[4]

There is yet another form of covert activity directed against tourists. This is the sexual humiliation of female tourists by men structurally subordinated to tourists. Glenn Bowman (1989 and forthcoming) recounts how Palestinian souvenir shopkeepers in Jerusalem 'seduce' tourist women, whom they then insult. He explains their behaviour by their subordinate status in geopolitical and local terms. Already second-class citizens in a city dominated by Israel, they were looked down upon by other Palestinians as touting for foreigners. They told Bowman that sexually humiliating foreign women, and cuckolding their rich husbands, made them 'feel good'. It also raised their status among colleagues, with whom they discussed their exploits in detail. Zinovieff (1991) found similar motives among the male 'harpoons' who hunt foreign women in Greece.

Such low-key, covert acts of defiance enable persons subordinated by their dependence on tourists to retain their self respect. Moreover, by these acts they keep alive the pilot light of resistance. Those who engage in such acts form a category of disgruntled persons who, if the occasions arises, can be mobilised into more active protest. The massive demonstration against new beach developments that Crain describes is an example (see also Davis 1975).

Hiding

In many societies, communities unenthusiastic about the presence of tourists have now taken to hiding aspects of their culture from visitors. Black discusses how her neighbours in Mellieha kept certain foods and spaces to themselves. Many communities hold celebrations at times and places that enable them to avoid the attention of outsiders (Boissevain 1992a). These are 'insider-only' celebrations.[5] They have a family resemblance to cast parties, when actors and (back)stage crew celebrate the end of a performance, well out of sight of the audience. Similarly, the inhabitants of tourist destinations withdraw to celebrate without tourists. Crain describes how Almonte villagers take part in a rigorous mid-August devotional pilgrimage, 'when the heat makes the tourists wilt and keeps them far away', to celebrate the Virgin of the Dew. This pilgrimage, the *traslado*, has become an insiders-only alternative to the traditional annual spring pilgrimage which has been partially expropriated by tourists. As aspects of this event become transformed into a mass spectacle, occasions for traditional devotion and comradeship have been reduced.

Insider events can also take the form of rituals celebrated *after* the tourist season. Examples of such events are the *fête du four* at Esclade, Cantal, during which neighbours share a meal of pig trotters and peas cooked in the communal oven, and the *Castañá* in Zahara, when neighbours meet on All Saints Day to feast on chestnuts, sweet wine, and soft drinks. These recent communal meals were explicitly designed to become part of the social calendar of a community of neighbours. In the words of one of Nogués Pedregal's informants, they 'created the *Castañá* to bring people closer to each other'.

Other insider events hidden from tourists are those that occur either before outsiders arrive or after they have left. Skyrians wait until the tourist buses have left the annual feasts of their Saints before they celebrate the 'real feast'. The members of the celebrating confraternities and their friends then relax, eat, drink, and sing together until morning (see Kenna 1992). Wild demonstrations of Maltese parish youths take place before the formal outdoor celebration of the parish patrons and after the official celebrations: before the arrival and after the departure of tourists. Tourists are not informed about these spectacular events (Boissevain forthcoming a). A Sardinian printer told Peter Odermatt that he advised clients ordering posters for village festivals that to keep foreigners away from their celebrations they should use the term *Sagra*, which attracted fewer non-Italian tourists, rather than the more commonly used *Festa*, which most foreigners knew.[6]

Natives cope with the growing participation of tourists in their formal, organised celebrations by arranging insider-only events where they can celebrate amongst themselves, hidden from the tourist gaze. This enables them to continue developing the major festivities which are important for their prosperity, without sacrificing the intimacy of celebrations among neighbours. These back-stage rites of intensification are increasingly important for maintaining solidarity in communities that are both overrun by outsiders and tied to a work regime that limits socialising for months on end. I would suggest that the scale of these back-stage celebrations will continue to grow as the relative importance of cultural tourism increases.

Another strategy for protecting local values from tourists is for guides to present different discourses to different categories of tourists. Dahles shows how a simple discourse protects Amsterdam's public image by hiding sensitive subjects. This discourse is given to undemanding tourists. More knowledgeable tourists – mostly Dutch and therefore partly insiders – are included in a discourse that involves sensitive topics such as prostitution, drug abuse, and poverty.

Fencing

Another way of avoiding the tourist gaze is to fence off private areas and events. The literature provides many examples. Roel Puijk notes that

tourists annoy Lofoten fishermen at work by taking pictures and specu-
lates that they may move their operations to areas less frequented by
tourists. However, above all Henningsvær women complain that tourists
roaming around the back of their houses to see how they live, often
interrupt them as they sunbathe. Increasingly they are having to fence
off their gardens to protect their privacy. Valene Smith (1989b) has
described the difficulties faced by the Kotzebue Eskimo of Alaska when
confronted with mass tourism. Inquisitive tourists annoyed them while
they processed their catch on the beach. Some tourists even took fish
from drying racks, sniffed it and threw it away 'as if it were garbage'
(1989b: 63). Above all they objected to being photographed at work by
persons whom they suspected were ridiculing them. They first refused to
be photographed; then they erected screens to shield their work; finally,
some hired taxis to haul the seals home so that they could process them
in privacy (1989b: 63-64). Poppi (1992) has also described how celebrants in the Italian Val di Fassa village of Penia physically barred outsiders – fellow Ladins from the lower valley as well as tourists – from the
hall where their Carnival masquerade reaches its climax.

Ritual

Ritual provides a well-documented means of coping with the stress
caused by uncertainty brought about by illness, conflict, and change
(see Turner 1957, 1969). Tourism, as will have become evident, is a
source of uncertainty. Over the past twenty-five years there has been a
striking increase in Europe of public rituals, particularly of insider
events celebrating community identity (Boissevain 1992a). I have
argued that this increase was a reaction to the rapid changes that have
swept across Europe since the 1950s and which are eroding community
identity. Tourism is one of these. This growth of public celebrations is
not limited to Europe. Roderick Ewins recently remarked on a similar
increase in Fiji. He links this to changes felt to be threatening to the
indigenous population's sense of identity. Of these, tourism is particularly prominent. He argues that the resurgence of Fijian rituals can be
viewed 'as an instrument used to mitigate the impact of external forces
which are perceived as culturally destructive, and to reassert indigenous
values and identity.'[7] Years ago, a Maltese priest, trying to explain the
expansion of local festivities, used similar words. He referred to the
social upheaval wrought in Malta by the Labour government during the
1970s, noting that 'these are felt by almost everybody, and we seek

opportunities to let off steam. But where do we look? ... We simply go back to our origins; we cultivate them again and complicate them' (Boissevain 1992b). The 'hidden' rituals described in this volume – the *traslado* in Almonte, the *fête du four* at Esclade and the *castañá* in Zahara – all help the celebrants reestablish the camaraderie and identity being worn away by changes, foremost among which is the influx of out-siders. The celebrations protect them against the impact of tourism and help them cope with these changes.

Organised Protest

Local citizens occasionally organise protest action against those market-ing their back regions and rights to the tourist industry without their consent. Odermatt, for example, details how Sardinian authorities expropriated a local monument, the *nuraghe* Losa. This neolithic tower had for most of the century given inhabitants of Abbasanta local, national, and even international recognition. Local residents had been content with the symbolic preeminence that their monument gave them and were pleased that tourists spent time and money to visit it. They had felt no need to market it, to highlight its monumental characteristics or in other ways to exploit it as a money-making asset. The regional archae-ological authorities thought otherwise. They set about improving access to the site, enclosing it, and clearing 'rubble', including, as it transpired, the complete Roman stratum of the site. When the mayor discovered this desecration of the community's heritage, he ordered the *Carabinieri* to stop the work. The irate regional authorities retaliated and closed the site, denying locals access to their monument. The continuing conflict resulted in both the museum department and the local community abandoning Losa. Thus by converting the nuraghe Losa from a com-munity symbol to a commercial symbol, the government destroyed its meaning for Abbasanta residents. Their response was first to oppose the government and then to boycott the monument. They defended their honour by neutralising the monument, at least temporarily, as a tourist asset. The whole episode illustrates the consequences of commoditising without the consent of the participants (Greenwood 1989).

Several other contributors describe action to defend community values threatened by tourists. Black and Zarkia describe how groups of concerned inhabitants dealt with the assault by scantily clad and topless tourists on their sense of decency, and thus on their sexual mores. Crain also details the steps in the successful struggle of residents of the region surrounding

Almonte to defend themselves against the onslaught by tourist developers
bent on expropriating their beach and forest heritage. In Malta there has
recently been a series of initiatives by environmentally concerned groups
to draw attention to threats to the island's culture and the environment
created by tourism (Briguglio 1994; Moviment Ghall-Ambient 1994).

Aggression

Occasionally people resort to violence to defend themselves against intru-
sive tourists. Some extreme cases have been recorded. A French tourist
was stoned to death by the villagers of San Juan Chamula in Chiapas,
Mexico for photographing their Carnival (van den Berghe 1994:124).
Deirdre Evans-Pritchard recounts how a furious Navajo shot out the tires
of the car of a tourist who barged into his hogan to photograph his family eating there. The indignant tourist explained his action by arguing
that his taxes had funded the Indians on the reservation (1988: 97)!

In Malta, too, tourists, encouraged by government brochures to
explore the countryside, are regularly menaced by hunters and bird trappers who object to foreigners invading territory they consider their
domain. They feel that tourists threaten their hobby, since foreigners are
usually critical of the large-scale shooting and trapping of migrating
birds (see Fenech 1992).[8] On the whole though, except for hunters,
trappers, and bus drivers (who, overworked and harassed by tourist questions, are often extremely aggressive and rude), most Maltese are quite
friendly to tourists. Nonetheless, I recorded the case of a tourist who was
punched by the boyfriend of the waitress to whom he had complained
about poor service. She and her friend felt that she had been insulted and
the latter took action to defend their honour (at least that is how I interpreted it). Nogués Pedregal describes how youths in Zahara destroyed a
shed that tourists had built to house their wind-surfing boards. The
young men objected to the way the shed, which had been erected against
a monumental palace, disturbed the village's historical environment.
Clearly, natives can be provoked to violence if they feel that their personal or collective rights have been violated.

Conclusions

Coping with tourists is a complex process. Destination communities
must adapt swiftly to derive profit and to prevent the erosion of their own

way of life. This is not only threatened by crowding and the 'liberated', occasionally rude, holiday behaviour of tourists. It is also jeopardised by authorities who offer local cultures to visitors without consulting those affected. Tourists seeking culture are potentially more difficult to deal with than sun-sand-and-sea tourists. Not content to stay by the shore, they roam about more widely in search of the grail of authenticity. This quest drives them to go beyond the staged front-area events and to penetrate private space, where locals shelter from the tourist masses. Even communities visited by tourists adjust and adapt surprisingly swiftly. They rapidly adopt business-like attitudes to maximise profits. They are creative in inventing and staging events that furnish entertainment and provide information on their culture. These attractions, while usually not explicitly developed to protect back regions, function to deflect the tourist gaze from private space and activities. Host communities take specific, active measures to protect their values and customs threatened by outsiders. The means they utilise include covert action, hiding from tourists, communal celebrations, fencing them out, organised protest and even overt aggression to protect their interests.

Host communities are often portrayed as passive victims of acculturation and the affluence and lifestyle of mass tourists (Turner and Ash 1975). Our studies show that the residents of these communities are in fact generally inventive and resilient. Tourism is one of many sources of change impinging upon them. It is something with which they must deal successfully, for increasingly they are economically dependent on it. The communities examined in this book appear to be coping with tourism, so far.

Notes

Thanks to Inga Boissevain, Nadia Sammut, Inge van Zoelen, participants in the Anthropology and Sociology of Tourism Seminar at Roehampton Institute, London, and the contributors to this volume for their most helpful comments on drafts of this introduction.

1. Cultural tourists are interested in the lifestyle of other people (whether at home or abroad, now or in the past), their history, and the artefacts and monuments they have made. Thus this category also includes what some have called ethnic and historical tourism (see Wood 1984; Smith 1989; van den Bergh 1994; van den Bergh and Keyes 1984). Cultural tourism may be contrasted with recreational tourism –

stereotypically focused on sun, sand, sea and sex – and environmental tourism. These categories are not mutually exclusive and usually overlap slightly.

2. Pro- and anti-development conflicts and progressive and conservative factionalism have been widely reported (see Epstein 1962: 129ff., 1973: 179ff.; Silverman and Salisbury 1978).
3. Stockfish is dried cod.
4. For other imaginative host reactions to patronising tourists see Evans-Pritchard 1989; Sweet 1989.
5. By 'insiders' I mean members of what could be called the nuclear community – its permanent residents. This excludes emigrants on holiday, visitors from nearby communities, and tourists, whether national or foreign (Boissevain 1992a: 12). Clearly, insider events take place in what MacCannell has called back regions (1976: 92).
6. Personal communication from Peter Odermatt.
7. Personal communication from Roderick Ewins.
8. Foreigners write regularly to the Maltese press to warn that they will not visit Malta (again) as long as the trapping and shooting of migrating birds continues.

REFERENCES

Bendix, R. 'Tourism and Cultural Displays. Inventing Traditions for Whom?' *Journal of American Folklore* vol. 102 (1989): 131-46.

Bergh, P.L. van den *The Quest for the Other. Ethnic Tourism in San Cristobal, Mexico.* Seattle: University of Washington Press, 1994.

Bergh, P.L. van den, and Keyes, C.F. 'Introduction. Tourism and Re-Created Ethnicity', *Annals of Tourism Research* vol. 11 (1984): 343-52.

Blok, A. *Wittgenstein en Elias. Een Methodische Richtlijn Voor de Antropologie.* Amsterdam: Athenaeum-Polak & Van Gennep, 1976.

Boissevain, J. 'Tourism and Development in Malta', *Development and Change* vol. 8 (1977): 523-38.

_____, 'Ritual Escalation in Malta', in Wolf, E., ed., *Religion, Power and Protest in Local Communities.* New York: Mouton, 1984, 163-83.

_____, 'Tourism as Anti-Structure', in Giordano, C., et al., eds, *Kulturanthropologisch. Ein Festschrift für Ina-Maria Greverus*, Notizien Nr. 30. Frankfurt: University of Frankfurt, 1989, 145-59.

_____, 'Introduction: Revitalizing European Rituals', in Boissevain, J., ed., *Revitalizing European Rituals.* London: Routledge, 1992a, 1-19.

_____, 'Play and identity. Ritual change in a Maltese village', in Boissevain, J., ed., *Revitalizing European Rituals.* London: Routledge, 1992b, 136-54.

_____, 'Discontent in Mdina: Some Problems with Cultural Tourism in Malta', *Tourism Concern* vol.12 (1994): 12.

_____, 'Ritual, Tourism and Cultural Commoditization. Culture by the Pound?', in Selwyn, T., ed., *The Tourist Image: Myths and Myth Making in Tourism*. London: Wiley, forthcoming a.

_____, '"But we live here!" Perspectives on Cultural Tourism in Malta', in Briguglio, L. et al., eds, *Sustainable Tourism in Islands and Small States. Case Studies*. London: Pintar, 1996.

Boissevain, J. and Sammut, N. *Mdina: Its Residents and Cultural Tourism. Findings and Recommendations.* (Report) Malta: Med-Campus Euromed Sustainable Tourism Network, University of Malta, 1994.

Bowman, G. 'Fucking Tourists: Sexual Relations and Tourism in Jerusalem's Old City', *Critique of Anthropology* vol. 9 (1989): 77-93.

_____, 'Passion, Power and Politics in a Palestinian Tourist Market', in Selwyn, T., ed., *Chasing Myths: Essays in the Anthropology of Tourism*. New York: John Wiley, 1996.

Brandes, S. *Power and Persuasion. Fiestas and Social Control in Rural Mexico.* Philadelphia: University of Pennsylvania Press, 1988.

Briguglio, L., ed. *Tourism in Gozo: Policies, Prospects and Problems*. Malta: University of Malta and Foundation for International Studies, 1994.

Brougham, J.E., and Butler, R.W. 'A Segmentation Analysis of Resident Attitudes to the Social Impact of Tourism', *Annals of Tourism Research* vol. 4 (1981): 569-90.

Cohen, E. 'Rethinking the Sociology of Tourism', *Annals of Tourism Research* vol. 6 (1979): 18-35.

_____, 'Authenticity and Commoditization in Tourism', *Annals of Tourism Research* vol. 15 (1988): 371-86.

_____, 'Primitive and Remote. Hill Tribe Trekking in Thailand', *Annals of Tourism Research* vol. 16 (1989): 30-61.

Crain, M. M. 'The Art of Selling an "Authentic" Ethnic Self: Native Women's Cultural Performances of Ecuadorean National and Transnational Consumption', in Howes, D., ed., *Commodities and Cultural Borders*, forthcoming.

Cruces, F. and Díaz de Rada, D. 'Public Celebrations in a Spanish Valley', in Boissevain, J., ed., *Revitalizing European Rituals*. London: Routledge, 1992, 62-79.

Crystal, E. 'Tourism in Toraja (Sulawesi, Indonesia)', in Smith, V., ed., *Hosts and Guests. The Anthropology of Tourism*, 2nd edn Philadelphia: University of Pennsylvania Press, 1989, 139-85.

Davis, N.Z. *Women on Top. Society and Culture in Early Modern France.* London: Duckworth, 1975, 125-51.

Dogan, H.Z. 'Forms of Adjustment. Sociocultural Impacts of Tourism', *Annals of Tourism Research* vol. 16 (1989): 216-36.

Droog, M. '"En Dan Word Je Weer Gewoon Mens." Het opleven van feesten in een Oostenrijkse dorp.' unpublished M.A. dissertation, Department of Anthropology, University of Amsterdam, 1991.

Epstein, T.S. *Economic Development and Social Change in South India.* Manchester: Manchester University Press, 1962.

_____, *South India: Yesterday, Today and Tomorrow. Mysore Villages Revisited.* Manchester: Manchester University Press, 1973.

Evans-Pritchard, D. 'How "They" See "Us". Native American Images of Tourists', *Annals of Tourism Research* vol. 16 (1989): 89-105.

Featherstone, M. *Consumer Culture and Postmodernism.* London: Sage, 1991.

Fenech, N. *Fatal Flight: The Maltese Obsession with Killing Birds.* London: P. Quiller, 1992.

Goffman, E. *The Presentation of Self in Everyday Life.* Garden City, N.J., 1959.

Graburn, N. 'Tourism: The Sacred Journey', in Smith, V., ed. *Hosts and Guests. The Anthropology of Tourism,* 2nd edn, Philadelphia: University of Pennsylvania Press, 1989, 21-36.

_____, 'The anthropology of tourism', *Annals of Tourism Research* vol. 10 (1983): 9-33.

Greenwood, D.D. 'Culture by the Pound: An Anthropological Perspective on Tourism as Cultural Commoditization', in Smith, V., ed., *Hosts and Guests. The Anthropology of Tourism,* 2nd edn, Philadelphia: University of Pennsylvania Press, 1989, 171-85.

Hermans, D. 'The Encounter of Agriculture and Tourism', *Annals of Tourism Research* vol. 3 (1981): 462-79.

Kenna, M. 'Mattresses and Migrants. A Patron Saint's Festival on a Small Greek Island Over Two Decades', in Boissevain, J., ed., *Revitalizing European Rituals.* London: Routledge, 1992, 154-72.

Leach, E. *Rethinking Anthropology.* London: Athlone Press, University of London, 1964.

Lett, J.W. 'Ludic and Liminoid Aspects of Charter Yacht Tourism in the Caribbean', *Annals of Tourism Research* vol. 10 (1983): 35-56.

MacCannell, D. *The Tourist. A New Theory of the Leisure Class.* New York: Schocken Books, 1976.

_____, 'Reconstructed Ethnicity. Tourism and Cultural Identity in Third World Communities', *Annals of Tourism Research* vol. 11 (1984): 375-91.

McKean, P. F. 'Towards a Theoretical Analysis of Tourism: Economic Dualism and Cultural Involution in Bali', in Smith, V., ed., *Hosts and Guests. The Anthropology of Tourism,* 2nd edn, Philadelphia: University of Pennsylvania Press, 1989: 93-107.

Moviment Ghall-Ambjent – Friends of the Earth Malta, eds, *Mediterranean Action Plan for Sustainable Tourism: Mellieha Workshop.* Malta: Moviment Ghall-Ambjent, 1994.

Pi Sunyer, O. 'Changing Perceptions of Tourism and Tourists in a Catalan Resort Town', in Smith, V., ed. *Hosts and Guests. The Anthropology of Tourism.* 2nd edn, Philadelphia: University of Pennsylvania Press, 1989, 187-99.

Pollard, J. and Rodriguez, R.D. 'Tourism and Torremolinos. Recession or Reaction to Environment?', *Tourism Management* vol. 14 (1993): 247-58.

Poppi, 'Building Differences: The Political Economy of Tradition in the Ladin Carnival of the Val di Fassa', in Boissevain, J., ed., *Revitalizing European Rituals.* London: Routledge, 1992, 113-36.

Sabel, C.F. *Work and Politics. The Division of Labour in Industry.* Cambridge: Cambridge University Press, 1982.

Scott, J. *Weapons of the Weak. Everyday Forms of Peasant Resistance.* New Haven: Yale University Press, 1985.

Silverman, M. and Salisbury, R.F., eds, *A House Divided? Anthropological Studies of Factionalism.* St. John's: Memorial University of Newfoundland, 1978.

Smith, V. 'Introduction', in Smith, V., ed., *Hosts and Guests. The Anthropology of Tourism,* 2nd edn, Philadelphia: University of Pennsylvania Press, 1989a, 1-17.

_____, 'Eskimo Tourism: Micro-Models and Marginal Men', in Smith, ed., *Hosts and Guests. The Anthropology of Tourism,* 2nd edn, Philadelphia: University of Pennsylvania Press, 1989b, 55-82.

Sofield, T.H.B. 'Sustainable Ethnic Tourism in the South Pacific: Some Principles', *The Journal of Tourism Studies* vol. 2 (1991): 57-73.

Sweet, J.D. 'Burlesquing "the Other" in Pueblo Performance', *Annals of Tourism Research* vol. 16 (1989): 62-75.

Testa, R.-M., *After the Fire. The Destruction of the Lancaster County Amish.* Hanover, New Hampshire and London: University Press of New England, 1992.

Tsartas, P. 'Socioeconomic Impacts of Tourism on Two Greek Isles', *Annals of Tourism Research* vol. 19 (1992): 16-33.

Turner, L. and Ash, J. *The Golden Hordes. International Tourism and the Pleasure Periphery.* London: Constable, 1975.

Turner, V. *Schism and Continuity in an African Society.* Manchester: Manchester University Press, 1957.

_____, *The Ritual Process. Structure and Anti-Structure.* Ithaca: Cornell University Press, 1969.

Weiler, B., and Hall, C.M., eds, *Special Interest Tourism.* London: Belthaven, 1992.

Wood, R.E. 'Ethnic Tourism, the State, and Cultural Change in Southeast Asia', *Annals of Tourism Research,* vol. 11 (1984): 353-74.

Urry, J. *The Tourist Gaze. Leisure and Travel in Contemporary Societies.* London: Sage, 1990.

Zinovieff, S. 'Hunters and Hunted: *Kamaki* and the Ambiguities of Sexual Predation in a Greek Town', in Loizos, P. and Papataxiarchis, E., eds, *Contested Identities: Gender and Kinship in Modern Greece.* Princeton: Princeton University Press, 1991, 203-20.

1. Contested Territories
The Politics of Touristic Development at the Shrine of El Rocío in Southwestern Andalusia

Mary M. Crain

*T*his chapter explores the manner in which religious, commercial and political elites in the *término* of Almonte (the municipality of Almonte and its outlying lands), have reformulated their municipality into a series of tourist sites.[1] I begin by examining three distinct but interrelated instances of touristic activity in this southwestern Andalusian setting. In order to account for the escalation of various forms of tourism during the past two decades, these activities are placed within a broader historical context. The sites of interest include the annual *romería* (pilgrimage) to the shrine of the Virgin of El Rocío, celebrated during the Pentecost, as well as the development of an international beach resort at Matalascañas on the Atlantic Coast, some seventeen kilometres south of the shrine. Finally, I investigate the growing popularity of ecological tourism at the nearby National Park of Doñana. Findings from this case study illuminate broader trends emerging within the Spanish tourism industry in general.

My analysis of the preceding touristic activities indicates that the response of local Andalusian hosts to the tourist gaze has not been a unified one. In fact, a range of host reactions can be detected. In what follows I delineate many of the diverse constituencies and outline their positions with respect to the impact of touristic developments. While certain hosts have been responsible for the amplification of tourism's presence in the region and have reaped a substantial portion of the financial rewards derived from tourist revenues, other hosts, from the communities of Almonte, Marisol, Pilas, and Villamanrique have contested the promotion of touristic developments. Their oppositional discourses, often formulated in a variety of overlapping idioms – economic, religious, and localistic – will be analysed. The promotion of tourism at all three of the above-mentioned sites has also incited debates regarding the compatibility of development with the conservation of natural resources, as even subtle alterations in the environment endanger the survival of the National Park of Doñana, presently one of Europe's largest wild game reserves.

In the concluding portion of this article, it is suggested that for many individuals who form part of this oppositional bloc (i.e., those who have contested touristic ventures), the complicity both of the local town council of Almonte and of many members of the founding brotherhood of Almonte in the commodification and massification of the *romería* of Pentecost is offset by their sponsorship of a second *romería*, known as *el traslado*, in which the effects of commodification and tourism are negligible. In comparison to the romería of the Pentecost, *el traslado* remains a celebration for insiders (Boissevain 1992). To date, sponsorship of el traslado has provided members of the relatively small Almonteño elite with the legitimation necessary to assure their continued control over the organisation of a cult, such as that of the Virgin of El Rocío, whose followers now greatly outnumber the population of the small pueblo of Almonte.

Touristic Texts

A large billboard mounted on the highway extending from the village of Almonte to the hamlet of El Rocío, both located within the *término* of Almonte, beckons the motorist with the following message: 'You have just entered the paradise of your dreams: The National Park of Doñana, the beach resort of Matalascañas, and the shrine of the Virgin of El Rocío all await you'. Ecological tourism, recreation and relaxation, as well as colourful ritual and cultural history, are all combined in this text. Emblematic of a new strategy pursued within the Spanish tourism industry, this multivocal text is designed to encourage *turismo integral*, or, multifaceted tourism. The aim of multifaceted tourism is to promote several diverse sites, all of potential interest to the tourist, within a limited geographical range. Such a strategy redirects touristic attention away from an exclusive focus on sunny, coastal Spain with its crowded beach resorts, towards the less developed interior regions. A decline in the number of foreign tourists frequenting the Spanish coast, partially the result of uncontrolled resort development, rising hotel costs, as well as the contamination of coastal waters, has prompted a search within the tourist sector for alternative strategies. The new focus on interior tourism promotes visits to picturesque rural villages, to areas of the hinterlands that contain historic sites and important monuments, as well as trips to observe festive celebrations and explore scenic landscapes and nature reserves.[2] One important advantage of these new sites is that they are not affected by seasonal fluctuations to the degree that beach resorts are. These forms of recreation provide greater possibilities for tourism to generate wage employment throughout the year, and to constitute an alternative source of income for the local population. Official spokespersons within the tourist industry argue that multifaceted tourism is designed both to recapture Spain's share of the European tourist market and to attract more affluent tourists by providing them with higher quality amenities ('Constituida' *ABC* 1991:77).

This shift both to interior and to multifaceted tourism can also be detected in the national tourism industry's creation of a new national logo to advertise Spain in 1992. The previous logo, 'Spain: Everything Under the Sun', intended to indicate the unlimited possibilities Spain offers to the traveller, graced the cover of innumerable tourist brochures and guidebooks, as well as posters announcing cultural events. However, in 1992, a new logo, 'Spain: Passion for Life' was established. An earlier focus on sun and beach culture was replaced by images and written texts that touted Spain's unique cultural and artistic heritage. This strategy redirected attention towards the nation's sophisticated urban centres and historic landmarks during 1992, a year in which Madrid was chosen as the cultural capital of Europe, Barcelona as the host to the summer Olympics, and Seville, as the site of the World's Fair.

Highly literary guidebooks describing Andalusia for the tourist have also begun to privilege interior routes for the foreign visitor, especially those that combine a diversity of sites. For example, in his recent handbook for a sophisticated, up-scale English-reading audience, author Michael Jacobs (1990) devotes considerable attention both to the Pentecostal pilgrimage to the shrine of El Rocío and to its counterpart, the Coto of Doñana. Emphasising the *romería's* local colour, its pageantry as well as its emotional pandemonium, Jacobs regards El Rocío as a venue for cultural tourism. His account of his own participation in this *romería*, in which he embarked upon one of the rigorous caminos, or pilgrimage routes to the shrine, encourages active touristic participation as well, in which elites may relish the experience of roughing it, or slumming. Furthermore, as in the previous example of the highway billboard, in Jacobs' text both the pilgrimage site and the National Park of Doñana are readily associated with one another. While for Jacobs the Coto of Doñana provides an idyllic background setting for the *romería*, evoking images of a remote wilderness paradise in which nature lovers may revel, his analysis of the celebration at the shrine of El Rocío pivots around those very structural contrasts that are characteristic of many touristic and festive experiences (Boissevain 1989, Falassi 1987). According to Jacobs, El Rocío offers the participant a chance to experience a different time and place, 'a time out of time', in which the *rociero*, (the steadfast pilgrim at the Rocío) temporarily leaves the twentieth century and enters 'the world of yesteryear'. The ritual context is represented as a realm of utopian possibilities in which play is elevated, and concerns for the social responsibilities of everyday life and the world of work are erased (Jacobs 1990: 161, Boissevain 1991). According to Jacobs, both places, Doñana and the Rocío, are unique. Doñana's relative isolation, combined with its unusual ecological conditions, veils it in a shroud of mystery, positioning it at the very margins of modernity's gaze. Similarly, the sandy trails encircling the shrine of El Rocío, which are packed with pilgrims as well as tourists mounted on horseback during the Pentecost, bears a resemblance to media images of dusty frontier towns, as depicted in Hollywood films about the Wild West.

Touristic Contexts

What are some of the features of the *término* of Almonte, the municipality which contains all three of these tourist sites? How have these sites emerged as touristic attractions? What are the various controversies surrounding tourism's impact both on various local 'host' communities as well as on the surrounding environment? These issues are considered below.

Almonte

Some 17,000 inhabitants reside in the town of Almonte; the municipal lands which encompass it amount to 950 square kilometres, making it one of the municipalities with the largest landholdings in all of Spain (see Comelles 1991). The majority of the inhabitants of Almonte combine several forms of livelihood, such as seasonal labour in agriculture, (rice, strawberries, melons, and flowers are produced both for the domestic market and for export) as well as work in tourist-related activities and in the construction industry. Complaining of a stagnant agrarian economy and high rates of unemployment and underemployment, many Almonteños demand preferential treatment in the acquisition of jobs available at the beach resort in Matalascañas, at the National Park of Doñana, and in tourist-related activities at the shrine of El Rocío.

Doñana National Park

Bordered to the south by the Guadalquivir River and to the west by the Atlantic Ocean, this national park is composed of three different ecosystems: great expanses of marshlands (known locally as the *marismas*), sand dunes, and finally, pine and eucalyptus forests.

During the fourteenth to nineteenth centuries the area which presently forms this national park was a royal hunting ground, or, *Coto Real,* controlled by the Kings of Castile. During this period, a large portion of the hunting reserve was awarded as a concession to the Dukes of Medina-Sidonia, whose principal residence was in the nearby coastal town of Sanlúcar de Barrameda. This family later constructed a palace and a hunting lodge in the *Coto.* Villagers from many of the bordering pueblos, such as Almonte, Villamanrique, Pilas, and Sanlúcar, performed services for the Ducal house (see map 1.1). Such servitude entitled them to customary rights of passage in an area in which game (deer, wildcats, rabbits, and lynx), birds (pheasants, doves, imperial eagles, egrets, flamingoes), and many kinds of fish, abounded. While in theory the ducal aristocracy imposed restrictions which prohibited villagers from hunting, in practice, such legislation was difficult to enforce and furtive hunting continues in this area up to the present day (see Ojeda 1987). For poor villagers, the *Coto* was also a source of charcoal, wild vegetables, (asparagus and mushrooms), pasture, and firewood, as well as materials (e.g., reeds and adobe) for the construction of huts and fences (see Comelles 1991, Ojeda 1987). Due to its unique terrain, much of the *Coto* was never suitable for intensive agricultural purposes.

In the twentieth century, several British naturalists demonstrated the importance of the Coto of Doñana as a crucial causeway for birds migrating from Western Europe to Africa. Many of these authors deplored the depletion of its wildlife and the over-exploitation of its natural resources, partially the result of private initiatives instituted at that time by the owner, a sherry baron. The latter sold large stands of the *Coto*'s forests as timber. In 1961, the World Wildlife Foundation was established in London. Partially as a result of international pleas to save the environmental wilderness of Doñana, in 1969, with financial assistance from the World Wildlife Foundation, the Spanish government created the National Park and Wild Game Reserve of Doñana. The Spanish state was placed in a tutelary role in the administration of the park. Bordered to the north both by the shrine of El Rocío and by the villages of Villamanrique, Pilas, Hinojos, and Almonte, and to the southeast by the beaches of Matalascañas, the initial surface area of the park was approximately 37,000 hectares (Ojeda 1987). This was increased to 50,720 hectares in 1978. The formation of the park placed a halt on the construction of a large highway which had been projected to cross this territory.

In 1969, the Spanish government declared the park a site of national touristic interest. During the decade of the 1970s, and more so throughout the 1980s, Doñana was promoted as a centre for ecological tourism. Much of this tourism is educational in its orientation. Guided tours of the park's wildlife in Land Rovers are offered twice daily. In addition, observation centres and nature trails provide detailed information regarding local flora and fauna and offer many opportunities for photographing the wildlife. The turn to ecological tourism was the result of the attraction of the rural at a time when Spain's population was becoming increasingly urban in its composition (Crain 1992). During the past two decades, abandonment of rural areas, growing contamination of the environment, as well as rapid social change has given rise both to a concern for the preservation of green spaces and to a cult of nature, especially popular among Spanish youth cultures and members of the urban middle and upper classes. Trips to the countryside on weekends as well as during longer holidays are a common practice for city dwellers in Spain.

Most recently, ecological tourism has been given further impetus by a national commission appointed by the Junta de Andalusia (the governing body of the autonomous region of Andalusia). The internationally renowned sociologist and urban planner, Manuel Castells, heads this commission. The April 1992 report released by the commission pronounced that further development, both touristic and otherwise, in the municipality of Almonte is compatible with the conservation of the park's natural resources. It also claimed that the number of tourists visiting Doñana can be increased without adverse effects to the park

(Amavizca 1992). However, the report did propose the discontinuation of any further build up, either of roads or of other facilities for mass tourism, along the Atlantic coastline, where the dune ecosystem is particularly fragile. Finally, it recommends further training of local villagers as professional nature guides, and the creation of additional environmental education centres, both at Doñana and in Almonte (*Punto de Vista*, 2 April 1992).

In May 1992, shortly after the release of Castell's report, Jacques Delors, President of the European Commission, visited Doñana and met with Spanish president Felipe González as well as Manuel Chaves, the head of the Junta of Andalusia. A propos the case of Doñana, the present Spanish head of state firmly maintained that his government was unable to finance the total projected costs for Doñana's conservation; costs which will enable future generations to enjoy the park. At the culmination of Delor's visit, it was announced that the European Economic Community would pay 50 million pesetas (roughly U.S. $500,000) in order to aid the Spanish government in the preservation of Doñana as European patrimony (Amavizca 1992). Part of this money will go towards subsidising economic activities for residents of Almonte, such as stimulating the production of pine nuts and other types of agricultural activities, primarily in those areas of the municipality that are most removed from the protected area of the park.

In summary, while proceeds from ecological tourism at Doñana bring a new source of revenue to residents of the *término* of Almonte, actual touristic policy at Doñana has been shaped by national and international priorities above and beyond the agendas of either local political entities, or, diverse inhabitants of Almonte. As will become apparent later in this discussion, conflicting opinions have emerged regarding the current status of ecological tourism in the *término*.

Matalascañas

Valued primarily as a site of recreational tourism, Matalascañas is the principal beach resort in the municipality of Almonte and also one of the largest coastal resorts in the entire Costa de la Luz (Coast of Light). This stretch of the Spanish coastline includes the western-most beaches of Spain, which extend all the way to the border of Portugal. Though they border Doñana, the urbanised area of Matalascañas and its adjacent beaches lie outside of the grounds of the national park (Bernard 1990). Not quite a town, Matalascañas is a touristic complex that is entirely

dependent on the town of Almonte, which lies some thirty-three kilometres to the north. The municipal council of Almonte is responsible for
the administration of Matalascañas. Initial development of this tourist
site occurred as a result of a private venture. An anonymous society
known as Playa del Coto de Doñana, composed of four large investment
firms, with funds from Germany, Catalonia, and Panama, was formed
during the late 1960s (Ojeda 1987). Intensive construction of tourist
facilities began during this time and continued more slowly throughout
the next decade. By 1980, and the onset of a financial crisis within the
private sector dominating tourism in this locale, the municipal council
of Almonte began to cover certain infrastructural costs in Matalascañas
(see Ojeda 1987: 366).

Matalascañas presently contains large blocks of hotels, condomini-
ums, restaurants, convention halls, camping sites, a golf course, discotheques, cinemas, and luxury boutiques. In July 1982, the municipal
council of Almonte opened its first tourism office there to promote local
facilities. In addition to several large campgrounds, there are presently
seven hotels in Matalascañas, the largest with a capacity of over 1,000
rooms. While this resort is particularly popular with Andalusian tourists,
German tour operators have tended to dominate the organisation of
mass tourism, booking charter flights for this resort. Prices during the
tourist season (May to September) are at least double those of the off-
season rates. During 1992, Matalascañas was advertised as the ideal site
for those visiting the World's Fair in Seville. Advertisements placed in a
nation-wide newspaper in May 1992 promised that tourists attending
the Universal Exposition in Seville could readily find tranquillity, a
beach-front setting, and convenient accommodations in Matalascañas,
located only forty-five minutes from the Exposition fairgrounds.

Besides the camping sites there are few inexpensive hotels in Matalascañas, as the beach resort atmosphere has driven prices up. Marisoleños
and other villagers from the surrounding area complain that although
they participate in tourism, and use the beach at Matalascañas by day,
they are unwilling to pay the expensive rates charged to spend a night in
a luxury hotel there, or, to dine in one of its restaurants. One night's stay
in a hotel may easily cost 10,000-18,000 pesetas (U.S.$100-$180) for a
family of four. As many villagers earn roughly 80,000 pesetas per month
(approximately U.S.$800 in 1993), several nights in a hotel could
quickly deplete their savings. As an alternative to the use of the expensive tourist facilities, Marisoleños who visit Matalascañas during the
summer months bring their own food with them to eat while at the

beach. For accommodation they choose to stay at the shrine in El Rocío, often spending as much as a fortnight there. Provided they are members of the brotherhood, they may sleep for free, either in bunk beds or on mattresses spread out across the floor, in the Casa de la Hermandad (Brotherhood House), near the sanctuary.

In close proximity to Doñana, uncontrolled touristic developments at Matalascañas can potentially cause the most harm to the park. Tourist facilities at the beach have depleted the underground water supply and sudden changes in this supply threaten the equilibrium of the neighbouring marshlands in Doñana, a protected habitat for birds ('Informe Sobre Los Problemas' 1977). Reports issued by Andalusian environmental organisations have noted a rapid deterioration in the tourist infrastructure in Matalascañas, and have also criticised the resort's sanitary conditions, the poor management of its waste disposal as well as a lack of proper zoning laws (Bernard 1990; 'Informe' 1977; Ojeda 1987).

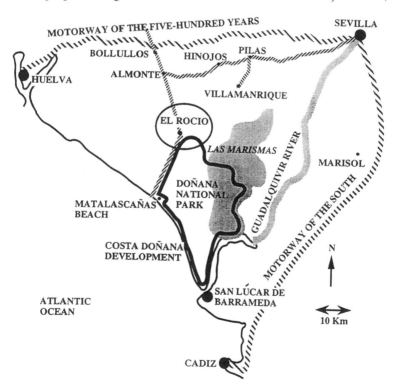

Map 1.1 Map showing the area surrounding the municipality of Almonte.

New beaches in Matalascañas, which opened to mass tourism in the 1970s, were closed during one summer due to contamination.

During the late 1980s, a proposed coastal resort known as Costa Doñana, received support both from the municipal council of Almonte as well as from the regional government of Andalusia and the socialist party (PSOE) presently governing in Madrid. Members of the municipal council were interested in creating another beach complex that would provide additional employment for Almonteños. The regional government initially viewed this project in a favourable light, claiming that it would absorb the increased number of tourists expected to attend Seville's EXPO (see Ojeda 1987; Bernard 1990: 155). Only a few kilometres south-east of Matalascañas, the proposed coastal resort was slated to have some fifteen hotels with a total capacity of 32,000 rooms (see map 1.1). Similar to Matalascañas, developments at Costa Doñana posed a serious threat to the conservation of resources at the National Park of Doñana. Plans for construction at this site were paralysed in 1990 as a result of protests from environmental organisations, both Spanish and international (Ordaz 1990: 2). In spring 1990 a coalition of Green parties organised a large demonstration in which some 8,000 people marched along the Atlantic coast to contest Costa Doñana. Participants included inhabitants of the cities of Seville and Huelva, individuals from neighbouring villages in the comarca (the region lying within a seventy kilometre radius of El Rocío), such as Pilas and Marisol, as well as some Almonteños. The recent report issued by the Castells' commission has also argued for a permanent halt to construction of this resort. While initially supportive of Costa Doñana, it is now expected that the Andalusian regional government will endorse the recommendations outlined in the Castells' report.

The Shrine of the Virgin of El Rocío

The *romería* (pilgrimage) to the shrine of El Rocío, located some sixty-five kilometres south of Seville, consists of a cult to the Virgin Mary who is referred to in this context as the Virgin of El Rocío, (the Virgin of the Dew). Debates continue regarding the origins of this particular cult. One authoritative account holds that during the thirteenth century, Alfonso X, King of Castille, ordered that a primitive sanctuary be constructed at the site and that a sculpted icon of the Virgin be placed inside (Archives of the Hermandad Matríz). Popular accounts dating from the fifteenth century, however, claim that the Virgin of El Rocío appeared before either a lowly shepherd or a hunter, who found her hidden in a wild olive tree in a dense thicket of the marismas (the area of marshlands created by the Guadalquivir river). According to the latter accounts, a brotherhood devoted to the Virgin was founded in the nearby town of Almonte, and a chapel was built at the site where the miraculous icon first appeared. In the late seventeenth century, affiliated brotherhoods representing distinct communities from Lower Andalusia, each subordinate to the founding brotherhood of Almonte, were formed. Every spring, during the Pentecost, the brotherhoods make a pilgrimage to the shrine, each following its own itinerary. Referred to as *el camino*, (the path, or, route), this journey is a strenuous undertaking: three days of travel, followed by two days at the shrine, and then three days to travel home. Each community carries its own emblem (embroidered banner) of the Virgin, travelling on foot, on horseback, in covered wagons, and in jeeps. In May 1989, when I first accompanied forty families from the community of Marisol to the shrine, there were a total of seventy-eight brotherhoods.[3]

Customarily, all of the brotherhoods arrive at the shrine by Friday afternoon. Saturday is dedicated to a colourful procession of each of the

Figure 1.1 Foot pilgrims en route to the sanctuary at El Rocío fashion walking sticks laden with wild flowers and sprigs of fresh 'romero' (rosemary). This herb is emblematic of undertaking pilgrimage.

37

Figure 1.2 With the sanctuary looming in the distance, various categories of pilgrims arrive at El Rocío on the Friday afternoon prior to Pentecost.

seventy-eight confraternities around the sanctuary. They file, according to seniority, before the Almonteño hierarchy, which forms a barricade at the door of the church, directly in front of the sculpted icon of the Virgin. On Saturday pilgrims also make individual visits to pay their respects to the Virgin, often leaving flowers, candles, or other votive objects for her. Saturday and Sunday night masses are held in honour of the Virgin. Immediately following the midnight mass on Sunday, a vigil begins, with the expectant crowd waiting for that precise moment between midnight and dawn, in which the Virgin, mounted on a pedestal, is taken out of the sanctuary and placed on the backs of the boisterous male youths of Almonte. The latter parade her around the shrine. Highly protective of their Virgin, these youths attempt to keep others from touching the icon. Even though it is considered a supreme honour for all local men to carry the Virgin *(llevarla),* and all men, women and children believe that grace is bestowed on those who are able to touch this sacred figure, during the celebration of the Pentecost, only a limited number of non-Almonteños are able to gain direct access to the Virgin.

According to Almonteños, the Virgin of El Rocío is first and foremost the patroness of Almonte, their corporate symbol, and an exemplary marker of village identity. Many Almonteños claim that the Virgin of El Rocío overrides all divisions within their community, such as distinctions based on class, gender, and political affiliations. However, members of the affiliated brotherhoods from nearby villages that lie outside the municipality of Almonte, such as Pilas, Villamanrique, and Marisol, are equally devoted to the Virgin. They frequently demonstrate this devotion through acts of faith. They undertake *promesas* (vows), make generous donations to the shrine, leave their ex-voto offerings for the icon, and also recount the numerous miracles that the Virgin has performed for individuals in their home communities. These villagers argue that the Virgin of El Rocío is the patroness of the entire *comarca*. Villagers of the *comarca* regard the Almonteños as overly possessive of the sacred female icon, which, in their opinion, belongs to all. Nevertheless, the Almonteños are quite intent upon demonstrating their ultimate control over this cult. During the past two decades, and in conjunction with various overarching agencies, the Almonteños have initiated a series of transformations at the shrine which have led to the commodification and massification of this Pentecostal roméria, thereby encouraging the attendance of the media, tourists, as well as other spectators (see Crain

Figure 1.3 During the Pentecost at the shrine, the Virgin of the Dew is removed from the sanctuary for approximately ten hours before being returned the following day.

Figure 1.4 Crowds of pilgrims, tourists and cameramen as well as other spectators assemble outside the chapel of one of the many brotherhood houses at the shrine during the Pentecost.

1992). Many of these changes have antagonised the inhabitants of the neighbouring villages in the comarca. A summary of several of these instances is provided below.

In 1969, the shrine of El Rocío was declared a site of national touristic interest. However, as early as the 1950s, Bishop Cantero of Huelva (the Spanish province to which the hamlet of El Rocío belongs), visited the shrine and foresaw the touristic benefits that could be obtained from this ritual celebration (Ojeda 1987: 335). As a result of the bishop's advice, the founding brotherhood began to issue a newsletter that promoted events at the shrine. Debates ensued in Almonte between two factions, the traditionalists and the developers, regarding whether one of the caminos, or customary pilgrimage routes to the shrine, should be replaced by a paved highway, thus facilitating the arrival of touring motorists. While those in the traditionalist/conservationist camp opposed this change, arguing that with the advent of a paved motorway, the Rocío would lose its essence and charm, modernising interests were finally victorious. A two-lane highway reached this area in the late 1950s.

Other innovations were to follow. Attention was directed towards the feasibility of constructing a new basilica at the shrine, large enough to house the growing numbers of visitors arriving during the Pentecost. The small primitive sanctuary was finally demolished in 1963 and construction began on the new basilica. As the *romería* continued to grow in size, and attracted a mass audience, the founding confraternity sought assistance, both financial and otherwise, from diverse institutions.[4] In the 1970s, entities such as the municipal council of Almonte and the Junta of Andalusia began to play a more active role in the co-sponsorship of the annual Pentecostal pilgrimage to the shrine.

During this same decade, there was a massive increase in number of private houses built in close proximity to the shrine. At present there are approximately 840 houses in El Rocío and the majority are owned by Almonteños. During the week-long Pentecostal celebration it is customary for the owners to rent their houses, often for large sums of money, with the most lavish going for as much as 400,000 pesetas (U.S. $4,000) a week, and others for U.S.$2,500 per week (Ojeda 1987). Increasingly, Almonteños are also able to rent these houses during the spring and fall, as tourists visiting the National Park of Doñana are in need of lodgings. The Rocío is only one kilometre from the park's main entrance and Information Centre. During the winter months, these same houses may be rented to migrant strawberry pickers, this time for as low as 30,000

Figure 1.5 Many tourists are attracted to the camaraderie characteristic of 'backstage' celebrations occurring at the shrine. This young girl dances 'Sevillanas' with fellow villagers inside the semi-private confines of her pueblo's confraternity house located in El Rocío.

Figure 1.6 Makeshift stands, such as these, which sell both
regional food and drink as well as tourist souvenirs, are one example of the
commercialisation occurring in close proximity to the shrine.

pesetas per month, or approximately U.S.$300 (Bernard 1990). Finally, while most Almonteños tend to occupy these houses at the shrine during the summer months, using them as second residences, there are some owners who have begun to rent their homes to tourists who want to spend their summer vacation at the beach resort of Matalascañas, some seventeen kilometres to the south.

Other construction has also continued at an unbridled pace at El Rocío. Upon leaving the sanctuary one is assaulted by an array of bars, *chiringuitos* (makeshift restaurants), and souvenir stands. The municipal council of Almonte charges these commercial establishments by the square metre for the rental of this space. Some pilgrims find this conglomeration near the shrine offensive. Others are not offended but do complain about the high prices charged by the merchants. Pilgrims argue that these stands are there for the convenience of the tourists and for the profit of certain Almonteños. The majority of pilgrims do not eat out while at the shrine. They bring a week's worth of provisions along with them and prepare meals and drinks in their respective Casa de la Hermandad (Confraternity House).

The *romería* to the shrine of El Rocío during the Pentecost is one of the most important celebrations in village life in the communities of Marisol, Pilas, and Villamanrique, villages in the *comarca* in which I have conducted fieldwork. For Marisoleños, the villagers whom I know best, it is both the Virgin's brief removal from the sanctuary and her entrance into public space, combined with their ancestor's customary participation in the celebration of this rite, which compels their attendance at the shrine year after year. For Marisoleños, sacred and secular practices are intertwined, as during this week of festivities communal eating and drinking are interspersed with singing and dancing *sevillanas* in praise of their Virgin. However, these villagers' forms of popular religiosity are not entirely compatible with the growing presence of tourists and other spectators at the shrine, who, instead of undertaking the arduous camino, arrive by aeroplane, bus, or car (see Crain 1992). For Marisoleños, these outsiders are individuals whose families and communities do not have a history of making a pilgrimage to this site. The arrival of the latter group is prompted more by television coverage or by tourist guidebooks than by village tradition or religious motivation.

With the massification of the Pentecostal *romería* in recent decades, many pilgrims now find that they are a minority at the shrine, overwhelmed in a larger sea of tourist-spectators. During many of the organised events, such as the famous midnight mass held on Sunday, the number of people partying at some distance from the shrine is much

Figure 1.7 A close-up shot of the Virgin of the Dew dressed as a shepherdess.
This particular costume is only worn every seven years during 'el traslado' in which
the sacred female figure is taken from the sanctuary and transported to the parish
church in the town of Almonte.

43

greater than the number of pilgrims attending mass. Pentecost is celebrated on the seventh Sunday following Easter, falling in either the
month of May or June. This date coincides with one of the peak periods
of the tourist season in southern Spain, especially in nearby Seville, as
spring time is an especially popular time for tourists to visit, prior to the
onset of summer's scorching heat. The mass media and local tourist
offices have advertised the Pentecostal festivities at El Rocío as a colourful folklore and heritage rite. In such touristic literature, both Seville's
Feria de Abril (April Fair) and the Pentecost at El Rocío are labelled as
the local rites of spring par excellence, rites which contain the passion,
exuberance, and love of pageantry for which Andalusians are reputedly
famous (see Jacobs 1990).

Development Debated: Diverse Constituencies and Voices

While they are separate entities that are distinguishable analytically, the
three tourist sites of Almonte under consideration here must often be
studied in relation to one another, as diverse interest groups have marketed these sites jointly as a tourist package. As was demonstrated in the
case of the billboard that reads 'Welcome to the Paradise of Your
Dreams' as well as in the case of other touristic literature, Doñana, El
Rocío, and Matalascañas are represented as interchangeable sites. Furthermore, as will be demonstrated below, activities at one site may have
profound repercussions on activities at the other sites. Hence the importance of studying their interdependence.

Those promoting touristic development in the municipality of
Almonte include a combination of parties, both local and extra-local,
such as the head of the Junta of Andalusia, the past and present mayors
of Almonte (both affiliated with PSOE, the Socialist Party that presently
governs in Madrid), particular members of the city council of Almonte,
owners of many businesses in Almonte, personnel in the tourism office
in Matalascañas, many members of the founding brotherhood of the
Virgin of El Rocío in Almonte, building contractors based in Seville, as
well as international investors. In addition, individual Almonteños who
work in the tourist trade – for example as guides in Doñana, hotel workers in Matalascañas, as well as those who rent their houses in El Rocío –
also lend their support to touristic endeavours. Those promoting tourist
ventures present them both as a panacea for a stagnating agrarian economy and as a deterrent to high unemployment rates. Figures from 1988

indicated that twenty-eight percent of the economically active population of Almonte was unemployed (Bernard 1990: 151). According to the rhetoric of the pro-development sector, these touristic ventures offer an alternative to seasonal employment in the agricultural sector and they will continue to provide jobs, thus guaranteeing the future security of the municipality.

It has largely been individual members of Almonte's middle, as well as its small upper, class that have benefited from the tourist trade. Poor Almonteños, such as itinerant workers, *jornaleros* (agricultural day labourers), and small agriculturalists, as well as many individuals from neighbouring municipalities in close proximity to Almonte, such as Villamanrique, Pilas, Marisol, and Hinojos, have been marginalised by the development process as it has unfolded at these three sites. Resentment has stirred among the latter group of villagers as Almonte is visibly more prosperous than it was a decade ago, with new homes, commercial establishments, and industries springing up everywhere (see Murphy 1990). Furthermore, individuals from these five villages traditionally enjoyed rights of passage both to the Coto of Doñana and to the shrine of the Virgin of El Rocío. Today, many of these villagers experience touristic developments at these sites as a conflict over space, as the said developments have brought greater privatisation, encroaching upon spaces that villagers regard as rightfully theirs. The latter view the growth of touristic ventures, and the greater state and international intervention in the area that has accompanied tourism, as restricting their access to the area's resources, both sacred and secular.

How have these villagers formulated their resistance to the tourist gaze and to touristic interventions at Doñana, at Matalascañas, and at El Rocío? Opposition to touristic developments has been couched in a variety of overlapping idioms: economic, religious as well as a discourse of localism that privileges village autonomy. As mentioned previously, Almonteños demand preferential treatment for all tourist-related jobs in the municipality. Consequently, few of the individuals who reside in villages that border Doñana, but lie outside the boundaries of the municipality of Almonte, can obtain jobs in Almonte's tourist trade, or receive any other economic benefits from this trade. Poor and illiterate Almonteños are also less likely to acquire jobs in this sector as these positions often require new skills or at least some training.

Foreigners, particularly those from other European countries, as well as individuals from other parts of Spain, are frequent visitors to the National Park of Doñana. Villagers' perceptions of Doñana's resources and the manner in which they should be utilised are at variance with those of tourists and those promoting tourist ventures. Many villagers complain that with the increased presence of tourists, new forms of legislation have been imposed, such as the establishment of visitation hours for the park, which discriminate against them by limiting their access to the *Coto*. For example, one villager from Villamanrique commented on the advent of tourism:

> We 'Manriqueños' do not think of Doñana as a park. What is a park? A park is for *forasteros* [outsiders] who come here as tourists. They take photos of the wildlife, go hiking and ride horseback during their vacation. Well for us, Doñana is not a park, it is 'the Coto' [hunting ground] and it is our Coto, to boot. All of the pueblos that you see around here have always lived from the Coto. If the Coto dies, our pueblos will die, too … Unlike some of the Almonteños, we don't see the profits from these forasteros. Those in favour of this tourism, certain Almonteños, the government, and now even the Europeans, they want to dress Doñana up like a woman, and show her off to all the new visitors. They begin by creating all these new rules.

In this context, 'forasteros' refers to individuals from pueblos outside the *comarca*, both to foreign visitors and to visitors from other parts of Spain. Opposition couched in an idiom of localism is also evident in this man's remarks regarding more encompassing political bodies, as from this villager's vantage point, local residents clearly do not consider themselves to be 'Europeans', or members of more inclusive communities, such as the EU. Traditions of village autonomy in Andalusia lead many villagers to fear the intervention both of a distant state and of the European Union in local affairs (see Pitt-Rivers 1974; Mitchell 1987). Rather than ensuring their rights to an area which they once regarded as their own backyard, villagers regard such hierarchical political systems as potentially disenfranchising them, as Doñana becomes the 'patrimony' not only of the Spanish nation, but of Europe, and eventually, of all of mankind.[5]

To date, the resistance of villagers in Villamanrique and Marisol to the new regulatory measures that define Doñana as a park and which promote activities such as ecological tourism, include oppositional practices, such as furtive hunting and the collection of wild vegetables in Doñana, as well as sneaking their animals into the pastures of the *Coto* at night. In early January 1993, the constituency opposed to Doñana's privileged status both as a park and as a protected nature reserve expanded to include a new faction: both large and small ranchers in Almonte. Ecological tourism, increasing perceived as a foreign discourse articulated and regulated by *técnicos* (technocrats), associated with the central government in Madrid and with the European Commission in Brussels, was rejected by these Almonteños when it conflicted with their perceived interests. During a period of prolonged drought, the latter demanded access to the Doñana's pasture lands and water for their cattle. Prior to the establishment of the park in 1969, local livestock had traditionally utilised some of this area for grazing. On 2 January 1993, approximately 200 Almonteños cut the wire fences, and with their horses and cattle, invaded the park. Before members of the Spanish national guard forced them to leave, the ranchers called for attention to their needs as well as the resignation of Jesús Casas, the park's director (Molina 1993). Negotiations between the Almonte ranchers, park personnel, the mayor of Almonte, and the head of the Junta of Andalusia continued for the next few weeks. By late January 1993, an agreement was reached in which local ranchers would be allowed to graze their cattle in specified areas of the park (Ordaz 1993: 29).

The resistance both of certain Almonteños and of other villagers of the *comarca* to the transformations accompanying touristic developments are also couched in religious terms, terms that are not easily disentangled from the preceding economic arguments. Villagers' access to the natural resources of Doñana as a means of subsistence, and their access to sacred spaces, such as the shrine at El Rocío, are increasingly jeopardised by the privatising initiatives supported by many ruling institutions in Almonte. In contrast to those Almonteños who focus their attention primarily on the site of the shrine, pilgrims of the *comarca* consider the entire area radiating out from the sanctuary, traversed historically by a dense network of pilgrimage routes, as a sacred space. For the latter group this landscape and its resources are laden with symbolic importance. Villagers argue that devotion to the land and to the Virgin are one and the same, and they back this assertion by referring to popular accounts of the Virgin's appearance as an integral part of the local landscape. According to these accounts, the Virgin's origins are tied to those of the humble folk of the *comarca*, as it was either a hunter or a shepherd who first discovered her hidden in an olive tree in the wilds of the marismas.[6] When an attempt was made to transport the icon to the town of Almonte, in order that the local authorities might witness this miraculous discovery, the Virgin outwitted them, and escaped back to her place of origin: the marshlands. While the founding brotherhood of Almonte now dismisses these folk accounts as myth in favour of the historical facts recorded in official documents, villagers steadfastly cling to these accounts, drawing on them to assert their demands both for equal participation in the cult of the Virgin of El Rocío and for a modicum of control over the management of resources at nearby Doñana.

Villagers' resentment towards the touristic transformations underway at El Rocío and in the outlying areas of Matalascañas and Doñana are fuelled by the belief that this land really belongs to the Virgin, and that local inhabitants, including the Almonteños, are merely its custodians. Following this logic, the shrine and a much wider surrounding area, is not readily available for anyone to commercialise at will. Thus, villagers contest the new definitions of the Pentecost at El Rocío, which market it as a colourful heritage rite, a media spectacle performed for absent television viewers, and finally, as a venue for cultural tourism (see Crain 1992).

As oppositional practices, Marisoleños, Villamanriqueños, as well as pilgrims from the community of Pilas have established their own set of counter-rituals in alternative spaces in which the tourist's gaze is circumscribed. While many of these pilgrims continue to attend the *romería* of Pentecost at the shrine, they now give priority to other ritual activities over which they have greater control, such as the camino. One elderly pilgrim from Pilas claimed that in the past the Pentecostal celebration at the shrine resembled a large family reunion in which everyone shared their food and wine. Increasingly, however, with over one million people concentrated at the shrine during Pentecost, it is the six days that pilgrims spend on the road, travelling with their respective brotherhoods to and from the sanctuary, that provides the sense of camaraderie and intimacy that villagers hold in high esteem. Thus, some pilgrims have expressed their desire to lengthen the camino portion of this *romería* and to establish 'restrictive communities' that would keep the participation of tourists and the media to a minimum.

Other pilgrims now refuse to attend mass events, such as the Pentecost, at the shrine. As an alternative, they demonstrate their devotion to the Virgin throughout the course of the year. They undertake minor pilgrimages to the sanctuary with family members, often to fulfil a vow, thereby thanking the Virgin for a favour granted. These pilgrims concentrate more on the sacred as an aspect of everyday life rather than as an event to be celebrated once a year at the shrine. Attention to the sacred in everyday life is primarily women's work. For example, in Marisol as well as in Villamanrique, it is village women who create altars for the Virgin of El Rocío, both in their homes and in the public plazas. When masses are held in honour of the Virgin of El Rocío, every fourth Sunday in the parish church, it is the women of Marisol who clean the church and bring new flowers to adorn the *simpecado* (the village's embroidered banner which bears the emblem of the Virgin of El Rocío).

In the eyes of neighbouring villagers of the comarca, there is one final rite which demonstrates the Almonteños' ability to truly honour and respect the Virgin. This rite is the *traslado*. This event restores the pilgrims' faith in the Almonteños, thus providing both the founding brotherhood and the municipal council with the legitimation necessary to assure their control over this cult, a cult whose followers now greatly outnumber the population of Almonte.

The *traslado* is a *romería* that occurs every seven years and is only fourteen hours in duration. The archives of the founding brotherhood of Almonte cite 1607 as the earliest recorded date in which a *traslado* was celebrated. It currently begins at approximately 4 p.m. on 19 August and continues until the next morning. This pilgrimage draws attention away from the comarca and underscores the Virgin's role as protectress of Almonte. Dressed as a shepherdess, during the afternoon of the nineteenth, the Virgin is carried out of the sanctuary, veiled, and hoisted onto the backs of the Almonteño youth. A long procession of followers preceding and trailing her, both on foot and mounted on top of tractors, accompanies the Virgin for some fifteen kilometres until she reaches her final destination in the town of Almonte. At dawn, when the first rays of light appear in the sky, there is an elaborate unveiling ceremony in the central plaza.[7] Shortly thereafter, the Virgin is placed in the parish church of Almonte, where she remains for the next ten months, in order to bestow grace on this pueblo.[8] The following spring the icon is returned to the shrine of El Rocío, prior to the celebration of the Pentecost.

Unlike the Pentecostal pilgrimage, the Almonteños exercise full control over this event. The *traslado* is deemed to be first and foremost a celebration of the Virgin of El Rocío, in her capacity as the patroness of Almonte. Members of the eighty-five affiliated brotherhoods as well as pilgrims from the comarca, are encouraged to join the Almonteños in this overnight procession on an individual basis. However, none of the brotherhoods can participate in an officially organised fashion, nor hold any positions as ritual specialists, as they are permitted to do during the Pentecost. Despite the restrictions on their participation, members of the affiliated brotherhoods, as well as pilgrims of the *comarca* comment positively on the sombre and sacred character of this event. They often contrast it with the *romería* at Pentecost, which is awash with commercialism. Unlike Pentecostal festivities, there are no rowdy parties, nor excessive drinking, and souvenir stands and *chiringitos* are not in evidence.

If the Pentecostal *romería* bears a certain resemblance to a media spectacle performed for outsiders, the *traslado* constitutes its antithesis. Among a crowd of some 320,000 pilgrims accompanying the *traslado* of August 1991, I encountered only two individuals who could be classified as tourists. Similarly, when compared to the Pentecost, the presence of the media was limited. At the sanctuary, before dusk, I encountered an amateur French camera crew, filming both the Virgin and pilgrims, before the all-night procession to Almonte began. For the majority of pilgrims who participate, the *traslado* represents an event for 'insiders', in which a spirit of fraternity reigns (see Boissevain 1992). In August of 1991, the crowd consisted primarily of Almonteños as well as other devotees, the latter drawn both from neighbouring pueblos of the comarca and from the two closest provincial capitals, Seville and Huelva.

Taking place in the excruciating summer heat of mid-August, the *traslado* is a *romería* for die-hard pilgrims. It demands perseverance and discipline to withstand the elevated temperatures, which may surpass 110 degrees fahrenheit. Consequently, much of this event, including the procession from the shrine to Almonte, occurs at night, when the heat subsides somewhat. Old-time pilgrims laugh and say that the heat makes the tourists wilt and keeps them far away. During the night-long procession it is possible for Almonteños as well as villagers of the *comarca* to walk close to the Virgin, as neither television cameramen nor obtrusive tourists block the pilgrim's access to the Virgin. What are other factors that presently seem to deter cultural tourists? Unlike the Pentecost at El Rocío, the *traslado* receives neither financial support nor publicity from a secular institution, such as the Junta of Andalusia, nor is it mentioned in any of the tourist literature. Newspaper coverage of the *traslado* is not national, but is confined to a limited number of Andalusian papers of the comarca. In addition, both the night sky and the great amount of dust that accumulates affect the visibility of the Virgin (the icon is covered with a protective cape throughout the fifteen kilometre *romería*). These conditions make it difficult for tourists with ordinary photographic equipment to get good pictures of this event. Similarly, the *traslado* necessitates movement; pilgrims must walk at a rapid pace to keep up with the Virgin, a factor which is not particularly appealing to many tourist spectators. Finally, the ephemerality of this event, its relatively short duration when compared to the week-long festivities of the Pentecost, deters large crowds.

Conclusion

During the past two decades diverse interest groups have promoted three different tourist sites in the municipality of Almonte. These groups present tourism as the salvation of the local economy, potentially resolving unemployment in a rural municipality that until recently constituted an isolated corner of the European periphery. As the findings in this case study indicate, some of the local strategies formulated in Almonte presently converge with the broader goals elaborated by the Spanish tourism industry, in which greater attention has been directed towards 'multifaceted tourism' and visits to 'interior Spain', with beach resorts serving as only one, of a wider range of centres of touristic attraction.

These new orientations in touristic practice, emerging both in Almonte and in other parts of Spain, can be fruitfully examined in light of Aeries (1990) analysis of changing trends in the tourism industry in the contemporary postmodern era. Extending from the decade of the 1960s up to the present, this period has been characterised by broad cultural and economic changes (see Harvey 1990; MacCannell 1992). For example, the service sector has undergone enormous expansion during this era, particularly in First World societies, with consumption partially supplanting production, as the economic *modus operandi*. At the same time, productive activities have been increasingly relocated to Developing World centres. According to Aeries, touristic practices are best analysed as part of this expanded field of consumption, with contemporary trends in tourism reflecting these broader cultural and economic shifts. Another key indicator of this shift is a movement away from earlier patterns of mass tourism. Today, touristic experiences are increasingly diversified, offering a vast array of personalised services, which are tailored to the tastes of different clienteles within a stratified tourist market.

A desire both to diversify touristic sites and to attract more affluent segments of the entire tourist market has characterised recent development planning in the municipality of Almonte. Institutions, such as the European Union as well as the national commission headed by Manuel Castells and backed by the Junta of Andalusia, maintain that financial dependence on tourism can be increased, and that, if properly managed, high-quality tourism is compatible with the conservation of the environment. However, such development policy has received mixed support in Almonte.

Additional constituencies, such as Andalusian environmental organisations and other residents of the comarca, also have reasons for contesting the endorsements of touristic ventures in the municipality. Villagers from neighbouring communities, such as Marisol, Pilas, and Villamanrique might currently hold more favourable views with respect to these ventures, if they had been able to obtain a greater share of the proceeds from tourism. As this has not been the case, many villagers claim that the transformations accompanying touristic developments have had a negative impact on their lives and the welfare of their communities. Their access to spaces, such as Doñana, where they once procured many of their subsistence needs, is now subject to new regulations. Similarly, massification as well as privatising tendencies at the shrine of El Rocío, partially the result of touristic developments, have hindered these villagers' access to the sacred, often making a travesty of their own understandings regarding the manner in which the Virgin should be worshipped. During the Pentecost at the shrine pilgrims are alienated by what they perceive to be a 'selling of culture', a practice condoned by certain Almonteños, that has resulted both in the over-commercialisation of this event as well as the presence of the media and enormous crowds. In contrast to the *traslado*, during the Pentecost pilgrims now constitute a minority at the shrine and the sense of conviviality they once experienced at this site has diminished. These villagers counter touristic transformations at Doñana with oppositional practices that defy Doñana's redefinition as a park. Similarly, they give less priority to Pentecostal celebrations at the shrine of El Rocío and have formed rituals in alternative spaces in which the tourist's gaze is circumscribed. For these villagers, it is their participation in acts, such as the *traslado* and the *camino*, as well as their affirmation of the sacred in everyday life, which restores a sense of intimacy and community that is now largely absent at the shrine.

With respect to those touristic developments in the municipality of Almonte which may potentially harm Doñana, members of various Andalusian as well as national environmental organisations have also voiced their doubts regarding the recommendations of the Castells' commission; recommendations which have also received support from the Spanish government. Environmental groups have opposed plans for the construction of a luxury hotel at the shrine, and have drawn attention to the manner in which the massification of El Rocío has resulted in the annual dumping of some 25,000 tons of garbage in the nearby park of Doñana ('La Asociación' *ABC* 1990: 39; Rivera 1991: 26). Although arguing from a vantage point quite different from that of Almonte's invading ranchers, these groups also question the promotion of ecological tourism. They ask whether it really constitutes a viable alternative and maintain that this form of leisure may also overtax Doñana's nonrenewable resources (*Punto de Vista* 1992).

NOTES

1. An earlier version of this article was delivered at the panel European Reactions to the Tourist Gaze, at the second meeting of the European Association of Social Anthropology in Prague, Czechoslovakia, in August 1992. It is based on fieldwork in Andalusia undertaken for a period of twenty-four months, between May 1989 and August 1992. The research was supported by two post-doctoral grants from the Wenner-Gren Foundation for Anthropological Research in New York City. I am most grateful to Wenner-Gren for their support of this project. In addition, I thank Jeremy Boissevain and Tom Selwyn for their comments regarding revisions of this publication.

2. In Andalusia, a regional network of rural lodgings as well as refurbished *cortijos* (extensive estates traditionally belonging to the rural aristocracy) is presently being established which will facilitate 'interior tourism'. Functioning along the lines of bed and breakfast inns in the United Kingdom, the Andalusian network will begin offering its services during the summer of 1992 (see 'Constituida', *ABC*, 1991, 77).

3. In 1991, despite the preoccupations of the founding brotherhood of Almonte regarding the expansion of the Pentecostal *romería* at El Rocío, the total number of affiliated brotherhoods had risen to eight-five.

4. While approximately 30,000 people attended the *romería* through the end of the 1950s, by 1990 it had attracted a crowd of one million (see Murphy 1990).

5. Political graffiti, seen in August of 1991, provided an ironic local commentary regarding the increasing control over the *Coto's* fate now exercised by governing bodies in Madrid. A road sign near the shrine of El Rocío, signalling both the distance and directions to the Coto of Doñana, was replaced by the spray-painted message: 'Coto de Felipe: 2 kilometres'. While the new message most surely made reference to the fact that the vacation residence of Felipe González, President of Spain, is located inside the grounds of Doñana, it also made an oblique reference to the interventions of the national government in 'local affairs'.

6. Competing folk accounts regarding the discovery of the Virgin also fuel the debate regarding which brotherhood and village should exercise control over this cult. While both accounts maintain that the Virgin was found in the *marismas*, one widely circulating account claims that she was discovered by a man from the pueblo of Villmanrique, whereas the alternative account maintains that the man was from Almonte.

7. See Driessen (1992) for a discussion of the rites, symbolism, and lore associated with daybreak in southern Spain.

8.   From the seventeenth to nineteenth centuries, the Virgin was brought to Almonte on an irregular basis, (i.e., not every seven years), during times of need. For example, she was brought to alleviate an epidemic, such as cholera, as well as during periods of drought and hunger. In 1809, she was brought to Almonte and successfully protected the town against an attack by Napoleonic troops, who occupied Spain (Infante-Galán 1971).

REFERENCES

'La Asociación Ecologista Agaden Denuncia La Construcción de un Gran Hotel en El Rocío', *ABC,* 12 May 1990: 39.

'Montaner Presenta Una Nueva Imagen de Andalucía para Recuperar el Turismo Aleman', *ABC,* 23 April 1991: 77.

'Constituida la Red de Alojamientos Rurales Andaluzas', *ABC,* 23 April 1991: 77.

Amavizca, E. 'González y el Presidente Europeo, en el Parque: Delors Afirma que la CE Asumirá su Responsabilidad para Proteger Doñana', *El País,* 12 May 1992: 27.

Archives of the Hermandad Matríz, Almonte, Andalusia.

Bernard, C. 'Agriculture et Tourisme Sur la Côte Atlantique Andalouse: La Costa de la Luz de Huelva.' *Mélanges de la Casa de Velázquez* Tome 26, no. 3 (1990): 151-73.

Boissevain, J. 'Tourism as Anti-Structure', in C. Giordano et al., eds, *Kultur Anthopologisch. Ein Festschrift Fur Ina-Maria Greverus* , Notizen Nr. 30, Frankfurt: University of Frankfurt, 1989.

_____, 'Ritual, Play and Identity: Changing Patterns of Celebration in Maltese Villages', *Mediterranean Studies* vol. 1 (1991): 87-100.

_____, 'Introduction', in J. Boissevain ed., *Revitalizing European Rituals,* London: Routledge, 1992.

Comelles, J. M. 'Rocío', in Jesús Contreras, Ubaldo Martínez Veiga, Isidoro Moreno and Joan Prat eds, *Antropología de los Pueblos de España,* Madrid: Taurus, 1991.

Crain, M. 'Pilgrims, Yuppies, and Media Men: The Transformation of an Andalusian Pilgrimage', in J. Boissevain ed., *Revitalizing European Rituals,* London: Routledge, 1992.

'Denuncia Sobre la Construcción de Un Knave Hotel en El Rocío', *El Pads,* Andalusian edition, 12 May 1990: 3.

Driessen, H. 'Celebration at Day Break in Southern Spain', in J. Boissevain ed., *Revitalizing European Rituals,* London: Routledge, 1992.

Falassi, A. 'Festival: Definition and Morphology', in A. Falassi ed., *Time Out of Time. Essays on the Festival*, Albuquerque: University of New Mexico Press, 1987.

Harvey, D. *The Condition of Postmodernity: An Inquiry into the Origins of Cultural Change*, London: Blackwell, 1990.

Infante-Galán, Juan. *Rocío: La Devoción Mariana de Andalucía*, Seville: Editorial Prensa Española, 1971.

'Informe Sobre Los Problemas del Parque Nacional de Doñana', *Boletín Informativo del Medio Ambiente*, N. 1, 1977: 191-218.

Jacobs, M. *A Guide to Andalusia*, London: Viking, 1990.

MacCannell, D. *Empty Meeting Grounds: The Tourist Papers*, London: Routledge, 1992.

Mitchell, T. *Violence and Piety in Spanish Folklore*, Philadelphia: University of Pennsylvania Press, 1987.

Molina, M. 'Vecinos de Almonte Invaden con Coches y Ganado Zonas de Nidificación del Parque Nacional de Doñana', *El País*, Barcelona edition, 4 January 1993: 1; 23.

Moreno, I. *Cofradías y Hermandades Andaluzas: Estructura, Simbolismo e Identidad*, Sevilla: Biblioteca de la Cultura Andaluza. 1985.

Murphy, M. 'Class and Costume in an Andalusian Pilgrimage', paper presented at the annual meeting of the American Anthropological Association, New Orleans, Louisiana, 2 December 1990.

Ojeda Rivera, J. F. *Organización del Territorio en Doñana y Su Entorno Proximo (Almonte). Siglos XVIII-XX*. Madrid: Ministerio de Agricultura, Instituto Nacional para La Conservación de la Naturaleza, 1987.

Ordaz, P. 'Lo Verde Vende: La Oposición Reclama en sus Programas la Paralización de Costa Doñana', *El País*, Andalusian edition, 10 June 1990: 2.

_____. 'El Ganado de Almonte Podra Pastar en el Parque de Doñana', *El País*, Barcelona edition, 22 January 1993.

Pitt-Rivers, J. *The People of the Sierra*, Chicago: University of Chicago Press, 1974.

'Reportaje Sobre La Comisión de Castells y El Parque Nacional de Doñana', *Punto de Vista*, television programme broadcast on TV 1 of Madrid, 12:45 a.m., 3 April 1992.

Rivera, A. 'Defensa de Un Territorio Acosada', *El País*, Barcelona edition, 22 December 1991: 26.

Urry, J. *The Tourist Gaze: Leisure and Travel in Contemporary Societies*, London: Sage, 1990.

2. Tourism and Self-Consciousness in a South Spanish Coastal Community[*]

Antonio Miguel Nogués Pedregal

> 'The camera and tourism are two of the
> uniquely modern ways of defining reality.'
> (D. Horne)

*I*n this chapter I will discuss increasing self-consciousness among hosts as a reaction to tourism in Zahara de los Atunes (population 1,183 in 1991), drawing on ethnographic data recorded between February 1991 and January 1993.[1] I will deal with those cultural manifestations which I consider to be representative of a general process of increasing self-consciousness.

Description of the Village

Zahara de los Atunes can scarcely be found on a map. To reach Zahara you have to know exactly where it is. You cannot simply pass by on the way to another location. Lying by the shore between two sierras and near the mouth of Cachón River where it empties into the Atlantic Ocean, there are only two roads which take you there. But you first have to see the traffic signs! This isolated community is a *pedanía*[2] of the municipality of

Barbate in Cádiz, the southern-most province of Spain. Closer to Africa than to Cádiz (64 km north), Zahara could be defined as a 'typical' Andalusian coastal village. Completely forgotten by national or regional institutions, it was 'discovered' for tourism when three German horsemen rode across Spain in the late 1950s.

Of the two roads that nowadays reach the village, the better known – the traditional one, built in 1916 – goes east to meet the N-340 from Cádiz to Málaga, through ten curving kilometres. It crosses La Zarzuela, a small hamlet (population 213) under the administrative jurisdiction of the municipality of Tarifa but belonging to the parish of Our Lady del Carmen, the patron Virgin of Zahara de los Atunes, as well as of fishermen.

Zahara is nine kilometres south of Barbate, the principal town of the municipality. There is nothing in between but a small military post where troops lodge while on manoeuvres in the Sierra del Retín. The Sierra was expropriated by the Ministry of Defence in 1981.[3] This fact was not important to Zahareños until recently when they became aware of the economic possibilities for touristic exploitation.

Communication with Barbate was traditionally by boat. The town lies by the Barbate River, which clearly separated the city from Zahara. In the past Zahareños had to walk along the coast – the shortest method – or along the dirt-road which ended at the military post, until they reached the river shore.[4] Once there, they had to boat across the narrow but deep entrance of the river. As the elderly still remember, 'We didn't go too much to Barbate. Why should we? What's in there? … Nothing but flies and dirtiness. It's like nowadays, I just go there once a month if at all.'

However, in 1972 there was a crucial investment in the infrastructure: a bridge was built over Barbate River. This new connection joined Barbate with its all but forgotten pedanía. Though the relations between these localities were not strengthened as might have been expected, the bridge improved Zahara's contacts with the outside world, and an emerging mass-tourism crossed it.

Before this second road was built in 1972, there was another one that crossed the rocky Sierra. Though it is still open, it is not usable due to damage caused by military vehicles and explosions.

Despite this much improved communication, a general perception of isolation persists among hosts as well as among guests in this coastal village. This particular point is underlined by the fact that Zahara is not a totally manufactured tourist environment. The image of the rather backward community offered to tourists is the one recognised by some groups of Zahareños when they state that, 'Well, it is true that this [the village] has changed, but it is no less true that there is still a lot to do here.'

In this sense, tourist brochures help us to understand guests' interpretations of Zahara:

> Enjoy the South's LAST paradise, RIGHT at the sea shore. If Atlanterra has conserved its original state, it is due to the fact that, fundamentally, it has remained on the margins of the major touristic zones of the Costa del Sol and the Bay of Cádiz, and that the primary road (A-road-carretera nacional) which unites the fore mentioned zones is at quite a distance from here. And, of course, if we wanted it to remain so, then one should keep the secret so it doesn't become fashionable. Do not tell anybody where you rest! (Original in English)

There is no industry nearby, and Zahara is not near any commercial town where commuting could modify the daily activities. Zahara has no economic external forces other than the seasonal or weekend arrival of tourists. The emphasis here on this general perception of isolation does not undervalue other cultural influences such as education, military service, television, or accessibility.[5] However, the reality of isolation perceived by the actors influences their self-consciousness.

A Question of Numbers: Is it a Cultural Question?

In order to be able to interpret tourism adequately as a cultural phenomenon, Smith (1977) and Cohen (1972) have suggested certain taxonomies. Though this is not the place to discuss their limitations, I will use them to explain the type of tourism and tourists that come to Zahara.

To define who is a tourist is not easy (Pearce 1982: 33). As MacCannell notes, 'so many tourists claim that they are not tourists themselves and that they dislike and avoid other tourists' (Crick 1989: 307).[6] Here we face one among many other paradoxes: while the guests are aware of being tourists (Feifer in Urry 1990: 100-101), and try not to act like tourists, they cannot evade the condition of being outsiders for villagers, as shown in tourist complaints: 'I know they charge more because we are not from here [Zahara], but what else can we do? I know that the people from here pay less than us'.[7]

On the other hand, from the hosts' perspective, the image of a tourist does not represent each individual but the whole, since for Zahareños a tourist is any person strange to the village cultural environment. In short, as the number of tourists progressively increases, tourists cease to be individuals and become stereotypes. This phenomenon is very important, for it not only generates a distinct host-guest relationship, but also creates a new internal social network: the opposition *we-they*. Tourism brings into the community the idea of otherness as an additional social classification, and this gives rise to a new conception of community.

Nonetheless, in Zahara it is important to distinguish the pre-bridge period (up to around 1973) from the post-bridge one. In the village most tourists are Spaniards who in the post-bridge period stay either in their own second residences or in rented houses.

1. Pre-Bridge Period:

Unfortunately, it is almost impossible to obtain even an estimated number of tourists for the pre-bridge period. Besides some historical descriptions of Zahara, the earliest touristic approach to the site was that of those first German adventurers:

> In a small village by the sea [Zahara], a little way north [of Bolonia], it was impossible to find an inn, until a Señora felt sorry and offered us a room in her house. 'In fact, there is another Señor in this room' she said, 'a smuggler. But just for one night you can stay here without any problem'. (Münchner 1960:16)

After their first trip to the small village, two of the three riders decided to create a tourist route that circled the province of Cádiz. Searching for lost paradises and experiencing traditional cultures alive, they always stopped by Zahara on whatever route they followed. Hence, in the early 1960s there was only one common type of tourist who, travelling in small groups with a guide and riding horses along the coast, usually spent the night in labourers' houses.

Nobody in Zahara seems to know how all this developed into the tourist site that exists today. Nobody mentioned any causal connection between those Germans and the actual tourist masses that now cyclically overcrowd the village during July and August and some fine-weather weekends. Despite this patent lack of a cause and effect relation, older Zahareños say that 'they came riding horses and went up there', while they draw an imaginary path along the coast which finally ends 'up there', in the Sierra de la Plata (Silver Sierra). The riders bought that stony area and began to build their expensive houses. This settlement includes a tiny bay which became known as Bahía de los Alemanes (Bay of the Germans).[8]

This settlement brings the cause and effect relation to hosts' minds, as they often show in their discourse: 'That's for sure, everything began up there'. But what is 'everything'? Though hard to explain, 'everything' is the mass tourism which according to my analysis started after the bridge was built.

This apparent contradiction with the aforementioned non-existent causal connection reflects certain features of Zahara's tourism. On the one hand, nobody blames those three first horsemen for bringing the actual masses. On the other, 'everything began up there'. Logically, there is a clear evolution between the three Germans, their first settlement, and the touristic boom. However, there is a sharp and crucial separation between the German neighbours and the other tourists. The German settlement is considered to be situated at the periphery of the symbolic limits of the village; while the new tourist constructions, as well as the rented houses, are just within the village's very private space.

2. Post-Bridge period

When the bridge was opened, tourists crossed it. Yet within this period there are two different stages, divided by the opening of the four-star Hotel Atlanterra in 1983. During the first stage the seasonal residents of the *Urbanización Atlanterra* (90 percent wealthy Germans) were rarely seen in the village along with the few Spanish tourists who rented their summer houses from the Zahareños.

In that early phase tourism did not challenge the cultural basis of the community. Only the new *Supermarkt* (ger.) began to import some European supplies which were adopted by the Zahareños. These early tourists influenced the way the youth dressed and what could be bought in the new supermarket.

Nevertheless, the processual changes initiated and promoted by the earliest German riders are somehow bound up with the general situation of Spain under Franco. It is easy enough to make broad generalisations about those forty years in the recent history of Spain, but in reality the issue is extremely complex.

Zahara had a mixed economic base of fishing and agriculture. Modernisation during the 1950s involved rural mechanisation. As a consequence of this, emigration affected many villages in southern Spain.

Zahara was not an exception. Even the fishermen abandoned their jobs during the crisis in the 1970s. Two factors encouraged the collapse of this important Spanish sector: on the one hand, the structural crisis generated by the internal contradictions and the fishing policy: on the other, the consequences of Northern African restrictions on international fishing areas (González Laxe 1983:189).

However, population rates did not decrease as expected, for tourism arrived as farming became increasingly mechanised and landowners needed fewer workers. A nascent, small, tourist-oriented local commerce arose. Construction and care of the gardens of Atlanterra's German mansions was an escape, not only for peasants but also for fishermen. In 1970 the construction of two hotels started. One of them, the four-star Hotel Atlanterra, was opened in 1983. The other, due to financial irregularities, was never finished. Together with the package tours of the Hotel Atlanterra, an emerging mass tourism developed during the next ten years. The Hotel was opened and international tour-operators came to Zahara. Along with these, tourists from Seville and Madrid came seeking tranquillity on what appeared to be the last virgin coast in Spain. Though from a urban point of view it is stereotypically quiet, the locals disagree: '*Veraneantes* [summer people] invade our streets, and do not let children play football, for it is really dangerous.'

Figure 2.1 An example of environmentally irresponsible construction. Compare the traditional house style with those beside it.

Zahara's unique type of tourism is purely recreational. Tourists look for sun, sea, sand, and silence. This homogeneity does not, however, simplify tourist representation. Categorising the types of tourists during the last eleven years means taking into account that these types 'are the result of the interaction of the tourists with the destination area and its residents' (Mathieson and Wall 1982:20). This important correlation between both the dynamic and static elements of tourism makes possible an explanatory taxonomy of tourists in Zahara.

Using Cohen's concept, 64 percent are institutionalised, organised mass tourists whose travel is typified and planned by the package and who do not expect surprises (see Table 2.1); 15 percent are non-institutionalised 'drifters', who plan their trips alone: the camp-site tourist. However, the remaining 22 percent are national tourists whose accommodation depends on either a second residence or a rented house.[9]

Table 2.1 Touristic Types According to Their Accommodation

Type of Tourist	Percentage
Residential tourists with property	4.34
Residential tourists in a rented house	17.36
Camping tourists	14.79
Hotel & hostel tourists	63.50
N = 21.288	100.00

Source: Own Elaboration, 1991.[10]

These residential tourists look for tranquillity and familiarity, and remain within the environmental bubble of home. Hence they furnish their second residences, or bring with them to the rental house some personal possessions. They are predominantly families who came from Seville and Madrid. They stay from fifteen to thirty days on average. Though these tourists actually live among the local population, they do not integrate in the local life.

However, there are distinct subgroups: the German neighbour, the ever-present Sevillano, and the rental tourist who does not come very often. Each behaves and is treated differently.

There is a certain respect for the German neighbours 'up there', for they brought progress to the village. Some of those Germans even have nicknames that are phonetic corruptions of their difficult-to-pronounce German names. The *alemanes* (Germans) are even considered by Zahareños as a proud achievement. The presence of Europeans has created a sense of Europeanness that links them with the European Union and, therefore, makes them different from surroundings communities.[11] A Neighbours' Association's staff member noted:

> How many German [in this case, synonymous with Western European] cars have you seen in Barbate? [...] The tourism in Barbate is completely different to the one we have. There, it is the typical Sevillano who wastes all of their savings in renting an apartment and later ... they do not have money for anything else, so they spend the holidays eating sandwiches by the shore with the family.

Or this *chiringuitos* owner's commentary:[12]

> We don't like either 'black feet' [hippies] or *windsurferos* [windsurfing tourists]. That's O.K. for Tarifa [south of Zahara], but not here .... Here it is different for we have always had foreigners ... though now it is changing .... There are more apartments, and the people begin to buy them or rent them [...] now it is becoming more familiar than before.[13]

A glance at Tables 2.2 and 2.3 will illustrate this last verbal account. The term 'outsiders' or 'tourists' refers to all kind of tourists except the German 'neighbours'. From the Zahareños' perspective, the Germans who 'went up there' stayed there. Though as seen in Carnival, this cordial attitude is being displaced by a disrespectful one.

The other two sub-groups of residential tourist, namely the Sevillano and the rental tourist, though not extensively described, are the main target of local reactions. That is to say that their authoritarian and dominant behaviour is the principal complaint of the natives. 'They pay and they think all is theirs' perfectly summarises hosts feelings against veraneantes.

The Rise of Self-Consciousness

Tourism is changing the 'Mediterranean-way-of-life'. 'There is no time to reinforce either family or neighbourly ties' (Boissevain 1982:56). Everybody is busy in summer. The *temporada* (summer season) drives every single Zahareño crazy. This is perhaps the reason why all the older people keep saying that there is no longer a community. 'The people do not help each other as before. Nowadays everybody plays for themselves. Even me.', said one of my oldest informants. Nevertheless, I recorded some communal self-consciousness as a negative reaction to Spanish tourists. Given the incipient stage of residential tourism, the signs of

Table 2.2 Population Composition in the Summer Season.

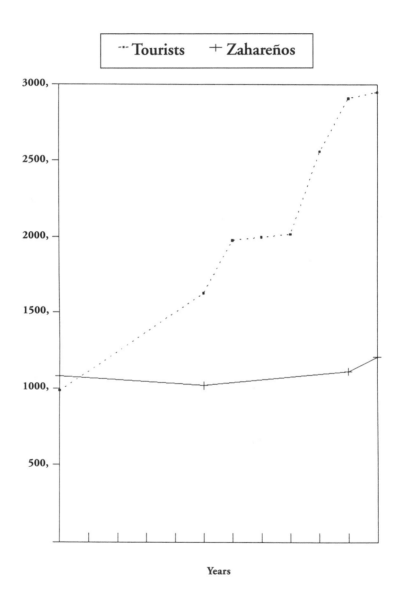

Table 2.3 Growth in House Construction in Zahara.

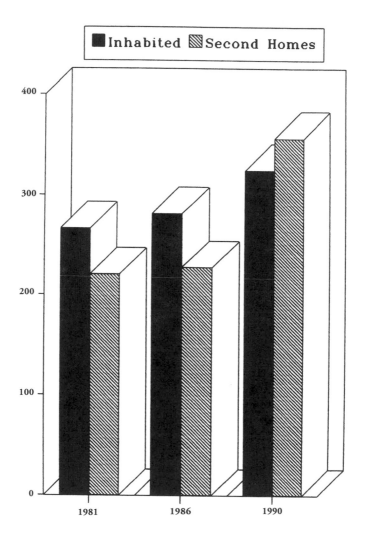

Source: Censo Población 1981, Padrón Habitantes 1986, and Censo Edificios y Locales 1990.

growing irritation are not yet institutionalised, mainly because the host-guest interactions seem not yet to be routinised.

Conceptualising institutionalisation as the process generated by the imposition of administrative rules that order and regularise popular cultural manifestations, I will classify some of the cultural expressions in Zahara in order to discern the impact of tourism on such manifestations, and therefore, on self-consciousness.

1. Festivals

Various scholars have noted the recent revitalisation of public celebrations throughout both industrialised and developing nations. Most of them identify secularisation, industrialisation, rationalisation of production, mass-media, among many others, as the factors accounting for the revival of rituals.[14] Though there are many circumstances that have affected communal attitudes, the demise of the post-war modernisation policy seems to be the most reasonable pattern to follow:

> A concern for a new concept, the 'quality of life', emerged [during the 1970s]. As a result of this reappraisal, the 'traditional' community-centred rural way of life, abandoned in the quest for modernisation, began to be rediscovered and idealised, along with an interest in the environment, organic foods, home brewing, and, of course, traditional rituals. (Boissevain 1992: 10)

Contributors to *Revitalizing European Rituals*, especially those interested in Southern Europe, highlight the return of emigrants as a central factor in this process of revitalisation. In the case analysed here emigration is not so representative. Emigration in Zahara has been neither quantitatively nor qualitatively significant. There is no clear connection between the decline of traditional festivities in the early 1960s and the moderate emigration flow of that period. Moreover, in Zahara the Golden Age of festivities coincides with the 1960s; yet, it also could be due to the personal involvement of the priest.

Whatever it was, during the next decade almost all religious festivities, including Carnival, vanished. As some studies have shown, the influence of the liturgical reforms of Vatican II, felt during the 1970s in Spain, generated a new more sober concept of religiosity. The Franciscans O.F.M., who implemented this new trend in Zahara, did not hesitate to eliminate popular worship by removing both ornaments and images from the church.

In any case, after Franco's death in 1975 Spain underwent a shift towards democracy. As a consequence of this political transition, the different cultures of Spain experienced a renewal of their celebrations and festivals, especially those linked with regional identity. Every single event was a political and cultural manifestation of the identity hidden for forty years. Zahara neither was nor is an exception. However, instead of returned emigrants or political interests, there are tourists searching for authenticity and local administrations becoming aware of this potential source of income. Independently of the motives of sponsoring institutions such as Andalusian nationalism, the people act and spontaneously ritualise the meaning of the celebration, allowing us to read the hosts' reactions for/against Others.

Does a festival become different depending on the degree to which it has been institutionalised? How much does the festival strengthen social identity? Let us take three examples, each one related to one mode of renewal.

A. *La Castañá.*[15]

This celebration is an *invented* one. That is, a completely new event, organised for the first time in November 1990 by the new Neighbours' Association. It is neither a commemorative feast nor a religious festivity, though it is held on All Saints Day (1 November). It is a purely communal celebration for 'insiders' only, meaning 'what could be called the nuclear community – its permanent residents. This excludes emigrants on holiday, visitors from nearby communities and tourists, whether national or foreign, and those who have moved from elsewhere.' (Boissevain 1992:12).[16]

The celebration is funded by the Neighbours' Association, which buys the chestnuts, soft drinks, and sherry, some individuals who provide coal, sweet-wine, and counters, and the school, which contributes the school courtyard.

Hence, the Castañá can be defined as a communal meal, where everyone can meet. I have been in the courtyard twice, and on each occasion was the only outsider. There is nothing to do but eat toasted chestnuts while talking with companions. However, not everybody meets at the Castañá. Top-families, even though they might have contributed with coal or counters, are not present. Despite this, the staff of the Association keep saying that 'we created the Castañá to bring people closer to each other, to bring them together.'

B. The Carnival.

This widespread celebration can be considered a *revitalised* one. It has had new energy injected into it. Under Franco's dictatorial regime Carnival was banned for several decades. This regulation mainly affected the southern province of Cádiz, where Carnivals were part of the cultural calendar of the people.

Carnival is said to be 'unique', 'the best', 'Zahara's main fiesta', despite the fact that *Virgen del Carmen*'s festivity is the most prominent of all. The ancient Carnival, though banned, was 'more fun', 'more intense', 'very much better'; that is, more playful.[17] The contrast between these adjectives and the former ones is illustrative, for it emphasises the existence of a clear division, or at least, of a degree of joy. Although 'whatever past time seems much better', as Jorge Manrique (Spanish poet, 1440-1478) wrote, I can recognise two periods: (1) when carnivals were banned by civil authorities, but still spontaneously celebrated by the people; (2) when democracy arrived, and popular festivals were organised and supported by local and regional institutions.

The classical Roman idea of *panes et circus* perfectly fits the institutional policy in Andalusia. Splendour and magnificence in festivals and celebrations are the finest election publicity; usually dressed and wrapped with a false interest in folk or legitimate culture. In Zahara inhabitants are very aware of this when they sing during Carnival: 'We don't need you [alluding to Barbate's mayor] to give us anything [ornaments and prizes for Carnival]. We don't need your money, to convince us.' (Carnival song, 1992)

Since political elections became a reason for cultural actions, the playful elements of the older Carnival became embedded in a highly ritualised parade, the outward aspect of the party. A sixty-year-old woman told me:

> Everything has changed, it is no longer the same, we all have to go in a line or on a stupid float ... you cannot have much fun now .... Well you can, but not as much as before. When Carnival was banned, once some friends of mine and I had to be taken out of the *cuartelillo* [Civil Guard post] by our fathers 'cause we were singing a funny song about something that happened to one of the *Trujillos* [landowners family].

Whereas people used to complain about the 'ritualisation' of Carnival, they have shifted their targets. While retaining social and political criticism, new themes and topics have arisen in the lyrics and costumes during the festival. Since the *chirigota*[18] was formally organised in 1989, tourists are very often represented in the songs. Though outsiders are not present during February in large numbers, and their lack of involvement is patent, their symbolic 'being' is shown not only in musical arrangements but also in costumes. An excellent materialisation of the concept of alienness among Zahareños was the costume that represented a UFO with a German licence plate during the 1992 Carnival.

The *we-they* opposition was musically displayed in a 1989 Carnival song:

> Just go to hell! // everybody who does not like the *levante* [19] // for this land has something // that it is not found anywhere else // a very strong little wind // and its name is *levante* // but a lot of people come here // and all they do is complain // and for those who reproach // I just say artistry // to those who do not like this wind // to reproach just go to any other place. [20]

Despite the evident references to both groups as being different, it must be said how important the levante is for the people of Zahara – just note the verse: 'that it is not found anywhere else'. As I have experienced, this wind, which reaches up to 100 kilometres per hour, is a cultural emblem. Constant allusion is made to it. To say that you hate the levante is taken as a statement that you do not like Zahara and, hence, Zahareños. The levante, along with an old sunken steam ship which foundered off-shore early this century; *El Palacio* (the Palace), the old *almadraba* [21] building, which was the first settlement in the area; the tall palm tree in the middle of the Palacio; and Miguel de Cervantes (1547-1616), who based part of his novel *La Ilustre Fregona* (1613) on his own experiences among the *pícaros* (almadraba's workers) at Zahara – these are thought by Zahareños to be the symbolic representations of the village.

Even though there is not a printed Carnival guide, no one misses any of the two major performances: the *Pregón* (inauguration speech) with the presentation of *La Reina del Carnaval* (Queen of the Carnival), and *La Cabalgata* (the parade).

C. *La Feria.*

This peculiar Andalusian festival is basically an evening entertainment. In Zahara, it was originally a festival held in honour of the village's patron on 16 July that was celebrated after the traditional procession had concluded. It was moved to the first week of August in 1969. Advertised as *Fiestas de Verano* (the Summer Festivals) in the leaflets and pamphlets, as if there were many such feasts, the current Feria is completely managed by the town hall. There is no feature of popular involvement left. The brochure is tightly ordered and scheduled, and consists of day-time activities such as sports competitions (tennis in the Hotel Atlanterra courtyards, football, and chess) and fishing contests.

At night during a feria there are very few special things to do other than drink or dance. The traditional dance of the area, the *chacarrá*, has been overwhelmed by the *sevillanas* (*flamenco*'s most famous and easy dance, originally from Seville). Aside from the above-mentioned organised ludic activities (which do not represent a 'play' dimension) there are also two recreational shows: (1) a flamenco dancing and singing contest where the locals are symbolically personified in the *cantaor/a* (singer), the *tocaor* (guitar player), the *bailaora* (dancer) and therefore staged to be gazed at; and (2) a *Miss Veraneante* election at 2 a.m. on Saturday (the third day of feria). Even the *pregón* (inauguration speech) is held at night and, incidentally, comes after the election of the *Reina Juvenil de las Fiestas* (Young Queen of the Summer Festivals) on the first day (Thursday) at 10 p.m.

With such a fixed agenda the result is a completely modern set of criteria demonstrating how authorities want others to see 'their others'. But there is also a clear division between generations: the youths opt for a new image, going to play tennis or chess; meanwhile, the older men ignore it and keep playing cards and dominoes at their traditional *tascas* (tiny bars). The older people cannot negotiate the new 'ritual'.

The Feria is not, from this point of view, an *innovative* revitalisation, for it does not innovate anything; nor is it a *retraditionalisation*, for no one had to learn anything from their elders; it is not even a *folklorised* festival, for Zahareños' involvement and participation is occasional – that is, the locals only take part in organised activities at the time and at the place where they are held with an entirely passive attitude. In any case, the festival was de-traditionalised when it was moved to August because it lost all of its original meaning, and was marketed as *the* traditional Feria of Zahara de los Atunes where guests can live out their touristic expectations.

Even so, there is no active reaction against this usurpation. There is only a common phrase left: 'the Feria is for young people, and for Sevillanos.'[22]

D. General comparison.

According to the degree of institutionalisation, la Castañá and the Carnival could be included in the more general trend towards the renewal of, in particular, winter festivals, though the Carnival has more town hall support (the parade and the queen election are good examples of this) than the Castañá. Note that while there is no official guide for these festivals, the programme of the Fiestas de Verano (1992) is a nine-page printed booklet with attractive colour pictures of Zahara, of the mayor heading his salutation, of the *pregonero*,[23] of the elected girls, of sponsors' advertisements, and one page of scheduled activities. Note too that while in Carnival there is an elected Reina del Carnaval (Queen of the Carnival), in Feria there is a Reina Juvenil de las Fiestas (Young Queen of the Summer Festivals).

Let us compare both elections. On the one hand, there is a Queen of the Carnival, who is usually a twenty to thirty year-old woman attired in

Figure 2.2 Traditional garments worn during the Carnival parade.

traditional garments. On the contrary, the Feria, which is organised and performed for outsiders and the younger generations, is represented in the teen-aged Young Queen of the Festivals, elected on the first day, and Miss Veraneante, elected at the weekend when the number of tourists increases. Their costumes are hard to distinguish from each other for they follow the tourists' models and manners of dressing.

Within the analytic framework of the degree of institutionalisation of festivals, the Feria scores highest. All elected summer girls (The Young Queen and her Ladies of Honour, *Damas de honor*) are sponsored by either the town hall, hotel owners, or restaurants. In 1992 and 1993 the Young Queen of the Summer Festivals was sponsored by Hotel Atlanterra.

On the other side of the coin is the uninstitutionalised Castañá. Invented in 1990, it can be analysed as an attempt to get away from the 'staged authenticity' (MacCannell 1989) of the Feria. If the Feria divides the community vertically according to the age of the actors, and the Carnival's social and political criticism has shifted towards new topics, the Castañá could be considered the recreation and performance of historical social divisions in Zahara.[24] Hence, the Castañá takes place in the 'backstage' of Zahara where the interactions between hosts and guests are minimised (MacCannell on Goffman's analyses, 1989:92).

While tourists look for sun, sea, sand, and silence, they are also interested in gazing upon 'living' museums,[25] for 'people increasingly seem attracted by representations of the "ordinary", of modest houses and of mundane forms of work' (Urry 1990: 130). However, this postmodern interest in the 'ordinary' is not reflected in the real touristic experience, since locals represent their romantic stage (unity of the community) in an unauthentic setting (Feria, or, in a smaller degree, Carnival), leaving aside the internal social tensions drawn during the Castañá.

Finally, the degree of institutionalisation of a festival is directly proportional to the possibilities of increasing tourist income during summer celebrations, and inversely proportional to the wastefull investments that the renewal or invention of non-summer insiders' celebrations implies. In other words, the more important tourism becomes in Zahara, the more interested local institutions will be in controlling summer celebrations – as sources of income, in order to avoid possible aggressive or negative actions which could threaten the Others, on whom they increasingly depend – and the less attention they will pay to non-tourist-oriented festivals.

Another side of this revitalisation and invention of non-summer celebrations is present in Boissevain's study: 'a new harmonization of ritual and productive cycles' (1992:12). In Zahara's case this would perfectly explain the invention of Castañá and the appearance of one and two day trips among Zahareños. These take place only when the season is over (end of September) and the productive cycle is ended, and they have money in their wallets, pockets, and purses. Zahareños can meet each other and reproduce their own inner identity. First, they will take a trip to a nearby town, or even to Portugal, to have a pleasant weekend. Later on, they meet at the Castañá, and perhaps begin to prepare Carnival songs and disguises.

2. Other Manifestations

Though festivals are good representations of communal feelings, there are many other situations that manifest negative or positive reactions to tourists. I will analyse two significant events. The first is related to festivals and the transformation of the traditional power structure: the creation and activities of the Neighbours' Association. The second includes some spontaneous negative reactions directed against the invasion of 'outsiders'.

A. The Neighbours' Association.

'El Palacio' is the only formal association in Zahara. It was founded in 1990 under the supervision and with the support of the new priest, whose arrival early that year accelerated the sudden interest in associations that appeared after the chirigota group was created in 1989. There was a general scepticism at the beginning, for Zahareños had no organizational tradition. The main concern of the Association was, and still is, to raise the standard of living in Zahara. In the words of the Association's president:

> We would like to be considered at least as a street of Barbate. We want to have water, and lights along the streets [...] Barbate gets a lot of money from us, and they don't give anything back. Have you seen the entrance to Zahara? It has four street lights and that's all .... They simply don't worry about Zahara .... But when the time for taxes comes ... ah!, then, of course, they do.

However, even though eighty percent of the population are members of the Association, the education and occupations of the main staff are not representative. There are six men and one woman who interchange positions (president, secretary, or speaker), whose educational level is higher than that of the average Zahareño (primary-school level). All but one have studied, at least in Secondary school, outside the village; and as they say proudly: 'we are the forty-year-old generation of Zahara, those who went out to study for the first time.' There is a teacher, a customs officer, a secretary, an economist, a clinical auxiliary, a clerk, and an unemployed person. Except for the last two, the rest work outside the village. They usually meet on Friday when all are at home for the weekend. From their outward appearance they are thought of as urban by the villagers. From my anthropological perspective, the staff members are new middle-class Zahareños.

The development of self-consciousness is linked to the emergence on the political scene of this new group, given their concern with Zahara's 'self-improvement'. In Zahara they are said to be *los de siempre*, meaning 'those who are always involved in everything and everywhere'. In this sense, the Association's staff created the Castañá and the only chirigota of the Carnival. It also happens that the most influential people on the Association's staff were members of the former *Juventudes Franciscanas* (Franciscan Youth Association).

If we think of festivals as vehicles and testers of an increasing self-consciousness, it could be said, referring to the Association's staff, that 'the animating agents are beginning to be individuals whose relationship with tradition is mediated by having lived or studied outside the community or belonging to cultural, recreational or religious associations through which tradition is interpreted and appropriated' (Cruces and Díaz 1992: 71).

The participation of this type of individual in every single activity ensures that the structure of identity in Zahara is based on the concept of being a villager, rather than on personalism or group interests. It is like saying: 'I am from Zahara'. There is no economic interest that unites them since they do not have any tourist-related professions. They do not have anything in common but the characteristic of being Zahareños; and this awareness comes from the fact that they have lived or studied outside the community. However, this variable does not necessarily lead to this new rise of self-consciousness. I must introduce the presence of the Other.

Given the expectations of tourism in Zahara (to become a rural Zahareño for a couple of weeks), tourists feel at home. Indeed, they behave as if they were at home, like the pregonero who had a lot of friends among Zahareños. Yet, there is a re-definition of Zahareño that obviously excludes the simple factor of having many friends or having spent many summers in Zahara. As one Association staff member (the 1990 pregonero) said in a passage worth quoting at length:

> In Zahara there are two types of Zahareños, the one born here and the one who has been coming here for several years and feels him/herself Zahareño, and some of these latter even want to be more Zahareño than those born here. Everybody says: 'I have been coming to Zahara since such a year, and I since another.' And the more years he/she has been coming here the better for them, and that makes us proud. But to be a Zahareño is something else, it is neither to have been coming here to *veranear* [spend the summer holidays] for many years nor to spend occasional weekends. To be Zahareño is as stated in the *copla* [popular song]: 'One cannot be Zahareño, if one has not been on the beach on a winter afternoon when the sea is really rough.' The summer is pretty, the nights of quiet *levante*, the festivals, the beach, but the year is very long, and the winters are hard and for some families almost unbearable .... [26]

Yet some changes have occurred. This individual symbolic strategy is being overtaken by economically interested social sectors. Once the entrepreneurs overcame their original distrust (remember that it was the first association of its kind) of the Neighbours Association, they realised how useful for their political and economic purposes the Association could be. Hence, recently there has been a move within the Association's staff to form an alliance with hotel owners. Both groups have achieved a certain degree of cooperation, especially in complaining to local, regional, and national administrations. Even so, along with this interest in the Association, there is a nascent feeling of identity.

For instance, hotels owners have exerted pressure through the Association in order to get chiringuitos torn down, for they disturbed the

Figure 2.3 Tearing down the chiringuito following pressure from the hotel owners.

tourists' peaceful rest. The Association and its new supporters show concern about night-time noise (caring for tourists' well-being) and drug consumption (caring about the insiders' unpleasant reality) that take place around chiringuitos. However, there are always comments such as the following that indicate a reaction against the coalition of the Association and hotel owners, i.e., social reactions against middle-class attitudes and the pro-tourist entrepreneurial class.

An eighteen-year-old girl told me: 'Well, if chiringuitos disturb the people, the only thing they [outsiders] can do is not to come to Zahara .... Nobody asks them to come here. If chiringuitos are not open, where are we [young Zahareños] supposed to go to have fun?' Three out of six stand holders are tourists (according to Zahareños) as they only come to the village during the summer. 'Yeah! they [outsiders] protest', a twenty-three-year-old man complained, 'but when they have the opportunity to open one [chiringuito] they don't hesitate .... They simply go there and build their shitty stuff.' 'They [the stands] bother me too 'cause I live by the beach, you know that, but the boys from Zahara need some money so they have to work wherever they can .... And if they [tourists] complain that much, then why the hell do they open chiringuitos too?' an old man sitting by his son's stand told me. The owner of a restaurant reported, 'I don't like them very much, but I understand that people from Zahara need the money .... One solution could be that the mayor allows two or three guys from here to build them [chiringuitos].'

The 'chiringuitos affair' enables us to understand some things about Zahareños self-consciousness. First, they are aware of the economic situation of the youth, and the serious difficulty of getting jobs in the village. Second, they realise the many means of income that tourism generates for 'the people of the *pueblo*.' Finally, it seems that Zahareños, while realizing their economic dependence on tourists, assume that the land and the benefits it provides, are a birthright. However, it is worth noting that all of these accounts refer only to complaints about tourists, not to Zahareños supposed objection to drug use.

Though with a profound economic base, the discussions about who could operate the chiringuitos show two complementary readings: the already explained feeling of self-consciousness and a curious paradox that contrast the hosts' perception of Zahara with that of their guests.

The paradox is born out of the main interest and activities of the Neighbours' Association. The Association is essentially a group of people who are trying to modernise the pueblo and have become aware of the new and powerful income that tourism brings to Zahara. This interest is based on a genuine desire to obtain more comfort for the town. It can, however, also be interpreted as a change in the hosts' self-perception. Though there is no obvious evidence of this shift towards a new self-perception, it is possible to link it with the 'chiringuitos affair' if I take it one step further.

At the beginning we noted some touristic perceptions of Zahara as a rather backward and tranquil place. This is why tourists went there. According to this view, it is a good idea to demolish the noisy night-time kiosks. At the same time, everybody recognised the difficulty young villagers had in earning money. Here is the paradox: Zahareños have begun to see their village through tourists' eyes as an undeveloped and peaceful community. Yet they want to pave and illuminate streets, while retaining the idea of traditional village, as shown in festivals and marketed in tourist brochures.

This awkward situation leads to strange and inconsistent actions such as paved streets without entertainment at night or summer festivals for villagers; and exploitation of tourism as the main economic force alongside the restrictions of jobs in chiringuitos for young Zahareños.

Perhaps it is for all these reasons that people in Zahara say that 'the Association [even if my informant is a member] has changed; now they are again helping those [i.e., hotel owners] who have always received help from whoever was in power.' Since certain actions were taken by the Association there has been an increased division between the staff and the members, who speak of the Association as though they were not members.

B. Two Spontaneous Popular Actions.

Some recent events indicate that a new feeling of a common cultural background is arising independently of associations or organised festivals.

Zahareños are well aware that tourists visit the village looking only for sun, sand, sea, and silence. In line with the national trend to search for historical identity, Zahara has also undertaken an action that can be understood as a rejection of that simple touristic image of quietness, backwardness, and virgin beaches.

One of the very first things that amazed me in Zahara was the constant reference to Miguel de Cervantes' works. Each time I mentioned that I was thinking about writing a book I was told, 'There is already a book written about Zahara. Cervantes wrote it, because he was here.'

During a conversation with two members of the Neighbours' Association, they told me, 'Don't worry if the people tell you something about Cervantes. They did not know anything about him until a couple of years ago.' The sense of this phrase must be understood from the speaker's point of view and, given the pejorative tone of his voice, was a disapproval of the new popular feeling about Cervantes. But for our purposes this can be read in a different way. I interpret this last advice as a sign of the increasing interest of Zahareños in their own history, indicated by their many references to Cervantes and to his works, in a large number of conversations.

On another occasion, I was told by an activist about measures taken against a construction that disturbed the historical environment of the Palace, the old almadraba building.

> It was three or four years ago … yes! 'cause the hotel [Gran Sol] wasn't constructed yet, and that was three years ago. Then some tourists came and began to build a kind of shed to put the windsurfing boards in, just by the wall …. Can you imagine all those guys climbing the wall just to protect their boards? Aren't the fishing-boats on the sand whatever the weather is, and nobody worries about covering them? … And we didn't like it, that's all. … So one day and spontaneously we threw stones and destroyed it [she described the action step-by-step]. The only problem was that there were a bunch of little kids who could be hurt. But nothing happened. We were acting together for almost the very first time. … I would like to know what a Sevillano would say if I went and built a shed by the Giralda. They wouldn't like it, so … neither do we.

There are other events that could also illustrate this recent historical awareness. I will report just one case that relates to the new historical interest, with a 'We' reacting against a 'They'.

In this example the area was the same: the Palace. The time was shortly after the above incident. The problem was quite similar, though with a higher sense of communal property. The legal owner of the Palace, who is from Barbate, decided to put a huge gate at one of the three entrances to the building. This is situated by the beach and a passage through the property had become another street of the village, since it was used by everybody to reach either the beach or their homes. Hence, one night a large group of villagers decided to remove the gate. They took it to the other side of the bridge over the Cachón River, that is, beyond the village's symbolic limits. This bridge is the entrance to Zahara, and it separates the pueblo from the rest of the world.

The best interpretation of this last episode, noting the bridge as the symbolic border between insiders and outsiders, is in another 1990 Carnival song called *La Muralla* (The Wall):

> If I had money // and I were a little braver // I would put a huge gate // with four or five locks on top of my bridge // who would I like would come in // 'cause this is quite clear // as we have seen, there are a lot of people // who are

not from Zahara // who accumulate all the resources and benefits [literally, cut the codfish] // dum, dum [knocking at the gate], who is there?, a tourist with a lot of money // open the gate // dum, dum, who is there?, Tato and Maribel [a couple of Zahareños] // they close the gate [to outsiders].[27]

Conclusion

The premise is that self-consciousness is a response to tourist arrivals. In support of this assertion, the idea of isolation of both locals and tourists is significant. Zahara is seen from the guests' mental construction as a peaceful place forgotten by tourist masses, and from the locals' view as an awkward place.

The emergence of self-consciousness among locals is examined via the degree of institutionalisation of festivals. The opposition between ritual and play, staged authenticity and backstage, and the renewal and invention of non-summer festivals are different features of a single dichotomy that reflects the dualism of the Self and the Other.

The Feria divides the community vertically (age); the Carnival initiates a symbolic two-fold division (1) between 'us' and 'them' and (2) among 'us', for it maintains the old function of inverting the social order, as well as confirming the Castañá picture and the recent cooperation between the Association's staff and hotel owners (i.e., the chiringuitos affair); and the Castañá reproduces – backstage – the social stratification of the community. In Zahara there is a specialisation of festivals that converges in the opposition self-other / us-them / locals-tourists / 'staged hosts '– 'true hosts' (hotel owners).

This dichotomy is also found in the novel Neighbours Association, the chiringuitos affair, the chirigota lyrics and the gate-bridge protest, which show Zahara's symbolic limits.

Though theorists could criticise how the use of the term 'tourist', especially when referring to the stand owners (chiringuitos), for they are not a leisure class, from the local perspective these holders are 'tourists' in a very strict sense. They were not born in Zahara and they only visit during the summer.

Here we face an interesting theoretical issue, namely, the disparity of criteria between social-scientific definitions, taxonomies, and denominations and the reality they aspire to explain. The locals have the authority to delimit the terms in which social definitions must fit, and we must give them such a possibility. Perhaps this is why Pearce (1982: 33) wrote that there was a great difficulty for researchers in defining a tourist, while everybody, Zahareños included, knew the definition perfectly well.

This chapter has also has examined two paradoxes generated by tourist space: (1) the tourist who does not act like a tourist while being treated as a tourist, and (2) the hosts who want to modernise the village – since they perceive their place through tourists' eyes – and thereby alter the attractiveness of Zahara. Both concern the alienation of actors within their own roles, generating a vicious circle, in which it is difficult to discern who/what modifies whom/what. Does the touristic space modify the actors' perceptions and behaviour? Or do the actors' actions recreate the touristic space?

Finally, the major practical point addressed in this chapter suggests both the importance and the necessity of analysing the interaction between tourists and the host community in order to understand the complexity of social and cultural expressions of the dichotomy Self-Other, where all the features examined converge.

NOTES

*   This research has been supported by two Ethnological Project Campaigns (1991 and 1992) from the *Junta de Andalucía* through its *Comisión de Etnología*.

1.   This article is a résumé of some parts of my PhD thesis entitled 'The Configuration of Reality: Hosts, Guests and Anthropologist' (Seville, 1995).

2.   Spanish words are italicised only on their first appearance in the text. *Pedanía:* a small population with limited administrative jurisdiction.

3.   The strategic importance of this geographical point is evident. Note that Spain signed its adhesion to NATO in May 1982.

4.   Usually, the *Guardia Civil* (Civil Guard) banned walking along the beach due to smuggling during the Franco regime.

5.   Boissevain asserts that we have failed in distinguishing the social consequences of tourism from other processes of change (Taken from Crick 1989:311).

6.   It is worth noting that among the fifteen traveller categories studied by Pearce, the tourist role is the one everybody avoids, given that it 'may have pejorative overtones' (1982:40). Obviously, people like to think of themselves as intrepid and brave explorers and romantic travellers, not as tourists.

7.   Notice the clustering 'we the tourists'. The notion of the cheated tourist is rooted in tourist perception; however, as in the case of Zahara, it does not exist very often. On the contrary this is one of the most common complaints among Zahareños: 'why should we pay as much as though we were tourists?'

8.   The Atlanterra Company, which developed the settlement, was founded in Zug (Switzerland) in March 1962. The capital was Swiss, and its aim was to promote the urbanisation of 'Silver Cap' on the Atlantic coast of Cádiz. The area is 2,926,219 m².

9. They do not match either Cohen's individual or organised mass tourists nor Smith's incipient mass or mass tourists (Cohen 1972: 167-68; Smith 1977: 9-10).

10. For a more detailed description, see Nogués Pedregal 1992:40-41.

11. Though Spaniards are geographically Europeans the idea of being European is something new for a vast majority of the population, mainly older and rural inhabitants.

12. *Chiringuito*: a kind of hut by the beach, where drinks are sold, specially at night. These are the places where youths meet every night during the summer season.

13. When using the adjective 'familiar' Zahareños mean exactly what has been described about tourism in Barbate.

14. I have drawn the main ideas of this whole section entirely from J. Boissevain's 'Introduction' to *Revitalizing European Rituals*.

15. Linguistic derivation from *castaña* (chestnut); accentuating the last syllable (castañá) means a huge amount of chestnuts to be delivered and eaten.

16. Though I have problems when dealing with concepts such as community or village given the possible confusion of identifying observed unity with analytical unity, I will accept Durkheim's view that the *fiesta* makes society, or at least 'creates the illusion of community.' On the identification between both unities applied to studies of communities in Spain, see Prat, 1992: 126-29.

17. The usage of the terms *ritual* and *play*, as well as their derivations, is based on this statement: 'Ritual refers to the celebration's formal, ordered events. These are characterized by rules, hierarchy, and constraints of time and place. Ritual is most often imposed and supervised by those with more power and reinforces their superordinate position. Play, in contrast, is associated with the negation of ritual. It is disorderly, innovative, egalitarian, improvised, and disrespectful of authority. If ritual is serious and solemn, play is joyful and silly' (Boissevain 1992: 13).

18. An all-male Carnival group that makes up and sings ironic and dirty songs about social, political, and economic issues.

19. East wind. It blows all year long, but it is especially undesirable when sunbathing on the beach.

20. Though the Andalusian accent (words in italic) is neither officially written (there is no uniformity in this respect) nor academically approved, it is not strange at all to find it in popular expressions. The usage of the vernacular is commonly accepted: ¡Que se vaya *a-ser* puñeta! // *to'*aquel que no le guste el levante // tiene esta tierra una cosa // que no la tiene otra parte // un vientesito *mu'*fuerte // y que se llama levante // pero vienen *musha* gente // y *na' ma' qu'acen* quejarse // y *pa' lo'*que protesten // les digo *con musho arte* // el que no quiera este viento // *pa'*protestar se vaya a otra parte.

21. *Almadraba:* Ancient Roman fishing system to capture tuna-fish (*atunes*) off the coast of Cádiz. The name of the village derives from this traditional industry: 'Zahara of the tuna fish.'

22. The *Sevillano* (from Seville), a term which has become a synonym of 'nasty and unpleasant tourist', represents 75 percent of recent tourism.

23. The person who gives the inauguration speech. It is usually a tourist. In 1992 he was from Seville and 'one of our most frequent veraneantes [...] who has many friends in our village' – meaning that he is not a stranger to the locals.

24. On this point, remember that though some individuals belonging to the upper classes provided coal and counters, they did not appear at that celebration.

25. Julio Caro Baroja writes: 'An Andalusian village is a living museum where can be found features from Neolithic until recent times' (1985:275).

26. En Zahara hay dos clases de zahareños, el nacido aquí y el que lleva años viniendo a Zahara y se siente zahareño, e incluso algunos quieren ser más zahareños que el nacido aquí. Todos dicen: 'Yo llevo viniendo a Zahara desde el año tal, y yo desde el año tal', y cuantos más años lleve viniendo, mejor para ellos, y eso es un orgullo para nosotros. Pero ser zahareño es otra cosa, no es venir desde hace años a veranear, ni pasar algunos fines de semana aquí. Ser zahareño es como dice la copla: 'No se puede ser zahareño si nunca ha estado en sus playas en una tarde de invierno estando la mar muy brava.' Es bonito el verano, las noches de levante en calma, las fiestas, la playa, pero el año es muy largo y los inviernos muy duros y para algunas familias casi inaguantables …

27. Si yo tuviera dinero // y fuera un poco valiente // pondría una buena cancela // con cuatro o cinco *candao* en lo *harto* de mi puente // entraría quien yo quisiera // porque esto es *descarao* // por lo visto hay mucha gente // que no son los de Zahara //los que parten el bacalao // dum, dum ¿quién es?, un turista con *parné* // abre la cancela // dum, dum ¿quién es?, el Tato y la Maribel // cierran la cancela …

REFERENCES

Boissevain, J., 'Variaciones estacionales sobre algunos temas mediterráneos', *Ethnica* vol. 18 (1982): 51-58.

_____, 'Introduction', in Boissevain, J., ed., *Revitalizing European Rituals*, London: Routledge, 1992, 1-19.

Caro Baroja, J., *Los pueblos de España*. vol. 2 Madrid: Istmo, 1985.

Cohen, E., 'Toward a Sociology of International Tourism', *Social Research*, vol. 39 (1972): 164-82.

Crick, M., 'Representations of International Tourism in the Social Sciences: Sun, Sex, Sights, Savings and Servility', *Annual Review of Anthropology* vol. 22, no. 5 (1989): 461-81.

Cruces, F. and Díaz, C., 'Public Celebrations in a Spanish Valley', in Boissevain, J., ed., *Revitalizing European Rituals*, London: Routledge, 1992, 62-79.

González Laxe, F., *El proceso de crecimiento del sector pesquero español (1961-1978)*. La Coruña: Caixa de Aforros de Galicia, 1983.

MacCannell, D., *The Tourist: a New Theory of the Leisure Class*. New York: Schocken Books, 1989.

Mathieson, A. and Wall, G., *Tourism: Economic, Physical and Social Impacts*. London: Longman, 1982.

Münchner Illustrierte, 16 January 1960: 10-17.

Nogués Pedregal, A.M., 'Cambio socio-cultural en una comunidad tradicional: el caso de Zahara de los Atunes (Cádiz)', *Anuario Etnológico de Andalucía 1991*, Seville: Consejería de Cultura y Medio Ambiente, 1992, 37-47.

Pearce, P., *The Social Psychology of Tourist Behaviour*. Oxford: Pergamon Press, 1982.

Prat, J., 'Teoría-Metodología', in Prat et al., eds, *Antropología de los pueblos de España*, Madrid: Taurus, 1991, 113-40.

Smith, V., 'Introduction', in Smith, V., ed., *Host and Guest. The Anthropology of Tourism*, Oxford: Basil Blackwell, 1977, 1-14.

Urry, J., *The Tourist Gaze*. London: Sage Publications, 1990.

3. A Case of Neglect?
The Politics of (Re)presentation: a Sardinian Case

Peter Odermatt

Introduction

*B*oissevain's statement that the complex nature of tourism and its impact on the host community can not be understood if we restrict our analysis to the 'very narrow concept of development in terms of economic growth and industrialization' (1977: 524) is now widely accepted. Nash's notion of a transactional imperialism (1978, 1989), for example, was a vigorous plea to broaden the research agenda by considering other aspects of the realm of social interaction. Nevertheless most studies still fail to go beyond the economic implications of tourism. This fact does not have to come as a complete surprise. By examining, for example, Nash's own premises it becomes clear that he restricts the objective of his sociocultural analysis to 'the development of a service economy and the necessary sociocultural changes to go with it' (1989: 51). In his widely celebrated book *The Tourist Gaze*, John Urry seems to go along with this bias. However, in his attempt to analyse the socially constructed character of the tourist gaze, he highlights both the production and consumption of the gaze. His notion of the tourist gaze seems to be a good

Notes for this section begin on page 108.

starting point to overcome the restrictions of a narrow, economically determined, host-guest perspective in tourism research. Gazing upon the Other, whether it be a human object, 'space, the wilderness, foreignness, the past, and so on' often means that we 'order, categorise, and consume it, and often show it off in museums' (Graburn 1983: 18). In the age of mass tourism the representation and staging of the Other often takes place in the tourist-receiving regions – the 'home-region' of the Other.[1] Through the act of staging (which implies selection, classification, description, enshrinement, etc.), what is for the tourist simply an object to gaze at on vacation can in the eyes of local residents become invested with new, controversial, and often problematic meanings. If the object of the tourist gaze is a historical shrine, the situation may be far more complex than the following statement of MacCannell suggests:

> Note … when historical shrines are the attraction, as in Philadelphia, they can be enjoyed by locals and tourists alike and augment the resources of the community's education system in a meaningful way. … (1984: 386)

It will be argued that for a deeper understanding of tourism, the non-economic implications of the tourist gaze have to be taken into account as well. This chapter is about the representation and presentation (referred to below as (re)presentation)[2] of the prehistoric past for touristic ends in Sardinia. The examples discussed have in common that they all deal with the (re)presentation of monuments of the Nuraghic-culture.[3] The material presented will provide evidence that a negative local attitude towards tourist development does not a priori have to be the *direct* result of a conflict about economic objectives and certainly does not have to be caused by any stressful relation between hosts and guests. The chapter will demonstrate, on the contrary, that a positive attitude towards tourism and tourists in general, and a local historical (tourist) attraction of national importance in particular, can change dramatically for the worse if the meaning the local residents attach to the object of the gaze is neglected, or even worse, transgressed, even if this implies that badly needed impulses for local economic development are jeopardised through the actions taken by local residents.

According to Graburn, there are at least two kinds of representations: 'public, put forward by the industry [and perhaps the hosts], and [the] private, those of the tourists themselves' (1983: 27). For the purpose of this chapter, this analytic dichotomy will be applied to the concept of (re)presentation. Given the limited space and scope available, the analysis will be restricted to public (re)presentation. The main purpose of this chapter is to draw attention to what has often been neglected in research about tourism: the relation between local residents and (re)presentations created to please the tourists. For that reason the usual host-guest perspective will be abandoned in favour of a perspective that highlights the relation between the hosts and the agents of (re)presentations.[4]

In order to do so, the development of the Sardinian heritage industry has to be dealt with. In the first section a more general development pattern will be outlined that finally will allow us to place the local evidence in a broader perspective. The starting point for the development under discussion was, appropriately enough, the foreign curiosity about Sardinian prehistory and its most popular remains, the nuraghi. Foreign travellers and scholars created, with some local support, what might be called a 'Sardinian prehistoric past'. In a later stage, particularly after the Second World War, indigenous and foreign scholars as well as local residents, later joined by an eager tourist industry, created jointly a '(re)presentable past'. It turns out that the development was a case of mutual benefit, and as such created no enduring stress between host and guests. Still, it is in the development described that the foundation is laid for a very destructive struggle on the local level; and it is here that we are at the heart of the matter. It is only by analysing the 'politics of (re)presentation' that one can make sense of the ongoing struggle concerning the development of one of the most famous tourist attractions in Sardinia, the nuraghe Losa near Abbasanta. Finally, some remarks on the subject of (re)presentation will be presented.

Cases of Mutual Benefit

During the nineteenth and early twentieth centuries, historians and archaeologists all over Europe, strongly reinforced by the national ideal, started to construct an official 'nation state monumental past' (Herzfeld 1991). In Sardinia, on the contrary, no monumental past came into existence until the second half of the twentieth century. Furthermore, it was not national ideology but the curiosity of foreigners and, most of all, the rise of mass tourism in the 1960s, that were the most important factors in the development of a monumental – nation state – conception of prehistory. As the archaeological and historical heritage became a weapon in the battle for tourists (it soon became the hallmark of Sardinia as tourist destination), the interest and the funding the indigenous history had received in the preceding centuries from foreigners, whether explorers, travellers or tourists, paid off in the end. New archaeological museums and sights opened annually.[5] In 1982, three quarters of a million people visited the archaeological parks and museums on the island. As a result most present-day archaeologists and the professionals who restore and preserve the antiquities experience tourism as a blessing for their profession.

The 'Making' of a Past

The nuraghi were first referred to in ancient writings by Sallustius, Solinus, Pausanias, and Pseudo Aristotle. From the sixteenth century onwards, the existence of the nuraghi was incidentally mentioned in travel accounts. However, it was some hundred years later that the first detailed description of the nuraghi appeared. Winkelmann's famous 1763 edition of *Geschichte der Kunst des Altertums* was the first book to explicitly draw the traveller's attention to the existence of these monuments. As such it can be considered as the first act of representation that was part of an effort to (re)present the nuraghi as a worthwhile object of the (future) gaze.[6] From that moment on publications on Sardinia more frequently contained notes on the nuraghi. But there were still no signs of real interest (either from foreigners or locals) in the history and prehistory of Sardinia and its material remains. Nor did eighteenth and early nineteenth-century travellers in Sardinia have an eye for the material heritage. Travel in this period was mainly practical. Expeditions searched for timber and ore or, like Nelson, examined the island from a strategic point of view.

The several travel accounts written in the 1850s and 1860s by two foreign explorers, Alberto Ferrero Della Marmora and Heinrich von Maltzan, both explicitly interested in the nuraghi, were a real turning point. Independently of each other but with the assistance of the same local scholar, Giovanni Spano, both men made several trips to the island and visited the prehistoric monuments. As a result of their work, Sardinian prehistory became an issue in its own right (see Brigaglia 1989: 31). The first real effort to investigate the archaeological evidence on the island by way of systematic and scientific research was made by Antonio Taramelli, a self-taught archaeologist from Sardinia who, after taking the chair of the new state-financed national board of antiquities, the Ufficio della Antichità, in 1903, dominated the archaeological scene on the island until his death in 1935. The creation of the Ufficio della Antichità was not, as one might expect, the result of a growing historical awareness in Sardinia, nor was it the result of a growing interest in the island by the national authorities. On the contrary, it was simply a measure to protect what belonged to the Italian nation (but what was ironically not yet appreciated as such). As knowledge of Sardinian prehistory, and especially the small nuraghic bronze figures (*bronzetti*), spread through Europe, the demand for the figures also grew. This demand then resulted in an appalling number of clandestine excavations.

While the rise of historicism in the nineteenth century resulted in a growing interest of the bourgeoisie in their own material heritage all over Europe (see Hunter 1981; see also Lowenthal 1981); the feudal economy and the poor living conditions in Sardinia prevented an autonomous bourgeoisie from coming into existence. Although Braudel is referring to sixteenth-century Sardinia, his remarks hold true of the island in the late nineteenth and early twentieth centuries.

> It was too lost in the sea to play an important role, too far from the enriching contacts that linked Sicily, for example, with Italy and Africa. Mountainous, excessively divided, a prison of its poverty, it was a self-contained world with its own language, custom, archaic economy, and pervasive pastoralism – in some regions remaining as Rome must have found it long ago. (1986: 150)

For most academics and intellectuals, a professional commitment to Sardinian prehistory was out of the question because of the poor employment opportunities on the island itself. A professional commitment to Sardinian prehistory would rule out a transfer to Italian institutions on the mainland, where the topic was not viewed as having any relevance. The discovery and the making of Sardinian history was thus reserved for local amateurs and foreigners. All this contributed to the somewhat esoteric and mythical nature of Sardinian archaeology at that time. The mystification of the nuraghic past for political purposes[7] on the island even further disqualified Sardinian prehistory in the eyes of the professional archaeologist on the mainland. It was only after the Second World War, when the overall economic, social, and political circumstances on the island slowly altered, that Sardinian prehistory finally became institutionalised and a serious effort was made to create an official monumental past.

In the aftermath of the Second World War, Italy found itself in a sorry state. The Fascist efforts to establish autarky had isolated the Italian economy and prevented it from functioning as a market economy.

The South, the Mezzogiorno, and the islands of Sicily and Sardinia were particularly badly affected. There the per-capita income was less than forty percent of that of the North (see Willis 1971: 103). The situation in Sardinia was even more serious than in the rest of Southern Italy. With respect to infrastructure, education, health care, and so forth, the island lagged far behind the rest of the Mezzogiorno. Although Sardinia was granted autonomy – a Sardinian parliament and government were established in 1946 – the development of the island was mainly planned, regulated, and financed by the Italian government. The most ambiguous development plan was a rebirth programme, *Piano di Rinascita*, to stimulate overall prosperity on the island. The success of the rebirth programme, and of all the programmes to follow, remained modest. As the economy on the island did not flourish, social unrest did. The 1960s were marked by an enormous boost of economically inspired banditry. As all the plans to industrialise the island failed, especially the plan to build a huge petrochemical industry in the island's heartland, all that was left was tourism.[8]

The Sardinian government established a national tourist board, the Ente Sardo Idustrie Turistiche (ESIT), in 1950. The main objective in the first fifteen years was to stimulate the development of tourist-related infrastructure. In the first period, the results were encouraging. There was a steady increase in the number of tourists, and a steady growth of tourist-related infrastructure. Whereas only 188,363 tourists visited the island in 1949, in 1956 the number swelled to nearly half a million (see Macciardi 1959: 6). In that same year, archaeologists on the island witnessed a clear commitment of the state to the material heritage. In 1956 a second archaeological department was founded for the two other provinces, Sassari and Nuoro. This further commitment by the state to the material heritage was closely linked to the state's efforts to promote tourism.

The 'Making' of a (Re)presentable Past

During the following years the presentation – the preservation and staging – of the material heritage became the primary task of the Sopritendenza alla Antichità.[9] It was not only by preservation efforts that archaeologists tried to serve tourism. In the 1980s, an agreement was reached that every province on the island should have an appreciable major nuraghic tourist attraction. To accomplish this, the Sopritendenza alla Antichità of Sassari and Nuoro undertook a major excavation, followed by a restoration project at the nuraghi Orrùbiu-Orroli in the province of Nuoro (Lilliu 1988: 587).

That the link of archaeology to tourism goes even further back is clearly demonstrated by the following. In 1962, a plan was developed that would alter the destiny of the island forever. The chairman of the Sopritendenza alla Antichità of Sassari and Nuoro announced the news at an international conference on tourism in San Remo. The government had agreed to sell 87 square kilometres of coastline on the northeast coast to a consortium headed by investor Aga Khan Karim. Within a few years, the coastline was transformed in a 700 billion-lire tourist paradise. The Costa Smeralda project alone created more than 37,000 jobs in the first few years (Bandinu 1980: 25). The private development plans were not restricted to the construction of hotels and beach accommodations alone. Roads were built as well as shops, garages, and theatres. In order to make it easier for tourists to reach the island, the harbours were modernised, airports were built, and a local airline – *Alisarda* – was set up. The Costa Smeralda project was soon followed by other projects and from that moment on, the authorities lost control of tourism-related development. From an active body that had tried to regulate and promote the development of tourist-related infrastructure, the tourist board turned into the promotion authority that it is today. Whereas the ESIT was condemned to stay on the sidelines with respect to the further development of the tourist infrastructure, archaeologists fulfilled an ever more active role in the transformation of Sardinia into a package-tourist destination.

Before the local evidence is examined it is necessary to return to the matter of representation, to say a few words about the general efforts made to represent Sardinian prehistory solely for touristic aims.[10] The first guidebook on Sardinia was published by the Italian Touring Club (TCI) in 1918. The *Guido Rosso* gained a reputation as the 'Italian Baedeker' because of his reliable information. Virtually all the guidebooks on Sardinia published before 1970 are based on information from the Italian TCI guides. It was only in the 1970s that comparable guides (in quality and reliability) were published on the island, strongly encouraged by the Sardinian government. As independent publishing houses consolidated their position on the island in the late 1970s and 1980s, the production of tourist-oriented information (brochures, guides, and postcards) was taken over by Sardinian entrepreneurs. Previous to this, the representation of Sardinia by means of print and photography had been in the hands of Italian and foreign publishers. There are even some guides that were only published thanks to the financial aid of investors such as the Costa Smeralda consortium. Again a clear case of mutual benefit.

Going into the subject of representation, here defined as 'providing information about the touristic Other', it is not sufficient to pay attention solely to the printed media. The influence of promotion tours or exhibitions abroad should not be underestimated.[11] To provide an example: in 1949 there was held an exhibition on Sardinian *bronzetti* in Venice, organised by an Italian archaeologist. Five years later this event was followed by another one in Milan. This time the exhibition was also sent to Zurich, Brussels, The Hague, Hamburg, Paris, and Lyon. It was this exhibition, and most of all the catalogue made by the Swiss photographer Christian Cervos, that was to attract the attention of a wider audience to the island. During the decades that followed, several more exhibitions on Sardinian prehistory were held in the United States, Germany, and other European countries. But it is again only recently that Sardinian authorities became involved in these manifestations. It is only since the late 1970s that the representation of Sardinia, and accordingly its prehistory, in print or by other means, has been problematised on the island.

The Local Perspective

The case of Abbasanta – a small village in the geographical centre of Sardinia – shows a remarkable resemblance with the general development outlined so far. It provides a clear case of a tourism-related devel-

Figure 3.1 Abbasanta.

opment pattern that can be generalised as being one of mutual benefit. Local residents, scholars, and tourists alike, who were all interested in one of the most famous Sardinian archaeological monuments, the nuraghe Losa, had the feeling that they, up to a certain point in time, gained by the arrangements made to (re)present the monument. It is this apparent success story that will provide us with the necessary clues to make sense of the disturbing events of the 1970s and later.

In the second half of the nineteenth century, the impressive nuraghe Losa, two miles east of Abbasanta, had been visited and described extensively by travellers. For example Della Marmora: 'Not far from Paulilatino, to the left of the road leading to Abbasanta, one can see an appreciable nuraghe called Nuraghe Losa: ... ' (Della Marmora 1971: 428; my translation). What follows is a lengthy description of the monument with some general remarks on its origin. In the course of the late nineteenth and early twentieth centuries, Losa became the best studied and most extensively described prehistoric monument on the island. The increasing fame of the nuraghe was not only the result of travel accounts, but also of scholarly activities and publications. In 1890 the monument was subject to the first scientific excavation ever conducted by a foreign professional archaeologist. Vivannet's project was followed by a second excavation in 1915, this time under the supervision of Taramelli. It was during this second campaign that the people of Abbasanta first experienced the difference between the archaeologists' perception of a monument and their own. To prevent shepherds from using Losa as a shelter for their flocks, Taramelli had a stone wall erected around the monument. By doing so, he was denying the local shepherds a right they had held for as long as they could remember. Although the ground of the nuraghe became private property in 1848, the owner had never denied them access. Even today there are nuraghi on the island that are still used by shepherds and have been rebuilt to meet their needs.

It is striking that although Taramelli built the wall to protect the nuraghe, he did not take any precautions to stop further the decay of the monument. Huge sections of the outer walls had collapsed and other parts were in very poor shape. In sharp contrast to what is common today, excavations at the time were not followed by restoration. The decay of the monument continued until 1930, when the local priest Salvatore Angelo Dessi devoted energy to its reconstruction and restoration. Assisted by his pupils from the local school, he continued his efforts until 1933. Although Dessi was a dedicated amateur archaeologist, the initiative was probably linked to an event four years earlier, and can be interpreted as the first conscious act of presenting the monument – i.e., investing in the staging of it – as something worthwhile to gaze at. In 1926 King Vittorio Emanuele III had visited the nuraghi with Mussolini. This visit, and the fact that both of these celebrities came again, Emanuele in 1937 and il Duce in 1939, filled local people with pride. Until the 1970s when the archaeological authorities removed them, a memorial stone and a marble table erected in 1926 in honour of the two were shown to every visitor. The 'king's table' was also a popular place for picnics, festivities, and family celebrations. But this was not the only way the people of Abbasanta became aware of the changing significance of the monument. The changing attitude was fostered by the fact that Losa had been used, in 1929, as a site for one of the first films ever made on the island. About this time, there was also a sharp increase in the number of family portraits taken in front of the monument.

Figure 3.2 Family portrait taken in front of Losa in 1936.

As a result of the increasing numbers of tourists visiting the nuraghe in the 1930s – a visit to Losa was warmly recommended in the first (1918) and second (1929) editions of the *Guido Rosso* – the first postcard was printed with a picture of the nuraghe and the words 'National Monument Nuraghe Losa, Abbasanta'. The postcard was ordered by a local shopkeeper who added a poem he had 'written' himself on the back.[12] This postcard can be seen as a local icon celebrating the changed significance of Losa.

Nuraghe Losa

O you majestic culturally valuable Nuraghe,
Your origins reaching back thousands of years;
You do not abandon the secret of your origin
Be it peace or be it war.

You puzzle the scientists
As well as the archaeologists and scholars;
They assume you are a tomb of a hero,
A tribal chief or a divinity.

Historians, celebrities and kings
All visit you with pleasure;
For centuries you have been loved.

Abbasanta is proud of you until eternity,
It's you that stands for the values of ancient Sardinia:
Nuraghe Losa you are a rare monument.
(Bonaventura Figus, Abbasanta; my translation)[13]

Before all the celebrities and scientists (and tourists) visited the monument, Losa had been one of many nuraghi near the village. Poems such as this prove that the people recognised that, to paraphrase Herzfeld, a national archaeological monument had been created out of what had been a place where residents, their friends, and their enemies had played and worked, lived and died. Phrases like 'Abbasanta is proud of you until eternity' make it clear to whom the national monument – according to the local residents – belongs to. Losa stands for Abbasanta and its place in the larger entity called Italy. An effort by yet another shopkeeper from nearby Ghilarza in the 1950s to order postcards that suggested a direct connection between the municipality of Ghilarza and the famous monument was met with the resistance of village authorities, who denied the photographer access to the monument.

It was in the interwar period that Losa – in the eyes of local residents – most deserved the label 'national monument'. In the 1920s and 1930s, it was a commonly-held conviction in Abbasanta that the village and its residents could catch up with the Italian mainland. This was not because of the national monument Losa, although the message of the repeated visits of heads of state should not be underestimated. The fact that local residents willingly connected Losa, and thus Abbasanta, with the Italian nation reflects the modernisation efforts Abbasanta was undergoing. At the time Abbasanta became one of the first villages in Sardinia to have electricity. Furthermore, it not only had access to the railway, but was connected to the Carlo Felice, the most important motorway on the island. With respect to education and medical health care facilities, Abbasanta outdid every village of its size on the island. With Losa, Abbasanta could finally offer the Italian nation something in return – a national tourist attraction. The label 'national' does not refer to a nation-state monumental past, but stands for the hopeful commitment of the local residents to the nation.

During the Second World War the monument belonged to the residents again. Losa fulfilled a role as a meeting point. It was to hold this position until the 1960s when, due to increased mobility, the beaches and cinemas in the nearby town of Oristano became more attractive. On Sundays families spent their leisure time together in the shade of the nuraghe. Relatives and friends from other villages as well as tourists were taken to the monument. It was then the presence of and the knowledge about the nuraghe that enabled the Abbasantees to come into contact with tourists.

Before and shortly after the Second World War, the (re)presentation of Losa for tourism was almost exclusively a local affair. Due to the shortage of accurate information, local residents voluntarily served as 'tourist guides' and were thus the main agents of the representation.[14] The continuing presentation of the monument was also only possible because of a local initiative to restore the monument. Although some local residents recognised that local control of the (re)presentation was only partial (see below), they still had the impression that by example, the local representation of the sight was evaluated by tourists and locals alike as being of equal if not higher value than the concise representation in guidebooks. Although Losa had a long way to go before it became the national icon it is today, [15] visitors from all over the world came to see it. And some of them were so charmed by it that they dedicated poems to the nuraghe. Take the English travel writer Ross: One of the two poems in the appendix of *South to Sardinia* is called 'Nuraghi near Abbasanta, Sardinia' (Ross 1960).

During my fieldwork, it was pointed out to me that there were many other publications mentioning either Abbasanta or Losa. In the 1950s and 1960s, there was clearly a notion about how the name Abbasanta made its way into the consciousness of the wider world. Ross himself

Figure 3.3 A nuraghe near Abbasanta.

noted what this probably meant for the local residents. Studying an English map of Sardinia during a train journey in 1951, he described the astonishment of his Sardinian fellow travellers when they discovered their own villages on the map. 'Michele Antonio! Alberto! Look! Santadi in English! And Barbusi! Fancy them knowing about Barbusi in England ... Barbusi, imagine Barbusi being minded about in England' (1960: 121-122). In a period when the whole island was trying to catch up with the modern world or at least with modern Italy and Europe, the existence of Losa allowed the residents to get a glimpse of this world long before most Sardinians. Sardinians knew about the mainland stereotypes depicting them as economically backward and socially anachronistic. In fact, for quite some time they took these stereotypes at face value and worked hard to overcome them, thereby endangering what was left of their social and cultural heritage. Even the shepherds with their mixed flocks and kitchen-gardens abandoned the domestic mode of production, extended families fell apart, and a tradition of great cultural diversity (language, folk-traditions) was given up in favour of a 'modern way of life'.

Local references to the monument in the 1950s and the 1960s were without the prefix 'national', which had seemed obligatory in the pre-war period. But this does not mean that Losa had lost its value with regard to the articulation of identity. It only implies that the symbolic significance had undergone some transformation. The role played by Losa in the articulation of identity was very ambivalent. In the confrontation with tourists and the modern world, Losa served as a symbol that could hopefully help to overcome borders. In the confrontation with residents from neighbouring villages, Losa was utilised to maintain the boundaries. Losa not only belonged to Abbasanta: more importantly, it *was* Abbasanta. It is significant for the argument under discussion that on the local level there was still no notion or reference made to the monument's historicity or its economic value as a tourist attraction. The monument's historicity played no role in the articulation of local identity, nor did the possible economic value of the tourist attraction appeal to local entrepreneurs and politicians. The only thing that counted was the presence of a famous monument which provided a significant way to distinguish oneself from one's neighbours and to bridge the gap with the rest of the world. What mattered was that others invested time and money to come and see a local object. As the act of gazing was not yet evaluated as another facet in the unbalanced power relation between the periphery and the metropolis, it was still considered something positive.

Although local residents were conscious of the appeal of the nuraghe to tourists, they did not invest in the monument except in symbolic terms. This was in sharp contrast to comparable tourist attractions like the nuraghe Su Nuraxi, also located in the island's interior. After the nuraghe Su Nuraxi was discovered under a hillock and was excavated in the 1950s, the population of Barumini systematically improved the tourist qualities of the attraction. This was not only achieved by governmental aid, although it played a very important role, but was also the result of the commitment to tourism made by some local entrepreneurs. A small museum as well as a snack bar, a restaurant, and a souvenir shop were built in the vicinity of the attraction. In the village souvenirs, such as wine and arts and crafts, are for sale everywhere. The municipality, in addition, in order to safeguard the investments, makes continuous efforts to improve the presentation of the nuraghe Su Nuraxi.

Cases of Neglect

Cases of neglect? Who is to be blamed for neglecting what? Are the local residents to be blamed for their failure to act according to the laws of maximisation? Are they to be blamed because they failed to exploit Losa other than symbolically? What about the defects of the heritage industry? And what to say about our – the scientists' – presumptions towards tourist development? In the second part of the chapter it will be argued that there is another kind of economics to be taken into account in the analysis of tourist development. A new and complementary kind of insight is to be gained by paying attention to the unbalanced access to the means of (re)presentation. If we only examine as Nash puts it 'the development of a service economy and the necessary sociocultural changes to go with it' (1989: 51), our analysis will fall short in cases such as that of Losa. It is only by analysing the 'politics of (re)presentation' that one can make sense of the ongoing struggle concerning the touristic development of Losa, and similar cases.

As the objectives of the local residents and those of the heritage industry seemed to diverse in the 1970s the local residents were denied any further active part in the (re)presentation of the attraction. When they were denied access to the monument, local residents were deprived of their prime means of representation. In addition, the local (re)presentation of the monument was deconstructed by removing core elements of the local presentation. This led local politicians to declare tourism and the nuraghe Losa, once a subject of enormous local pride, a topic *non grata* in Abbasanta. As a consequence, up to the 1990s, the (re)presentation of Losa does not fulfil the expectations of either the local residents, the heritage industry, or the tourists.

The Politics of (Re)presentation

Since local residents in Abbasanta made no efforts to highlight the official monumental qualities of the monument, ensuring that the monument was properly (re)presented to tourists, the Sopritendenza alla Antichità in Cagliari became involved. The (re)presentation of Losa became an issue of contest. During two campaigns in 1971 and 1972 the accessibility of the site was adjusted to meet tourist demands. A street was built and huge amounts of 'rubble' on the site itself were cleared. When the rubble later turned out to be the complete Roman stratum of the site, the local mayor stopped the work by a dramatic action. He ordered the *Carabineri* to use force if the Sopritendenza employees continued the 'clearing'. The conflict escalated and as a result, Ferruccio Barreca, the director of the Sopritendenza, closed the monument to the public for two years. He was able to do so because of a fence that had been erected around the whole site. In practice, this meant that local residents and independent tourists were denied access, whereas organised tourists obtained permission to visit the nuraghe. In 1990 a local resident expressed his feelings to me: 'Twenty or thirty years ago Losa was our symbol [*simbolo proprio*], we were proud of it, we showed it to friends and tourists and often visited it ourselves, but then it became a commercial symbol [*simbolo commerciale*].'

By denying local residents and independent tourists access to the monument, the Sopritendenza denied the Abbasantees an active part in the (re)presentation of Losa. In addition the former (re)presentation of the monument was deconstructed by removing the 'king's table', a core element of the local (re)presentation. The people of Abbasanta may have noticed the parallels with the economic and political situation at the time. The failure of state-financed development projects was already obvious. Politicians and academics were publicly blamed for overlooking local interests. Evidence of failed efforts to develop and industrialise the island were all over the island. The factories, which had cost billions to build, were abandoned to fall to ruin, but not without having first destroyed the subsistence economy of the shepherds. They are now referred to by Sardinians as *Cattedrali nel Deserto*. Ironically, from the top of Losa, one has an excellent view of Abbasanta's *Cattedrali nel Deserto*. In the south-west one can get a glimpse of what was supposed to be a huge pig stock-farm. Turning one's gaze to the south-east, the buildings of an abandoned chicken farm come into view.

The recent development at Losa provided still more proof of Abbasanta's subordination, the very subordination that the people had hoped to overcome in the first place. This time local residents refused to cooperate with the authorities. Up to the 1990s, a tourist in Abbasanta had a hard time finding a postcard, souvenir, or any information about Losa.

In the 1980s, the clash with the archaeological authorities and the alienation of the local people from the monument continued. As part of my fieldwork, I showed people all over Sardinia photographs of the most famous nuraghi on the island in order to identify them. As I expected, Losa and Su Nuraxi turned out to be the two best-known monuments of their kind. Around eighty percent of the people interviewed were able to identify Losa. Strikingly enough, the percentage among the Abbasantees population living two miles from the monument was not significantly higher. Most of the people had not visited the monument since the 1970s. And in the 1970s and especially the 1980s Losa became one of the best-known tourist attractions on the island! The image of Losa appeared extensively on the covers of travel guides. Moreover, the national tourist board had launched an international promotion campaign in the 1980s using the image of Losa. The representation of Losa no longer exclusively referred to the monument. Yet, it is not uncommon for teenagers in Abbasanta to visit the monument for the first time during school-organised activities. What happened?

As the flow of visitors to the island steadily increased in the 1970s, the authorities in Cagliari again made funds available to improve the quality of the monument. Whereas the main objective of the campaigns in 1971 to 1972 had been to increase the accessibility of the site, the goal of the second campaign in 1975 was to improve the tourist quality of the monument itself. During the campaign, it came to yet another clash between archaeological and local authorities. Unlike the first time, it was not the way the archaeological authorities were dealing with the local heritage that led to the actual dispute, but the disproportional use of scarce resources. Until then, visitors had to take a torch if they wanted to enter the nuraghe. To remedy this unsatisfactory situation, the Sopritendenza decided to install lighting inside the building. In addition, four gigantic spot lights were planned to shine upon the monument at night, so people could enjoy the silhouette of this national monument while passing by on the Carlo Felice. At the same time the municipality of Abbasanta was involved in an ongoing struggle to get funds to provide the main parts of the village with public lighting. For years the requests of local residents and local authorities had been met with indifference in Cagliari. The mayor of Abbasanta then threatened to cut the electricity supply for Losa if the spot lights were erected before the village received public lightning. To make sure that at least the lighting of the inner part was assured, the Sopritendenza decided not to place the spot lights.

It was the second time in the history of the village that the subject of electricity had symbolised a fundamental change in the relation between the locals, the nation, and the monument. In the 1920s and 1930s, the connection to the electricity system had been seen as a sign of the incorporation of the village into the nation, but the recent incident demonstrated to the people of Abbasanta that the incorporation has not made much progress. When it pertained to a matter of 'real' national importance – the (re)presentation of Losa – the rights and objectives of the local residents turned out to be of a secondary importance. While local residents had been eager to (re)present the national importance of Losa in the 1930s and the 1950s, their attitude turned into one of neglect and rejection once the state authorities took possession of the monument.

At the national level, tourism became of the utmost importance in this period. As politicians and most of the people in Sardinia finally realised that the economic 'rebirth' of the island had failed, the government and many local authorities finally decided to invest in tourism. Not so in Abbasanta.

Due to repeated resistance by local authorities (exclusively Christian Democrats) to measures concerning the (re)presentation of the monument, state authorities finally decided not to invest in Losa any longer. This was in contrast to many other nuraghi of comparable size and condition, which were transformed into tourist attractions in the 1980s, strongly fostering local economies.

As a consequence, local Christian Democratic politicians, who had ruled community affairs since the 1950s, themselves unable to attract further financial aid for tourist-related developments and in particular the improvement of Losa, made tourism a topic *non grata* in Abbasanta. While Losa, or rather the representation of Losa, became a national symbol, this time because of the combined efforts of the national history-makers and the national tourist authorities,[16] the local residents' attitude towards the monument can best be characterised as one of indifference. When Losa turned from a *simbolo proprio* into a *simbolo commerciale*, they were not able to keep up with the change in meaning. Unable to invest in tourism and lacking national support, they left Losa for what it was – a huge heap of nicely arranged pieces of rock that, strangely enough, attracted tens of thousands of visitors every year. All over the world Losa, or rather its image, gained more and more fame (there was also a disproportionally high increase of Sardinian tourists visiting the monument), but local residents showed no interest in the historicity or the economic potential of their monument. Incidental efforts by local entrepreneurs and non Christian Democratic politicians to profit from the increasing flow of tourists on the island were met with indifference (no public aid or assistance whatsoever) and sometimes even with active opposition on the part of the municipality; especially when it concerned the representation of Abbasanta.

At one point the mayor prevented the distribution of a brochure, titled 'Abbasanta Tourism', that was meant to promote Abbasanta. One reason for this step might have been the fact that the brochure was prepared by several local entrepreneurs and amateur historians connected to the opposition (see below). On another occasion, when the local station-master invited all the villages in the area to represent their potential tourist attractions in the railway-station, Abbasanta was the only municipality to ignore the invitation. Two years later, when Abbasanta finally furnished a poster, it was not Losa that was represented as worthwhile visiting, but the local park.

It was only in 1988, when two of the main opposition leaders of the village, the number-one candidates of the Partito Sardo d'Azione (PSd'A) and the Partito Socialista Italiano (PSI), organised a widely-praised photographic exhibition on the local monumental heritage, that things began to change. By means of 120 photographs, the local residents 'rediscovered' Losa and other prehistoric monuments they themselves had proudly shown to tourists and relatives twenty or thirty years earlier.

In the local election campaign in spring 1990, the opposition tried to tap into the tourist development by investing the local material heritage with a tourist value. It harshly criticised the ruling Democratia Cristiana (DC) for its neglect of Losa. Due to this, the DC, for the first time in fifteen years, was forced to take a position regarding the town's material heritage and tourism. This resulted in what seems an unintentionally ambiguous statement in the local election campaign:

> We have to become aware that for many decades, Losa has represented the image of the Sardinian interior in Italy and abroad. In fact history books at school and tourist brochures contain photographs of Losa. The *neglect* by the authorities does not take into account its importance. (DC: la proposta amministrativa per gli anni '90, my emphasis, my translation)[17]

The statement, so it seems, could as well have been a statement by the opposition. But as it was an election statement of the DC, we wonder who was blamed, and for what? In private conversations, DC officials in Abbasanta were well aware that the past opposition of the DC-ruled municipality had been responsible for the neglect by the authorities. But this was obviously not the message they wanted to get across. This statement was really about the failure to take into account the non-economic implications of the tourist gaze. The blame for that lay not only with local politicians or the heritage industry.

The effects of the politics of (re)presentation not only changed the attitude of the local residents towards Losa. It also had far-reaching consequences for the local attitude towards the heritage industry as well as towards local historical heritage. Encouraged by the success of the 1988 exhibition, the organisers kept stimulating the newly aroused historical consciousness of their fellow villagers. One way of doing this was by organising archaeological outings. The discussions and events that took place before and after of one of those occasions, an outing in May 1990,

Figure 3.4 A Sunday visit to a prehistoric grave near Abbasanta.

illustrate how locals are willing to sacrifice convictions or economic gains in order to remain in charge of the (re)presentation. In some cases efforts might even be combined to obstruct any further act of (re)presentation in order to prevent the loss of control over the (re)presentation.

The object of the organisers was to visit several less known but quite extraordinary monuments near Abbasanta. About seventy people participated in the day-long programme. Its highlight was the visit to three *Domus de Janas* (prehistoric rock-cut graves) situated at a plot (Mura Iddari) owned by a local butcher. In contrast to the other monuments on the programme, the participants knew a good deal about the graves, though most had never actually seen them. The graves, together with Losa, had been highlighted during the 1988 exhibition. Many people still possessed a set of prints of Losa and the three graves, published for the occasion. As they played such a central part in the representation of local history, even the DC could not help expressing deep concern about their future. Recognition that the local heritage consists of more than the (temporarily) despised nuraghe Losa thus found its way into the DC election programme of 1990: 'The magnitude of the nuraghe Losa does not belittle the importance of the other countless testimonies of our historic legacy' (ibid.; my translation).[18] The DC thus maintained that actions must be taken to secure the future of the local heritage. As far as the three graves are concerned: '[t]his interest has to be transformed into the purchase of the plot(s) where the archaeological monuments are situated … The importance of that monument hails from the fact that it is one of the very few examples in Sardinia where three Domi are located near to each other without showing any resemblance to one another' (ibid.; my translation).[19]

During preparation for the outing, the organisers visited the site and discovered that the graves restored only two years previously were in very bad condition. The owner of the site had transformed one into a dog kennel. The condition of the other two was even more deplorable. The organisers publicly declared the state of the monuments was an absolute disgrace. This judgement was broadly shared in Abbasanta. The huge turn-out for the outing may partly be the result of the commotion caused by the report of the amateur historians. After seventy villagers had actually seen the graves, the butcher had an even more difficult time explaining, even to his own friends and relatives, his treatment of the local heritage.

About a month later, the butcher invited a couple of old men, his family and friends and some acquaintances such as myself, to help shear his sheep and celebrate the end of the herding season at Mura Iddari. After his sheep were sheared, tables were set up and a tremendous meal was served, in clear sight of the demolished graves. The day was very

Figure 3.5 Celebrating the end of the herding season at Mura Iddari.

pleasant. After we had enjoyed the meal the company delighted in drinking and singing. Around six o'clock in the evening, as people were preparing to leave, a car appeared suddenly on the dusty road leading to Mura Iddari. It stopped in front of the party and, paying no notice to the people present, three men crossed the fences and headed directly towards the graves. The butcher finally addressed them with a slightly rhetorical question: 'Would it not be proper to ask the owner of the site, since he is present, for permission to enter his property?'. The reply was sharp: 'A person who deals with the cultural heritage the way you do, has lost all right to speak'. Furthermore, the visitors said, they intended notify the archaeological authorities about the matter. The butcher became enraged. The threat of violence persuaded the three to leave. The guests then discussed the incident. People who previously had been outraged by the state of the graves, changed their attitude completely (also in private conversations afterwards). In their eyes it had now become a different matter. The rights of a friend, or at least a fellow villager, were at stake here. The right to use his property as it pleased him and, most important of all, his right to be in charge of any measures concerning the (re)presentation of the graves should by not be restricted by outsiders, authorities, and certainly not by the heritage industry. He was advised to take precautions to prevent uninvited visitors or tourists visiting the graves. As news of what had happened spread through the village, accusations against the butcher vanished. A kind of common opinion evolved that it might be best not to invest in the (re)presentation of the graves at all. The story of Losa seemed to repeat itself.

Most of the time local residents must accept the (re)presentations created by others as well as the consequences arising from the actions taken. The dynamics of the next case to be presented will for that reason look far more familiar. Although Sardinia has the remains of seven thousand nuraghi, the representations aimed at tourists are drawn from no more then twenty nuraghi. Being photogenic or picturesque is often the only quality that seems to entitle certain nuraghi to be part of the set. A fine example is a nuraghe situated next to a small church, located near the village Silanus, twenty kilometres from Abbasanta. Local residents call it simply 'Nuraghe Silanus'. The red TCI from 1967, however, mentions two names: 'Nuraghe S. Sabina' and 'Nuraghe S. Sarbana'. The fifth (1984) edition reduced this to a single one: 'Nuraghe S. Sabina'. Locals do not accept this name. Santa Sabina is the patron saint of Silanus. The parochial church, and only the church, and certainly not a heathen monument in its vicinity, should bear the name of the saint.

The naming policy adopted by the TCI established the standard subsequently used by outsiders for the (re)presentation of the nuraghe. This practice insults the villagers. Still, the representation introduced by the TCI seems to have so much authority that even a local shopkeeper finally went along with it, publishing a series of postcards using, or should one say abusing, the name of the patron saint. He still had in stock several thousand postcards referring to the Nuraghe Silanus but that did not appeal to the tourists. They came looking for S. Sabina and that is what they finally got. Although the local community had, through the local entrepreneur, access to the means of representation, they still lacked the power necessary to be in charge of its content.

Some Remarks on the Subject of (Re)presentation

The representation of the Other is a well-established subject in anthropological discourse. It was Dean MacCannell (1976, 1989), the most frequently quoted scholar on tourism (see Cohen 1988: 35), who successfully situated the (re)presentation of the touristic Other (all the objects, material or immaterial, dead or alive, which tourists gaze on) on the research agenda of the social scientist. MacCannell's main aim, however, was simply to understand the role of the tourist in modern society (1976: 10). The core of his argument was that the idealised expectation of the tourist can neutralise or at least obscure the experience of reality. The representation of the Other in tourist-generating regions can, as far as the tourist is concerned, take precedence over the actual *presentation* of the Other. So it comes as no surprise that MacCannell and his successors frequently failed to address the other end of the human equation in tourism, namely the host. For other scholars, it might just have been the innocent appearance of the tourist gaze, its assumed lack of transformative power, that kept them from investigating the relation between the tourist gaze, the (re)presentation, and the hosts.

The general conclusion of this chapter is, however, that the politics of (re)presentation is not as innocent as it might appear. It is just a continuation of the unbalanced power struggle between the metropolis and the periphery (see also Pratt 1992). At present, though, it seems that more and more Europeans in the periphery (often tourists themselves), have become aware of the content, the mechanisms, the efficiency and the deficiencies of (re)presentations. As a result the politics of (re)presentation, the control of the (re)presentation, and therefore the control of the tourist gaze, become a matter of local concern. Ignoring or even violating the right of the host to be in charge of the (re)presentation, and thus the tourist gaze, can have far-reaching consequences. The case of Abbasanta makes this clear. I believe the struggle about (re)presentation will become the most significant hallmark of European reactions to the tourist gaze.

Let me finish by giving two other examples of a people becoming aware of and dealing with different aspects of the politics of representation. To put the subject in a even broader perspective my examples come from other parts of the world. In August 1992 the *U.S.* multinational Coca Cola launched a new advertising campaign in *Italy*. The advertisement used showed the *Greek* Parthenon. The temple's original fluted baseless columns were replaced by columns resembling the world's most famous bottle. Whereas it took the Greeks almost 180 years to launch a protest against the theft of the sculptures of the Parthenon by Lord Elgin, their reaction was now of another order. The Greek public and the archaeological authorities were infuriated by the tasteless representation. As the national archaeological authorities were preparing to sue, Coca Cola offered its excuses to the Greek government.

There are also signs that the hosts' growing consciousness of the politics of (re)presentation have already altered the unbalanced power relations in Developing World countries where the industry's objectives have been met with passive obedience. Take the case of Sri Lanka. The government of Sri Lanka founded a Ministry of Tourism in 1989 with the aim of attracting 600,000 tourists annually. After just one year, despite the bloody civil war, the number of tourists coming to Sri Lanka had already doubled from 200,000 to 400,000. It was not because of the favourable consequences but because of the non-economic effects of the gaze, that an opposition leader welcomed the government initiative: 'It is a very unpleasant experience for tourists to be confronted with dead bodies while travelling. We hope the presence of the tourist might put an end to the killing' (De Moor: *De Volkskrant,* 23 February 1991, my translation).[20] It may provide some food for thought to know that, according to the same newspaper article, a couple of German tourists complained to their tour operator that 'their vacation was ruined by dead bodies insolently drifting down the river.'[21]

NOTES

1. In contrast with the period of European conquest, when world fairs brought the Other into the home-regions of the gazers.

2. The term 'representation' is used to refer to information about the touristic Other. The term 'presentation', refers to the actual staging of the 'real' object. '(Re)presentation' then refers to the combined efforts of the tourist industry to make the touristic Other.

3. A indigenous bronze and iron age culture (1800 BC – 238 BC) named after its most famous remains: the *nuraghi*. The nuraghi are towers commonly with two or more storeys built of cyclopean masonry. Some of these towers, their cyclopean walls sloping inward towards the top, originally reached a height of up to twenty metres. At present most scholars agree that the nuraghi is an indigenous Sardinian product dating back to the second millennium BC. Today there are more than 7,000 remains of these towers, most of them in very bad shape. It is estimated that when the Romans finally conquered the island in 238 BC, more than 20,000 had been erected on the island. The nuraghi constitute one of the major tourist attractions on the island.

4. The absence of the tourists in the argument presented does of course not do justice to the actual situation at the tourist site, although the size of the tourist flow is temporarily affected by the struggle about representation. Nor does it, in general, do justice to the importance of the host-guest relation.

5. The fourth edition of the Sardinian travel guide by the Touring Club Italiano from 1967 mentions four museums with an archaeological collection. The fifth edition from 1984 already mentions fourteen museums devoted to archaeology. In the period 1984 to 1989 another six museums concerned with the island's past opened their gates.

6. We have to keep in mind that, as yet, no effort has been made to actually present the past – meaning to stage the remains in order to please gazing visitors. This seems to be a common feature of the first phase in the genesis of a naturally evolved tourist destination. Acts of presentation occur only after a long period in which the existing – authentic -qualities of a destination, that might appeal to tourists, have been represented as worth visiting. Only later on, or when a clear model is at hand (as is the case with the creation of new modern tourist resorts in remote areas), does it become possible to create an attraction out of nothing (i.e., without any previous act of presentation).

7. In the immediate aftermath of the First World War, war veterans constituted the first Sardinian Party – the Partito Sardo d'Azione (PSd'A). PSd'A politicians made Sardinian under-development a political issue. Since than it has been known as *La Questione Sarda*. Campaigning for independence, they used a mystified image of nuraghic culture to prove the viability of a Sardinian nation. The party was incorporated into Mussolini's Fascist Party immediately after his take-over in Rome, then reinstated after the Second World War. Its members are now mockingly referred to by the left as *I nuraghisti*.

8. For a detailed discussion about the relation between tourism and economic development in Sardinia see Odermatt 1990.

9. The former Ufficio della Antichità.

10. The appearance of publications solely dedicated to tourists normally indicates that a mature stage in the genesis of a given tourist destination has been or soon will be reached. The case presented makes clear that this can still take nearly up to fifty years.(For a comprehensive discussion of this matter see Odermatt 1994).

11. See for example the vast body of literature on fairs, most notably the work of Burton Benedict or most recently Rydell and Gwinn 1994.

12. Bonaventura, the true author of the poem, was one of the most famous folk poets in the area. Until the 1960s it was a Sardinian custom to organise poetry contests on religious and village holidays. At such occasions, three or more poets, without any time for preparation, were given a theme they had to elaborate on. According to Bonaventura's daughter, the poem must have been a product of such a contest because until 1950 her father never created a poem at his desk. Interestingly enough, the custom of poetry contests was revitalised in substantial parts of the island in the 1980s. Now the whole thing is highly commercialised. The best poets can earn a month's salary in just one evening.

13. Nuraghe Losa

O maestosu, artisticu nuraghe,
D'origine millenaria portentosu;
Non isvelas su tou misteriosu
Fundamentu, si po gherra o puru 'e paghe.

A s'Iscienza meraviglia faghe
Et a ommi Archeologo istudiosu;
Ti cren tumba de Capu virtuosu,
O cumandu 'e Tribù, o de Deidade.

Istoricos illustres e regales
Visita ti rendene benigna;
De seculos antigos tantu caru.

Abbasanta, origogliosa in sos annales,
Hat su valore antigu de Sardigna;
Nuraghe Losa, monumentu raru.

14. The act of representation does not necessarily involve printed material but can also be achieved by means of oral performances; see Fine and Speer 1985.

15. At present Losa qualifies as touristic landmark more than any other tourist attraction on the island.

16. In their combined effort to (re)present Sardinian prehistory the tourist authorities and the national history-makers can at that stage best be referred to as the heritage industry.

17. 'Dobbiamo ricordaci che alcuni decenni fa il Nuraghe Losa era l'immagine che rappresentava l'interna Sardegna sia in Italia che all'estero, infatti sui testi scolastici e sui programmi turistici c'era la foto di "Losa"; il suo abbandono da parte degli organi preposti ha fatto scordare la sua importanza.'

18. 'L'importanza del Nuraghe Losa non mette in secondo ordine altre numerose testimonianze di cui é ricco il territorio comunale di Abbasanta.'

19. 'Tale interesse di interventi lo si dovrà concretizzare con l'acquisizione di quei terreni su cui insistono i monumenti archeologici ... i terreni dove si trovano le "Domus De Janas di Mura Iddari", uno dei rari esempi in Sardegna di tre Domus vicine tra loro ma con caratteristiche particolari che ne evidenziano la singolarità.'

20. 'Voor toeristen is het niet prettig om onderweg voortdurend op lijken te stoten. We hopen dat door hun aanwezigheid een einde aan het moorden komt.'
21. '... hun vakantiepret bedorven werd door lijken die zo onbeschaamd waren om in de rivier voorbij te drijven.'

REFERENCES

Bandinu, B. *Costa Smeralda. Come nasce una favola turistica*, Milano: Rizzoli, 1980.

Boissevain, J. 'Tourism and Development in Malta', *Development and Change* 8, (1977): 523-38.

Braudel, F. *The Mediterranean and the Mediterranean World in the Age of Philip II*, vol. 1, Glasgow: Fontana Press, 1986.

Brigaglia, M., ed. *Tutti i libri della Sardegna. 100 schede per capire un'isola*, Cagliari: Edizione Della Torre, 1989.

Cohen, E. 'Traditions in the Qualitative Sociology of Tourism', *Annals of Tourism Research* 15, (1988): 29-46.

Della Marmora, A. *Itinerario dell' isola di Sardegna*, Cagliari: 3T, 1971.

Graburn, N.H.H. 'The Anthropology of Tourism', *Annals of Tourism Research* 10, (1983): 9-33.

Fine, E.C., and Speer, J.H. 'Tour Guide Performances as Sight Sacralization', *Annals of Tourism Research* 12, (1985): 73-95.

Herzfeld, M. *Place in History: Social and Monumental Time in a Cretan Town*, Princeton: Princeton University Press, 1991.

Hunter, M. 'The Preconditions of Preservation: A Historical Perspective', in D. Lowenthal and M. Binny ed., *Our Past Before Us. Why Do We Save It?*, London: Blackwell Press, 1981: 22-31.

Lilliu, G. *La Civiltà dei sardi dal paleolitico all'età dei nuraghi*, Torino: Nuova ERI Edizioni RAI, 1988.

Lowenthal, D. 'Introduction', in D. Lowenthal and M. Binny ed., *Our Past Before Us. Why Do We Save It?*, London: Blackwell Press, 1981: 9-16.

MacCannell, D. *The Tourist: A New Theory of the Leisure Class*, New York: Schocken Books, 1976.

_____, 'Reconstructed Ethnicity: Tourism and Cultural Identity in Third World Communities', *Annals of Tourism Research* 11, (1984): 375-91.

_____, *The Tourist: A New Theory of the Leisure Class*, 2nd edn, New York: Schocken Books, 1989.

Macciardi, L. 'Balancia turistica della Sardegna', *Prospettive meridionali* 5, no. 12 (1959): 643-55.

Nash, D. 'Tourism as a Form of Imperialism', in V.L. Smith ed., *Hosts and Guests. The Anthropology of Tourism*, Oxford: Basil Blackwell, 1978: 33-48.

———, 'Tourism as a Form of Imperialism', in V.L. Smith ed., *Hosts and Guests. The Anthropology of Tourism*, Philadelphia: University of Pennsylvania Press, 1989: 37-52.

Odermatt, P. 'Tourism and Sardinian Development' in L.F. Bruyning and J.T. Leersen eds, *Yearbook of European Studies 3. Italy – Europe*, Amsterdam: Rodopi, 1990: 161-78.

———, '*Een hard Sardisch gelag: Toeristische attracties systematisch bekeken*', Amsterdam: Het Spinhuis, 1994.

Pratt, M.L. *Imperial Eyes: Travel Writing and Transculturation*, London: Routledge, 1992.

Ross, A. *South to Sardinia*, Hamisch: Hamilton, 1960.

Rydell, R.W. and Gwinn, N., eds *Fair Representations: World's Fairs and the Modern World*, Amsterdam: VU University Press, 1994.

Urry, J. *The Tourist Gaze. Leisure and Travel in Contemporary Societies*, London: Sage, 1990.

Willis, R.F. *Italy Chooses Europe*, Oxford: Oxford University Press, 1971.

4. NEGOTIATING THE TOURIST GAZE
The Example of Malta

Annabel Black

*T*his chapter examines some of the ways in which the people of the Island of Malta have responded to the ever-encroaching presence of tourism over the last twenty years. Much of my material is drawn from fieldwork in Mellieha, a village-turned-tourist resort in the north of Malta. However, the idea for writing about this arose from the experience of working as an information officer for the London Tourist Board over one summer. This brought home to me, arguably more than any research ever could, what it feels like to act as a host. I was struck by the number of ways in which one becomes involved in colluding with a remarkably strict set of expectations and ideas about one's own culture. These may bear little resemblance to the parameters which structure one's world outside the context of acting as a host, and yet they somehow make sense, or at least contain an internal logic, irremovable from the spaces marked out and sometimes constructed through tourism.

Whilst working as a host my sense of the geography of the U.K. became structured around the itineraries of the various coach tours on offer, and my sense of time organised according to the opening times of museums and the hours when attractions such as the Changing of the Guard would be 'performed'. Away from the office my senses became rapidly restored to the prosaic: un-hostlike elbowing for space on delayed buses and the like. Both worlds were equally real but, in this experience, often entirely separate. However, this is not always the case with hosts and more often it is a question of how and by whom the boundaries between host and guest become established. This is especially true in situations such as in the Maltese village of Mellieha where there appears to be a considerable collision between the worlds of the tourists and their hosts. I therefore came out of this experience interested to relate it both to my material on Malta and to the literature on the cultural interaction between hosts and guests.

An important preliminary question is what we mean when we talk about culture and cultural interaction in this context. It has sometimes been pointed out in the literature that anthropology and tourism tend to fit very uncomfortably together (e.g., Boissevain 1977, Nash 1981). Concerned with appreciation and communication between cultures, anthropologists tend to be squeamish when it comes to the idea of this communication either originating or resulting in direct financial profit as it so often does in the hands of the industry's organisers. Also, highly tuned to the nuances entailed when dealing with the concept of culture, anthropologists may often have ideas which differ profoundly both from the changing ways in which the cultural domain is defined by the controllers of the industry and from the tourists themselves. There is also the question of the extent to which the above range of definitions corresponds to the hosts' ideas about their own culture.

An example of this dilemma arose during fieldwork whilst I was interviewing British tourists on their opinions about Malta. Repeatedly, following positive comments on how friendly and hospitable the people were, and how easy it was to feel at home in Malta, they would say 'but they don't have much *culture* here, you know crafts and that...the people are very nice of course, but they seem to lack imagination – initiative – I mean they don't make much of what they *do* have, do they?'

This statement puzzled me at the time; I was entrenched in fieldwork and trying to come to grips with a totally new language and an alien moral code. As far as I was concerned the Maltese 'had', if anything, rather too much culture and the tourist gaze seemed somewhat myopic. I was tempted to interpret such views as reflecting two main things. First, they sounded like an echo of the way the country had been viewed by the British authorities in the context of colonialism – that somehow, the island's very adequacy as some kind of extension of home (but now one free from the normal constraints of working life) was matched in equal measure by the inadequacies of its inhabitants to appreciate and develop their own environment. Second, that the views expressed seemed to reflect the way in which certain types of tourism literally do package a place into a framework in terms of which the only possible means of perceiving and 'thinking' culture are stripped down to their barest minimum; indeed virtually to a checklist of material artefacts.

However, the problem is of course more complex. Given the different ways culture can be conceived and experienced, in this type of discussion one is caught up in dealing simultaneously with a number of different and maybe conflicting discourses surrounding the definitions of the areas of life this term should cover. The question then becomes the extent to which these conflicting notions can be seen to fit together in tourism studies. Reading through the current literature, one finds few clues as to how to set about such a reconciliation. One reason for this may lie in the lack of communication between the two, very different tendencies in the literature on the cultural aspects of tourism.

One deals with more traditional questions, focusing generally on acculturation and culture change and more specifically on the cultural outcomes for the host community of the host-guest encounter. The second focuses on the behaviour and motivations of tourists and upon tourism itself, involving topics ranging from the nature of authenticity and the idea of tourism as ritual and pilgrimage, to tourism within the world economic system (e.g., Allcock 1988, Brown 1988, MacCannell 1984, Urry 1990). For all that this, second focus uses an interesting mixture of theoretical ideas and methods, providing insights into the guests' experiences, it tends to ignore those of the hosts. To date there have been few attempts to bring together these two sets of concerns, and the first trend in the field particularly suffers as a result. It is useful to describe briefly this aspect of the problem before turning to my own suggestions and material on Malta.

When studies of the outcomes of the host-guest encounter were first made in the mid-1970s they were very much influenced by the debates taking place in the sociology of development at the time. The focus of debate on the economic aspects of tourism was mainly upon the benefits versus the costs of tourism to developing countries (Diamond 1977, Evans 1975, McKean 1976; for positive views; Schneider and Hanson 1972, Bryden 1973, and Turner and Ash 1975 for the negative). Many social scientists writing on the cultural effects took their cue from this debate. This resulted in two tendencies. First it led to an over-emphasis on measurement, quantification, and taxonomy, the assumption being that cultural effects could be studied in a kind of ascending scale – the greater the number of tourists, the greater the cultural effects. For instance, Doxey (1976), in discussing the cultural effects of tourism in Barbados and Long-Mile Island, drew up an irritation index, arguing that in the initial stages hosts heartily welcome their guests, but as more tourists come the host population becomes increasingly sour, passing through the stages of apathy and antagonism to downright xenophobia.

There is a certain neatness to this model and it struck some chords during my London Tourist Board experience. During our training, we were frequently impressed with the need to treat every customer as an individual, and shown John Cleese videos to push the lesson home; but as numbers mounted during mid-July, we all ended up urgently in need of a refresher course! However, the very neatness of this kind of model belies the fact that host reactions to the effects of mass tourism can often be extremely mixed and ambivalent. Furthermore, the model could in no clear way have been applied to the Maltese case.

In 1983 nearly 500,000 tourists visited the Maltese Islands against a total local population of just over 300,000. In Mellieha there were three large hotels containing between them enough beds to accommodate over 1,500, a holiday complex under construction to sleep a further 600, and countless holiday apartments to cater for the tourists who came to visit the area each year. According to Doxey's model, one would expect the Maltese population to be well on the way to xenophobia, but the situation was not nearly as straightforward as this. Thus, the problem with such models is that they tended to substitute taxonomy for in-depth analysis, and in failing to take sufficient account of the overall context in which tourism developed they were often silent on its differ-ential effects upon different sectors of the population. However, later studies do not fall so easily into this trap, and writers have become more careful in qualifying their conclusions (see Samarasuriya 1983).

A second outcome of the early influence from the economic field has been more long-lasting. This lies in the tendency to assume that the eco-nomic inequalities upon which tourism exchanges are so often premised (both on an inter-personal and an inter-regional level) are inevitably and very directly paralleled when talking about the cultural aspects of such exchanges. A misleading corollary to this is the assumption that the poorer and smaller the population of the host region, the weaker its cul-ture, whilst the more economically powerful the country or countries of origin of the guests, the 'stronger' their culture will be and the less able the hosts will be to resist the worst outcomes of tourism.

A concept that draws heavily on the above assumption is that of the demonstration effect: that exposed to the consumption and behaviour patterns of their guests, members of the host population at first feel resentful and suffer feelings of inferiority, but later want to 'jump on the bandwagon', in order to obtain the material means necessary to copy the consumption patterns of their guests, and adopt what J. and P. Schneider (1972 and 1976) have termed 'distorted metropolitan lifestyles'. Turner and Ash describe the demonstration effect as 'tourism's main weapon, an instrument of slow torture, through which tourists almost inevitably impose their values upon the societies visited' (1975: 197-98). Here again, my primary objection has lain in the fact that my own material fits uneasily with these predictions – by now we would expect the Maltese population to have long since taken to guzzling Watneys, to parading around topless and to eating the ubiquitous 'English breakfast', advertised in almost every café in the tourist areas. All of these they have cheerfully resisted.

Therefore, although the idea of the demonstration effect may be appropriate in certain contexts, it can contain in-built assumptions as to the frailty of the host culture, on the basis of which writers speak of the urgent need to intervene and defend the hosts from inevitable obliteration. In spite of worthy intentions, there is the danger of presenting stereotyped and somewhat idealised pictures of the host cultures and of begging rather than addressing some of the key questions that need to be asked as to the historical and social forces at work within the host communities; forces that may contain the potential to resist the ideological encroachments of neo-imperialist forces such as tourism. Represented in this manner, host cultures are almost inevitably viewed as lacking an internal dynamic and become blank screens upon which to project ideas about a 'lost past' and to reflect upon the social ills of the developed world. In the meantime, the voices of the people upon whom all these ills are supposedly working often remain completely absent.

Furthermore, as pointed out by McDonald (1987) in her discussion of cultural tourism in the Monte D'Arrée region of central Finistere in Brittany, one key fact overlooked by those who express fears concerning the disappearance of authenticity is that it is often *through* tourism that a recognisably traditional world exists. She points out how in recent years the region has come to appear 'traditional' precisely as a result of the intervention of tourism, which has demanded and conjured up this world. There has been a proliferation of culture as certain customs, rituals, crafts, and forms of speech that were previously falling out of use come to be re-evaluated and re-established in the new context and economic structure of tourism.

As a result of the organisation of tourism around such categories, the guests may well be able to return home content that they have experienced authenticity. However, the consequences may not be so straightforward for the bearers of this authenticity. As Bruner (1991) observes, although tourist discourse claims that the tourist self is transformed through travel with the native self remaining unchanged, in experience the reverse may well be true – it being the hosts who are forced to change and reassess their self-worth and that of their culture in the light of tourist expectations.

The above comments provide insights that can be applied more generally: this conjuring up of traditional worlds is by no means restricted to cultural tourism. It is significant that even tourists at the more unsophisticated end of the market, who take their holidays in the cheaper resorts of the Mediterranean, are led to, and do, expect very specific things. At the very least, an outdoor café life will be expected. This is surely a part of 'Mediterranean' life and something must be amiss if it is not found. Yet there are areas where this was and is not the case at all. In Malta, until quite recently, any café life that existed at all was extremely restricted and its custom mainly confined to members of the urban elite (themselves expending considerable resources and energy upon living up to a particular interpretation of how elites *should* behave in sophisticated European circles).

As travel to southern Europe has become more common, such expectations have obviously tended to gain momentum. Customs that are found in one Mediterranean country (for instance the existence of a dance tradition in Greece) tend to become defined as the whole Mediterranean package, as a cultural requirement. Here too, as is the case with cultural tourism, demand can easily outstrip supply, leading to the need to conjure up ever more items of 'culture'. Thus in Malta it has become popular to stage performances of 'traditional' dances which are mostly only a few years old.

Therefore, more thought needs to be given to the assumptions made when assessing the cultural influences of tourism upon host communities and more energy into capturing the ambiguity of the processes that condition the host-guest encounter. There are a number of ways in which this could be done, but here I shall restrict myself to exploring two suggestions.

First, I would suggest that in specific cases we need to look at the communicative messages that lie behind the encounter itself, with attention to how an area comes to be packaged for tourism. What is it that guests are told to expect, and do expect of a place they visit for a holiday, and in which ways do these perceptions and expectations correspond to or differ from what the hosts themselves hold of value in their own culture? Second, how do host perceptions of their guests and of themselves change over time as they become more productively involved in tourism? Important here are the strategies available to the hosts to mark the boundaries between their own cultural expectations and perceptions and those of their guests.

Maltese Tourism: Background and Development

For much of the nineteenth century and for the first part of the twentieth, the Maltese economy was totally geared to the country's role as a British armed services base. When the decision was made in the mid-1950s to run down the base and naval dockyard, it became obvious that the legacy of a totally undiversified economy posed a severe problem – in 1958 unemployment rose to forty-eight percent of the population. Tourism was introduced in the Development Plans of the early 1960s together with an extensive emigration scheme[1] and a series of measures to entice foreign manufacturing concerns to establish factories on Malta; these included the granting of a tax holiday and the letting of sites for factory and tourist development at peppercorn rents. The idea was to generate foreign exchange earnings, encourage infrastructural development and provide much-needed employment. This strategy was not without its drawbacks. One of the immediate consequences was a rampant boom in building and land speculation, involving much economic activity but little actual development. Also, tourism was expanded at a time of tremendous political uncertainty centred on competing definitions of what exactly constituted the Maltese nation and national cultural identity. This coincidence raises a wider set of questions concerning the cultural implications of tourism in a post-colonial context and its effects upon the host's freedom to develop and maintain a sense of cultural integrity.

Meanwhile there was the problem of how to market the Islands as a tourist attraction, because although there had long been a close connection between Malta and Britain, up until then this link had been premised on the Island's exploitation as a military base; it contained few obvious attractions as a tourist resort. Indeed if we look at the way in which Malta was perceived by the British during the colonial period, it enjoyed little of the praise and attention lavished by poets, novelists, and travellers upon the more recognisably exotic and impressive outposts of Empire. And if Byron's comment on Valletta, the capital city, as a 'city of bells, yells and smells' is anything to go by, it seems that the island contained little to excite the Romantic Imagination.

Rather, it was the island's role in the eyes of the British administrators, as little more than a military fortress that was most frequently reflected in the eye-witness and travel reports of the nineteenth and early twentieth centuries. Descriptions tend to stop short once they have described the Grand Harbour, the fortifications, the baroque architecture of the Knights of St John, and the gardens created by the British for the enjoyment of their senior administrators and servicemen. Observations of the local environment and population are largely restricted to complaints about the wind, comments on the *Faldetta* (the costume that used to be worn by Maltese women) and remarks about the intense Roman Catholicism of the population. These comments are sometimes supplemented with observations about the diligence of the people, but more often with expressions of exasperation at their rather gloomy countenance and fatalistic disposition (e.g., Badger 1838, Senior 1882). This was seen to be possibly due to the excessive influence of the Church, plus, in the words of one author, 'a streak of oriental acquiescence'. During the second half of the nineteenth century, Malta's role as a provider of services intensified, and in a sense this role reached its height during the Second World War. After the war Malta was awarded the George Cross for valour and it was very much in terms of its role during the war that Malta was perceived by the British in the following decade.

The Development of a Tourist Image for Malta

It can therefore be seen that those who wished to develop a new image for the island as a holiday resort during the 1960s and 1970s found themselves involved in something of an exercise in symbolic transformation and reversal.[2] Lacking the stock of sumptuous images and adjectives used to describe more exotic resorts, promoters relied upon a rather mixed bag of attractions. The beauty of the island's unspoilt coastlines was stressed and coupled with its as yet undiscovered charms. These were listed as Malta's friendly, hospitable population, its lace and metal crafts, traditional religious festivals, and so on. In addition, the island

was promoted as a home away from home, although within a discon-
nected and disconcertingly quaint frame of reference, including fragments of information such as the fact that 'they drive on the left', 'have'
English telephone boxes and 'especially welcome the English'.

This message has changed surprisingly little over the years in the
tourist brochures and newspaper copy promoting Malta to the U.K.
market. Brief resumés of what one brochure refers to as Malta's 'speck-
led' history are followed up by reassurances that 'the famed Maltese hospitality and friendliness makes you feel welcome' (Aquasun 1992) and
that 'a wealth of historical interest and the lovely weather are equalled
only by the welcome you'll receive from the Maltese people' (Horizon
Winter Sun Selection 1992/3). The 'home from home' aspect is still
stressed: 'Apart from the hot and dry weather and the Arabic looking
buildings you could imagine you are at home here. There are British
looking cafés, pubs and fish'n'chip shops and just about everyone speaks
English' (Holiday Mirror 1993). And tourists are assured that 'many
things will be familiar – English spoken everywhere, driving on the left,
red pillar boxes for your postcards and your money in pounds, albeit
Maltese!' (Horizon Winter Sun Selection 1992/3). The old-fashioned
quaintness of the island is also still emphasised, for instance in relation
to transport: 'The local transport system is rather vintage but faithful –
you can't go anywhere without seeing the green and white Leyland buses
which commute between the Island's resorts' (Med Choice 1992); and
'you have never seen so many old British cars from the 50s and 60s still
on the road...they are enough to remind your dad of his student and
courting days' (Holiday Mirror 1993).

Fulfilling the set of promises contained in this chameleon role as a
sunny, semi-exotic anglophile home away from home has resulted in
some interesting cultural manifestations. Apart from the new 'dance tradition', an equally new glass-making industry has been established (originally set up by an enterprising Englishman) along with one turning out
entire suits of knights' armour in every conceivable size. There has also
been a noticeable proliferation of signs advertising that 'English breakfasts are served all day' in certain areas of the country.

The efforts of the tourist promoters have not gone unrewarded, and
apart from a few setbacks in the late 1970s there has been a steady rise
in tourist arrivals from the late 1960s onwards, rising to 1,002,381 in
1992. To a large extent the promises seemed to have been delivered in
the eyes of the guests. In the survey I undertook of British visitors'
impressions of Malta (many of whom were small traders and some of

whom had been to Malta as servicemen during the war), a striking feature to emerge was the very uniformity of the responses. Almost unanimous approval was expressed about the friendliness of the people, in comments that could well serve as copy for a tourist brochure: 'you know it is really possible to feel at home here, they really like and welcome us; there's no language problem like in Greece or Spain and they don't go in for all that olive oil either!' This sense of affinity with the local people was given as the main reason why many came to Malta regularly for their holidays. It is important that this sense of affinity was and is shared by the Maltese. Many Melliehans still hold almost affectionate memories of the war when many servicemen were billeted there, and more recently long-lasting friendships are often established between local people and tourists. The fact that British tourists actively seek to meet people and make friends with them is an aspect of tourism which the Maltese enjoy and appreciate.

However, local responses to the comments about Malta 'lacking culture', which I related at the beginning of the article, were and remain far more mixed and ambivalent. Some would say that this just revealed the ignorance of their guests. Indeed, I was often surprised at how little the tourists generally knew about basic facts such as the religion and language of the people, for instance by presuming that the language was some sort of Italian (Maltese is a Semitic language, closely related to Arabic). Others take the tourists' point but would not attribute Malta's lack of culture to the same causes, blaming not absence of local initiative but rather the island's history, or want of direction from government. This whole topic deserves deeper examination. So I shall now look in greater detail at the local development of a tourist culture in Mellieha and at how Melliehans have come to negotiate and cope with the demands placed upon themselves and their environment by tourism.

The Development of a Tourist Culture: The Example of Mellieha

When tourism was first developing many Maltese held rather ambivalent attitudes towards foreigners; particularly towards the British and the Italians. While feeling some resentment and suspicion towards outsiders due to centuries of external domination, many people, especially those amongst the elite, also made constant claims of identification with the cultures of more powerful outsiders. People would often speak of the

Figure 4.1 The village of Mellieha.

problem as a kind of national inferiority complex – the feeling that everything *ta'barra* (from abroad) was inevitably superior and more desirable than anything produced at home. In the more sophisticated urban centres this expressed itself most poignantly through language, especially in the dialect spoken by the Sliemese (the inhabitants of Sliema, which used to be a smart suburb of Valletta and the home of the section of the upper class who most identified with, and sometimes married into, the British colonial elite). This dialect was, and still is, a distinctive combination of Maltese and English, with the latter predominating. At first hearing it sounds to the English ear extremely affected – as though the speakers are simply refusing to speak either language correctly. However, this dialect is really an integral part of Sliemese culture, the product of generations of children being brought up to look down on the Maltese language and discouraged from speaking it, while never being taught to speak English 'correctly' as a separate language.

However, in the more remote villages such as Mellieha, the experience of colonialism and attitude to things *ta'barra* was rather different. Located some way from the administrative arms of the colonial government, Melliehans prided themselves on the way that they developed a reputation for their 'awayness' from other parts of the island. This extended well beyond the colonial period and again was reflected partly through language. Shunning the city ways of the Sliemese, Melliehans prided themselves on their distinctive dialect, similar to that spoken by Gozitans – who to this day are considered decidedly different and a little distant by many Maltese. Melliehans were also proud of their ingenuity in coping with their land and environment and of the fact that other Maltese perceived them as being set apart. When I first moved there from one of the suburban areas close to Valletta, Melliehans were often very amused when I told them of the horror expressed about my move by 'city' friends in remarks such as 'but Mellieha's so far away!'

This did not mean that things *ta'barra* did not hold a fascination, and for a time tourism and its works fell into this category. I once went off on a womens' coach trip organised by the local branch of the Labour Party to visit some of the more recently established factories. We visited the Mdina glass works, and following the various explanations and demonstrations, we were invited to buy souvenirs. Most in our party enthusiastically followed this up, but a few showed no interest whatsoever. Alert to any signs of local people rejecting these 'unauthentic' manifestations of the new tourist culture, I asked the women about their lack of conformity. In fact, their forbearance bore witness to Melliehan parsimony rather than anything else. I was told that these things were lovely of course, something different, but they had already obtained their purchases on the trip organised the previous year!

Meanwhile, the initial stages of tourist development within the parish boundaries were comparatively self-contained and in many respects nonintrusive upon village life. Located on the lower slopes of two steep hills and the valley between them, the village was originally a compact settlement, dominated by the parish church, with small single-storey houses stretching out neatly from the main square. The hills above and the valleys leading down to the sea were taken up by the patchwork of tiny terraced fields so characteristic of the Maltese countryside.

Building began in the mid-1960s and by the mid-1970s there were three distinct areas of new development. First there was a large villa estate, built on Church land and tucked away on one of the valleys leading to the sea. The building plots and villas were largely sold off to property speculators and British expatriates. This development earned a rather notorious reputation in local history. There was a series of scandals surrounding the dealing in the plots of land at rapidly inflating prices and it is said that a barrier was originally placed at the entrance forbidding access to locals to what had previously been good agricultural land.

The second development was on the ridge of one of the hills above the village and contained some plots sold off to local people for housing as well as some for tourist flats. Finally, there was some development down on the wide bay about two kilometres below the village itself and reached by a winding road. This consisted of a restaurant, a few beach bars and a large hotel owned by Thomsons. Nearby, there were two more large hotels, one owned by an Englishman and another by a local entrepreneur. Although these new developments generated a new source of employment for villagers, at this stage the overall appearance and atmosphere of the parish was not greatly changed. Even during the late 1970s much of the land was still cultivated and the village still retained its reputation for being a distant and rather remote place. Furthermore, the tourists themselves and the people living in the expatriate villa community were still considered a rather strange and exotic species. Local people may have been happy to visit and make purchases from the Mdina glass works, but when the first two supermarkets were opened (both by returned emigrants) to cater to the tourists and expatriates, these were mainly seen as places to visit out of curiosity and to remark in horror at the high prices being demanded for imported goods.

Increasing development over the last fifteen years has brought about dramatic changes, most noticeably in the geographical distribution of tourism. All of the building developments described above have spread out, and not only to provide accommodation and services for tourists. Increased prosperity over the last decades has enabled many more young people to build or buy themselves new homes upon marriage. It is now common for young couples to establish homes in the areas previously marked out mainly for tourist developments. Also, people both from Mellieha and from other parts of Malta like to use their money to build, buy, or rent small holiday houses or flats down on the bay.

The twenty kilometres or so from the island's capital no longer seems such a distance, and during the summer a bustling seasonal community becomes established in the housing that is gradually spreading upwards towards the village from the coast. It includes a mixture of foreign tourists, Melliehans and people from the urban and suburban districts of the Island. The crowded shelves of the supermarkets, which have mushroomed to cater for the demand, reflect this new mixed clientele: cans of baked beans and bottles of tomato ketchup now jostle for space with Maltese staple foods such as packets of pasta and tins of tuna fish and tomato paste.

By now, the originally distinct areas of development have almost merged, virtually obliterating much of the landscape around the village and in many ways seeming to cancel out the features that used to characterise the area. It would be tempting to conclude from this that developments associated with tourism have, as seemingly in so many parts of Malta, literally swamped the village and villagers alike, robbing them of their space, integrity, and privacy. However, people's responses to these changes are again mixed.

For all that the village has been transformed geographically and economically through tourism, and the inhabitants have become increasingly involved in catering for the industry in one way or another, Melliehans have not become sour or xenophobic. Rather, they have managed to maintain clear ideas both about what they choose to incorporate from tourist culture into their own lives and about what marks off their own cultural identity from that of their visitors. Given this, I would suggest that a great deal of negotiation and adjustment is taking place, producing results more complex than can be explained in terms of the simple effects of tourism upon a passive local culture. To illustrate this, I shall begin by looking at some of the spatial aspects of the changes brought about through tourism and then move to a more general discussion of the interplay between tourist and local cultural values.

Figure 4.2 A view across to the cramped beach of Mellieha Bay.

Tourism and The Allocation of Space

Many local people do feel sadness and resentment at the almost total reallocation of their land to the services of tourism and the inevitable destruction of the features that once made the landscape both beautiful and agriculturally profitable. Furthermore, the fact that the road along the bay which used to be fairly clear throughout the year is now crammed with hired cars throughout the summer, can be a source of frustration and annoyance. Another source of complaint is the plain ugliness of much of the new development, and for this people blame the chronic lack of effective centralised planning control on the part of the government. Yet, the same people actively welcome the increase of facilities brought about by the developments. This is partly due to the fact, pointed out by Boissevain (1989), that in some ways tourism has reinforced and accentuated local culture and values, important amongst which is enjoyment of the seaside during the summer months. He remarks how 'the swimming, feasting, sporting, partying and romancing that tourists come to Malta to find are also the elements Maltese themselves consider essential in the summer'.

Figure 4.3 A day by the seaside, Maltese-style.

This is very true of Melliehans; it is not uncommon for families to move down to small houses near the coast during the summer months and many have some kind of room or boathouse to which they decamp on Sundays and feast-days. I have even seen a group of nuns from the local convent following suit and cooling off from the heat by taking a dip in the sea (preserving their modesty by remaining dressed in their habits whilst in the water). This correspondence between local and tourist tastes has certainly led to overcrowding in some areas but not necessarily to resentment. There are three main reasons for this.

The first reason lies in subtle but important differences in the way locals and the tourists use the seaside. Most tourists, and indeed some local people, head straight for the few areas of sandy beach and the coastline stretches with bar, sun-lounger, and swimming pool facilities. However, a good many local people are more adaptable, or rather better adapted to their environment, often preferring the far more extensive rocky areas of coastline as a base for the day. Indeed, Melliehan friends have often expressed a healthy suspicion of the sandy beach on the bay, warning that it is a dirty place, harbouring all kinds of infection. Therefore, surprisingly large areas of the coastline remain relatively uncrowded and freely accessible to all. Second is the fact that it is becoming increasingly common for people to possess boats. For many local men, fishing has always been an important (and sometimes lucrative) hobby, and setting off to quiet and hidden spots along the coast and out to sea is seen as an excellent way of relaxing. These days, the prosperity brought about through tourism has meant that more people than in the past can afford to buy larger boats; and one of the simplest ways of avoiding crowds is to set off and visit the many small bays on the islands still inaccessible to tourist hire cars.

However, the local people do not spend their whole time trying to escape from their tourist guests. The third reason for the lack of resentment is that they like to share in some of the new facilities. For instance, partly as a result of tourist influence and partly because of increases in wealth, local people have taken to going out for a meal or a drink in the evenings and at weekends and enjoy the greater choice that the new pizzerias and cafes along the coast offer. Amongst the young, the opening of a couple of discotheques has certainly been popular, as it saves them having to go to nearby Bugibba and St Paul's Bay or to St Julians for an evening out dancing.

A final factor, which in part operates to protect Melliehans from feeling overrun by their tourist guests, is that even today both the old part of the village and the newer areas of residential building remain surprisingly removed and private from the main areas of tourist activity. Sparsely clad tourists passing through the village on their way to the beach often stop to visit the many souvenir shops, boutiques, supermarkets, and cafés that now line the main street connecting the village with the rest of the island and running down to the sea. Even so, within the space of a few metres all the bustle gives way to the relative calm of the small streets of the old part of the village. Although many now live in the more newly established residential areas, this part of Mellieha is still the focus of many key areas of local social life. The two band clubs, the headquarters of the various lay religious associations, the local school and, of course, the parish church are all located here.

The days have long since passed when the parish square was the main meeting place and the church the central focus of public social life. Indeed, over a decade ago, a leader of one of the lay associations mentioned productive involvement in tourism as one of the main causes for a drop in membership. Yet, this area of the village retains its importance as a cultural reference point, and as a place to escape from exposure to the tourist gaze. Whether this will remain so for much longer it is difficult to tell, as the brochures have recently begun mentioning the villages themselves as one of the island's attractions; one brochure mentions how 'the old town of Mellieha itself is a network of intriguing narrow streets and peaceful squares' (Horizon Winter Sun Selection 1993/93).

Where Culture is Unmarked/Unshared

Turning to a wider discussion of the interplay between tourist tastes and values and those of their hosts, a useful way to begin is to explore a little further the implications of the British tourists' comments about the island 'lacking culture'. When pressed for examples, the tourists would sometimes mention the lack of 'development' of the numerous temple sites on the islands. In a sense this observation was accurate. Dating from 2,800-2,000 B.C. and in some cases in a remarkably good state of preservation, these temples are extremely impressive, with a form and construction unique to the islands. Yet, compared to equivalent sites elsewhere there have been only limited efforts to 'organise' the heritage they represent into a full-blown tourist attraction. Indeed the same could be said of many facets of local culture, for instance the older 'quaint' parts of the villages such as Mellieha, mentioned above; many of the Renaissance buildings originally occupied by the Knights in Valletta and elsewhere on the island; the spring-time *Mnarja* festival; the traditional Maltese song-form (*ghana*); and, until recently, even Maltese cuisine.

Focusing on the example of the temple sites, this observation can be pushed a little further by recalling MacCannell's (1976) argument concerning the relationships that become established between signifier/ied in the links between sight markers and the sights themselves. MacCannell points out that for an attraction to be recognised as such within the cultural space we occupy as tourists, at least some degree of marking is necessary. He outlines the various stages of such marking,

Figure 4.4 The busy main street of Mellieha.

Figure 4.5 A quiet and 'picturesque' village street.

within the overall process that he describes as site sacralisation, as involving naming, authenticating, framing, and enshrinement. He argues that, ultimately, the stages mechanical and social reproduction might be reached, whereby reproductions and representations of the original sight become themselves objects of display (against which the significance of the Real Thing becomes even more enhanced), until finally groups, cities, and regions begin to name themselves after the famous attractions.

If we accept the intimate relationship between marker and sight put forward by MacCannell as representing the core of what constitutes cultural recognition in the context of tourism, it can be argued that the comments of the tourists were in fact well observed. Although several of the sites on Malta and Gozo have long been named and authenticated, until recently few have been framed, let alone enshrined and so on. Lacking the necessary markers (including signposts on the road!) this aspect of culture was in a sense 'absent', and the Maltese – at least those organising the industry on the Islands – did not make very much of what they had. In a drive to encourage tourists to visit the islands at all times of the year rather than mainly in the summer, more stress is now being placed on 'developing' the image of the islands' historical and cultural heritage. The sites are now advertised in the brochures and reproductions of the 'fat lady' statues found at the temples of Hagar Qim and Tarxien can be found in souvenir shops. Even so, little has been done to develop, or indeed to conserve, the sites themselves.

As to what the hosts make of the observations of their British guests, there are some ways in which they would agree. In the decades since independence there has been a considerable backlash against the attitude of looking down on Maltese culture and language. This is reflected, amongst other things, in the growing number of poets and novelists writing in Maltese, in the trend amongst architects to draw upon traditional Maltese building styles and designs, and in the growth of local lobby groups wanting to protect the environment and the islands' cultural heritage. It is significant that these concerns are incorporated into the programme of the only new political party to have emerged in the past two decades (Alternattiva Demokratika). People in sympathy with these views express frustration at the lack of energy put into conserving archaeological sites and other monuments and disappointment at the fact that tourists do not always see the best side of Malta, and say that they feel ashamed when showing guests round the sites. It is interesting that, in this context, a friend mentioned her annoyance at the fact that when choosing their routes some of the tourist guides select, not according to the most historically interesting itineraries, but according to the location of the souvenir shops from which they might gain a cut of the profits. To a degree, this local reappraisal of Maltese culture is certainly due to the influence of tourism, both in the positive sense of wishing to share it with tourist guests and in the negative sense of wanting to find some protection against any further destruction of the environment as a result of industry.

However, this is not the whole story. There are many areas of Maltese culture and way of life that remain totally 'unmarked' by the tourist operators and organisers. This may well act as a further mechanism to protect the Maltese from feeling swamped by tourism and tourists. We have yet to see what the consequences will be if culture-hungry tourists do start to swarm into the 'intriguing' village back streets.

Meanwhile, there are some ways in which local people feel that the opinions of the British tourists express more the limitations in the latters' range of expectations than any shortcomings in Maltese culture and its presentation. Indeed, friends have often commented that although they feel friendly towards the British, finding it no effort to joke with them and to live up to the hospitable image expected, they also find them very conservative and unsophisticated in their tastes and demands. They still tend to come expecting a sunny 'home from home', and this is just what they do find, at the expense of exploring other aspects of the islands. This has become increasingly obvious since more people have started visiting Malta from other northern European countries, free from the preconceptions held by the British and with more varied expectations.

One important difference between the guests' tastes is, predictably, over food. Although the cases where 'English breakfasts' (and sometimes *only* English breakfasts!) are served all day are rather extreme examples of the contrast that Maltese sometimes perceive between their own and British eating habits, only recently does the food served to tourists bear any resemblance to that eaten by the Maltese themselves. There still tends to be a tremendous lack of variety in tourist menus and, ironically, this was sometimes mentioned by tourists as an example of the local peoples' lack of enterprise and imagination. However, three observations follow from this.

First, the serving of bland food in many tourist establishments partly reflects the fact that the Maltese are shrewd judges of their market, certainly when it comes to their British guests; for all that they might express a vague wish to sample local cuisine, many British tourists do seem remarkably conservative in their tastes and preferences. Second, whilst Maltese food combines elements from North African, Italian, and British cuisines it is also distinctively Maltese and many of the best dishes and foods rely upon ingredients that are only locally obtainable and therefore only in seasonal and limited supply. Also, several of the best locally produced foods such as *gbejnit* (a small round cheese) or *ftira* (a type of bread made in a ring or disk) used, until recently, to be sold only through limited outlets, and Maltese friends would go to some effort to find a good local supplier. Such channels of supply and consumption fit into a wider pattern of reciprocity, food-sharing, and organisation of inter-personal relationships that are all essential to the fabric of Maltese life – again it is an area that is quintessentially 'cultural' but not one that the local people have, until recently, felt compelled to package and exploit for mass consumption.

However, a final important observation is that in response to an increasing demand from tourists for more in the way of local cuisine, several restaurants offering authentic Maltese food have now opened. This reflects a change not only in the tourist market but also in local tastes. The Maltese appreciate the new value placed on local cuisine and visit these restaurants along with the tourist guests. In time, maybe even the British will be weaned off their conservative tourist diet of fish, chips, and English breakfasts.

This final observation draws attention to the question of the interplay between changing tourist tastes and those of their hosts. As tourism has changed in Malta, so have the Maltese themselves. Local people no longer see tourists as an unvariegated 'species apart', and the previously very marked differences perceived between hosts and guests have become less pronounced. This is partly because, as mentioned earlier, more and more of the visitors are themselves Maltese coming out from the suburban areas to resorts such as Mellieha for the summer months. Friends with shops down on the bay report that they rely upon these customers for a considerable proportion of their trade.

Also, the increasing number of people coming from all over Europe has, as we have seen, generated a fresh appraisal of what the local culture and environment has to offer. For their part, the Maltese welcome the new curiosity of their guests and as they have become more involved in dealing with tourists, they appreciate how this increased contact with other Europeans opens them up to a wider range of opinions and views. This is particularly true of younger people, who feel that in the past their worldview tended to be too parochial and narrow-minded. This appreciation has taken on new dimensions recently, with Malta wishing to join the European Union. Maltese people, Melliehans included, are keen to develop their contacts with other Europeans and their knowledge of Union affairs.

Meanwhile, the prosperity on the islands over the last few decades has meant that there has been a considerable change in local consumption patterns. These days many imported goods are readily available and even the careful Melliehans have become far more inclined to spend their money on personal luxuries and their homes than in the past.

However, whilst many feel enriched by these influences, the Maltese have neither simply absorbed the behaviour and consumption patterns of their guests, nor have they taken to 'mirroring' what is expected of them. They feel, and indeed seem to be, well-equipped to negotiate their relationships with foreigners and to exercise some choice and control as to where the lines of influence become drawn. The reason for this may lie precisely in the fact that they have for so long been subject to influences from outside, often less friendly and certainly less lucrative than that of tourism. Maltese ideas about themselves since independence have developed so as to allow an openness and flexibility towards foreigners and foreign influence, but one tempered by healthy suspicion and a subtle awareness of a set of ideas and behaviour patterns that mark off their own cultural identity from that of their guests. These ideas still stand as measures against which to judge both their own self-respect and status and that of others. They focus on many areas of life and include judgements about particular patterns of reciprocity, forms of loyalty, prescribed forms of conduct towards the opposite sex, and customary ways of timing and pacing activities both on a daily basis and in relation to the yearly calender. In terms of these, the behaviour of tourists is either seen as irrelevant or rather bad.

Religion and the Guardianship of Cultural Integrity

Local values and judgements are informed by a range of influences, extremely important amongst which is the Roman Catholic faith. This is worth examining in a little detail, as religion has for so long played a key role in shaping local ideas about cultural integrity and identity. In the many centuries of occupation and rule by foreign powers, the Church consistently acted as a source of authority, legal control, and moral guidance to the population and as such its role provides important clues to the context within which the influence of tourism has developed in Malta.

133

Throughout the period of British colonial rule, the Church guarded its own extensive institutional interests in Malta and on several occasions became active in defining and protecting local interests against infringements by colonial rule. As a result there developed a close identification between national culture and Roman Catholicism. This identification operated, and continues to operate, both on a political and a more general cultural level. Of particular interest when looking at the effects of tourism is the way this strong and multi-levelled influence of religion has continued to permeate everyday life; the ideas and symbols connecting individual and social identity are still often organised through a religious idiom. Meanwhile, in spite of secularising influences such as tourism, there remain key areas of life in which religion acts as a major force in defining the limits of legitimate social activity. As such it has operated as a force in conditioning the development and effects of tourism.

One important area of life where religion and the church have recently intervened to 'organise' the effects of tourism is the recruitment of women into the workforce. It has been noted in other contexts (e.g., Goddard 1987, Samarasuriya 1983) that the conditions under which women are recruited into the workforce are strongly influenced by ideological constraints relating to the wider roles assigned to them within the society. In this context, the role played by Catholic ideology is important, for one of the key areas in which religious control is maintained is in matters relating to marriage, family, and moral conduct – particularly in relation to young women. Also, although women are very important both as a source of labour and as partners in running local enterprises connected with the tourist industry, making up over a third of the official workforce, it remains the case that their ability to perform their expected roles as wives and mothers and as guardians of the moral welfare of the community remain important measures against which they are judged by others and by which they judge themselves.

Thus a high premium is placed upon behaving according to the rules of correct moral and social conduct, and such rules apply not only to sexuality but also very strongly to neatness and cleanliness, specifically within the home. I have been told that to suggest that somebody has an untidy or dirty home is tantamount to an accusation of improper sexual conduct. Whilst not wanting to stress this 'cleanliness is next to godliness' point too strongly, one anecdote might serve as an illustration of how such attitudes mark off local behaviour from those of guests. Once, when visiting Malta for a holiday, I stayed in a cheap holiday apartment 'complex' in Bugibba. It seemed fine, and certainly very clean to me.

However, perhaps inspired by sentimental fieldwork memories, I found myself vigorously sweeping and mopping the floors very soon after my arrival. A small audience of Sliemese children appeared, nodding in approval and informing me that when they arrived here their mother spent two whole days undertaking a thorough cleaning of their holiday quarters. Chatting to my British neighbour next day, she could not help but remark quizzically on my apparent enthusiasm for housework.

Given these constraints, women who go out to work or run a business at the same time as having to maintain a house and family can suffer extreme work and moral pressures. In the past, the situation was possibly hardest for the many young women working as hotel chambermaids, as here there was the added problem of there being a stigma attached to this work. Chambermaids suffered the danger of becoming victims of gossip since they were seen as risking intimate contact with tourist guests of the opposite sex and in danger of being led astray. In a sense it seems that by performing a service so closely tied up with womens' duties *within* the home, but for strangers outside it, these women carried the danger of contaminating their own moral purity and that of their families.

In this context, the role of the church hierarchy in the person of the parish priest became important, for it was to some extent possible to redeem the situation by using the priest as a mediator through whom to find employment. This aspect became obvious to me whilst I was inter-viewing the local hotel owners and managers. I was often told that in the earlier stages of tourist development women were reluctant to work as staff in hotels, and the solution found was to work through the parish priest and/or through kin networks of families 'close' to him. This method of recruitment was reflected in the way management/staff rela-tions were regulated: I heard of several cases in which the parish priest was called in to mediate disputes.

The local representatives of the church hierarchy also intervened in a more general way, through keeping an eye on the behaviour of the young girls and women in the village. Until recently teenage girls lived very shel-tered lives under the strict supervision of church and family – indeed few social activities took place outside these contexts. This is no longer so true: girls are now allowed to go out; rules as to when they should return home have become more relaxed. In this connection, it is interesting that Boissevain and Serracino-Inglott (1979) have commented that increased contact with foreigners through tourism has widened the marriage mar-ket considerably. This does not seem to hold true in Mellieha. The few Maltese girls that I have known to go out with foreign visitors have been those drawn from the local elite, who have a tendency to make a point of *not* conforming to, or identifying themselves with, the rules and values that govern the rest of the community. For the majority of unmarried girls, the relationship appears, if anything, to be one of avoidance.

Before leaving this topic it should be pointed out that the concern felt by young women to protect their reputations is not matched by their male contemporaries. Indeed one serious example of resentment towards tourists is that felt by young women towards foreign females who engage the attention of local youths during the summer months. This resentment is well-founded – whole groups of young men between eighteen and twenty-four seem to disappear down to the beach for days on end between May and September.

The issue was raised some time ago in an article in a local magazine that deals with social problems. It contained several interviews with these self-labelled 'sharks' and their 'defence' was that foreign women are far more spontaneous, available, and sexually aggressive. Indeed, the young men interviewed had the gall to explain their behaviour by blaming Maltese girls for being too proud and cautious. One commented that 'it's not that Maltese girls can't talk with you, but they keep a certain distance. Invite them somewhere for a drink and they won't come because they think it's for a purpose' (Anon. 1983). He saw the reason for this gulf between the sexes as lying in the strict upbringing of the girls, which he in turn blamed on the Church. However, I have found that in nearly all cases, provided their Maltese girlfriends are prepared to put up with their behaviour, the young men drop these activities after a few seasons and do not choose to marry foreigners. On the contrary, foreigners' attraction lies in the fact that their relationships with them are often transitory.

A further area in which the Church has been very active in combating the potential influence of tourism is in the matter of dress, and to some extent the official views of the church are felt also by the villagers. There is one particular local priest who has made it almost his life's mission to protect his flock against the immoral evils of indecency. Although his views are rather extreme – when bikinis first came into fashion he is reputed to have held up a specimen in church and delivered a passionate sermon on how the 'two-piece' was the work of the devil – villagers do respect his views and feel offended when tourists come into the village and walk around without putting on t-shirts or only wearing their bathing costumes. Meanwhile, the whole issue of female topless bathing continues to cause considerable debate (on holiday in Malta in 1992 I heard a long radio discussion programme devoted to the topic). Not only are tourists warned against this practice on all flights to Malta, but should they insist upon removing their tops, they are liable to be caught by the police patrols that watch over the beaches and are supposed to fine people on the spot for infringements against the rule. Recently there was also a very active campaign against topless bathing run by the Social Action movement, complete with large and graphic posters.

This part of the discussion has shown some of the areas in which the Church and religion have been influential in ensuring that a certain separateness is maintained between the behaviour of the tourists and what is felt to be culturally appropriate for the local population. Such maintenance of a set of standards indicates, certainly to the anthropological eye, the existence of a very strong local culture; but culture in a sense far removed from the meanings employed by the tourists I originally interviewed.

I have been exploring some of the ways in which the local inhabitants have succeeded in retaining their integrity in the face of the considerable influx of tourists. I have stressed that there are several areas of local culture which, by remaining in a sense 'undiscovered' and sometimes unaffected by mass tourism, have acted to separate the cultural universe of the hosts from that of their guests. There is of course a possible corollary to this, that instances where aspects of indigenous culture *have*, for a long time, been incorporated into the tourist package could reflect or have led to a simultaneous erosion of local values in some respects. Again, I do not think that such a conclusion necessarily holds true in this case.

Culture as Commodity?

The local religious festivals have for a long time been seen as a part of the tourist package and it has become common practice to advertise as tourist attractions both the annual *festas* that are held in all the villages and the processions and celebrations held in some parts of the islands at Easter. This has coincided over the last two decades with a considerable increase in the scale of the celebrations and the amount of money spent on providing new statues and costumes for the processions, etc. This coincidence could be read as a sign that these festivals have become commoditised, with the 'spectacular' aspects taking over from the more devotional and more overtly religiously meaningful aspects of these events. Believing this to be true, Vassallo (1979) has argued that the fact that *festas* have become tourist attractions has caused them to grow out of all proportion and that they are little more than 'spectacles as com-modities', divorced from the symbolic universe surrounding them. Boissevain (1984, 1992) disagrees with this, arguing that Maltese cele-brations have been growing 'because they express the desire of people buffeted by waves of radical change and political divisions to play and so to re-establish their identity and contact with one another and to achieve, momentarily, the peace of communitas' (Boissevain 1992: 152). He has also argued (1984) that the increase in money spent on the *festas* reflects the increase in prosperity on the island but does not nec-essarily mean that this has led to an alienation of the villagers from their symbolic universe.

In Mellieha the *festa* falls on 8 September and celebrates the Nativity of Our Lady; this is also one of Malta's National days when the victori-ous ending of two sieges is celebrated. It is an important event on the local ritual and social calendar, and the decorations and festivities (par-ticularly the fireworks) have become heightened over the years.

Decorations and fireworks are provided by a range of local patrons, including the two village Band Clubs, local hotel and restaurant owners, building contractors, and local professionals and politicians. During the *festa* the largest donations are listed and displayed along with the names of the donors. It has also become fashionable for owners of catering establishments and for prominent citizens of the village to decorate the facades of their buildings with light bulbs resembling the shape of Christmas trees (by night these landmarks provide a strikingly accurate map of the village's economic development through tourism). Such ges-tures obviously provide the dual purpose of advertising the generosity and status of those contributing as well as drawing their establishments to the attention of the many tourists and visitors (emigrants returning to their families for a holiday frequently time their visits to coincide with the *festa*). They also reflect the fact that public claims to wealth, privilege and the capacity to dispense with patronage are still, as in the past, expressed in important ways through religious channels and institutions.

However, I would follow Boissevain and argue that the escalation of the festivities and the increasing number of tourists attending them need not be interpreted as reflecting mere commercialisation. There are two main reasons for this. First, an important distinction that retains its sig-nificance for villagers is that between the two 'sides' of the *festa*; between the outdoor events – *il festa ta'barra* – and those surrounding the series of religious devotions within the church leading up to the actual proces-sion of the statue of *Maria Bambina* around the village – *il festa ta'gewwa*

– the *festa* 'within or inside'. Many tourists attend and take photographs of the outdoor events and hence obviously swell the crowd and indeed the custom of the street vendors who crowd into the parish square at this time. However, the events inside the church are also extremely well and enthusiastically attended, but this time almost exclusively by the villagers themselves. Aware and appreciative of the complementary yet separate sides of the *festa*, I do not believe that they suffer feelings of contradiction when it comes to separating out the noisy, often frivolous external manifestations of the event from the meanings it holds for them in terms of personal devotion.

The second reason for disagreeing with the 'ritual as spectacle/commodity' argument is that it also seems important to take account of how such festivities fit into a whole yearly social and cultural calendar. In Malta it is striking how even young and/or anti-clerical people (the two quite often go together of course) who claim that they 'have little time for religion' are still strongly influenced by the way the yearly cycle of ritual events governs the pace of social and domestic activities. Many aspects of behaviour are influenced by this theological and saintly cycle: from visiting more distant relatives and paying ground rents, to preparing certain types of food; buying or making new clothes; changing from summer to winter curtains and floor coverings and back again; and even when to start and finish bathing in the sea. People vary in how scrupulous they are in organising their activities in these terms, but a shared awareness exists of how the most mundane aspects of life are linked, however distantly, to the more obvious and direct manifestations of religious faith and practice.

Conclusion

The final points made above bring the argument to its conclusion and, I hope, illustrate the main observation I wish to stress: that when talking about the cultural effects of tourism we should not be tempted to accept simple and one-sided definitions of what we know to be a shifting and highly negotiable concept. As an industry, tourism often does require 'finished', marked and recognisable pieces of culture in order to market its destinations, and when we behave as tourists we require this. There is a danger when writing about the subject of including hosts and guests within the same cultural universe and of paying insufficient attention to the untidier and less easily compartmentalised areas of host experience. I have tried to illustrate how in the case of Malta and Mellieha, the local experience of tourism cannot be understood unless we look at how the linkages between culture, meaning, and value are maintained and transformed through a whole range of often flexible behaviour patterns and attitudes.

NOTES

1. The number of people who emigrated to Australia, Canada, the United States, and the United Kingdom between 1948 and 1967 amounted to thirty percent of the population as it had stood in 1948. (Source: Population Censuses of the Maltese Islands for 1948, 1957, and 1967)
2. In some cases the reversal was literal, as in the attempt to convert an ex-military barracks into a holiday complex.

REFERENCES

Allcock, J. B. 'Tourism as a Sacred Journey', *Society and Leisure*, vol. II, no. 1 (1988): 33-48.

Anon. 'Sharks Cry', *Tomorrow*, July 1983.

Aquasun Holiday Brochure, 1992.

Badger, G. P. *Description of Malta and Gozo*. Malta, Valletta, 1838.

Boissevain, J. 'Tourism and Development in Malta', *Development and Change*, vol. 8 (1977): 523-38.

_____, 'Ritual Escalation in Malta', in E. R. Wolf ed., *Religion, Power and Protest in Local Communities*, New York: Mouton, 1984.

_____, 'Tourism as anti-structure', in C. Giordano, W. Schiffauer, H. Schilling, G. Welz, and M. Zimmermann eds, *Kultur anthropologisch: Eine Festschrift für Ina-Maria Greverus*. Frankfurt: Institut für Kulturanthropologie und Euoropäische Ethnologie, Universität Frankfurt am Main, 1989.

_____, 'Play and Identity: Ritual Change in a Maltese Village', in J. Boissevain ed., *Revitalizing European Rituals*. London: Routledge, 1992.

Boissevain, J. and Serracino-Inglott P. 'Tourism in Malta', in E de Kadt ed., *Tourism: Passport to Development?* Oxford: Oxford University Press, 1979.

Brown, G.P. 'Observations on the Use of Symbolic Interactionism in Leisure, Recreation and Tourism', *Annales of Tourism Research*, vol. 15, no. 4 (1988): 550-52.

Bruner, E. M. 'Transformation of Self in Tourism', *Annales of Tourism Research*, vol. 18, no. 2 (1991): 238-50.

Bryden, J. M. *Tourism and Development: A Case Study of The Commonwealth Carribean*, Cambridge: Cambridge University Press, 1973.

Diamond, J. 'Tourism's Role in Economic Development: A Case Re-examined', *Economic and Cultural Change*, vol. 25 (1977): 539-53.

Doxey, G. V. 'When Enough's Enough: The Natives are Restless in Old Niagra', *Heritage Canada*, vol. 2, no. 2 (1976).

Evans, N. 'Tourism and Cross-Cultural Communication', *Annual Meeting of American Anthropological Association*, 1975.

Goddard, V. 'Honour and Shame: The Control of Women's Sexuality and Group Identity in Naples', in P. Caplan, ed., *The Cultural Construction of Sexuality*, London: Tavistock, 1987.

Greenwood, D. J. 'Culture by The Pound: An Anthropological Perspective on Tourism as Cultural Commoditisation' in V. Smith ed., *Hosts and Guests*, Oxford: Basil Blackwell, 1978.

'Holiday Mirror, 1993', in *Daily Mirror*, 2 January, 1993.

Horizon Winter Sun Selection, October 1992-April 1993. Thomson Co., 1992.

MacCannell, D. *The Tourist: A New Theory of The Leisure Class*, New York: Schocken Books, 1976.

———, 'Reconstructed Ethnicity: Tourism and Cultural Identity in Third World Communties', in *Annales of Tourism Research*, vol. 11, no. 3 (1984): 375-91.

McDonald, M. 'Tourism in Brittany', in M. Bouquet and M. Winter eds, *Who From Their Labours Rest?*,. Aldershot: Averbury, 1987.

McKean, P. F. 'Tourism, Culture Change and Culture Conservation in Bali', in J. D. Banks ed., *Changing Attitudes in Modern Southeast Asia and World Anthropology*, The Hague: Mouton, 1976.

Med Choice Holiday Brochure, 1992.

Nash, D. 'Tourism as an Anthropological Subject', *Current Anthropology*, vol. 22, no. 5 (1981): 461-81.

Samarasuriya, S. *Who Needs Tourism? Employment for Women in The Holiday Industry of Sudugama, Sri Lanka*, Research Project Women and Development, Colombe-Leiden, 1983.

Schneider, J. & P. and Hanson, E. 'Modernisation and Development: The Role of Regional Elites and Noncorporate Groups in The European Mediterranean', *Comparative Studies in Society and History*, vol. 14 (1972): 328-60.

Schneider, J. & P. *Culture and Political Economy in Western Sicily*, New York: Academic Press, 1976.

Senior, N. W. *Conversations and Journals in Egypt and Malta* (2 Volumes), London: Simpson Low & Co., 1882.

Turner, L. and Ash, J. *The Golden Hordes: International Tourism and The Pleasure Periphery*, London: Constable, 1975.

Urry, J. *The Tourist Gaze: Leisure and Travel in Contemporary Societies*, London: Sage Publications, 1990.

Vassallo, M. *From Lordship to Stewardship: Religion and Social Change in Malta*, The Hague: Mouton, 1979.

5. Philoxenia
Receiving Tourists – but not Guests – on a Greek Island

Cornélia Zarkia

'Xenos (dans le monde grec) indique des relations de compensation entre hommes liés par un pacte qui implique des obligations précises s' étendant aussi aux descendants.' Benveniste (1969, tI: 94)

'La notion de *philos* [friend] en société homérique énonce le comportement obligé d'un membre de la communauté à l'égard du *xénos* de l'hôte, de l'étranger.' (Ibid.: 341)

*T*he following discussion presents the case of a Greek island that has recently entered the tourist market. Since 1973, the year of the opening of the airport, Skyros has turned its development expectations slowly but methodically towards tourism. Since then several phases can be distinguished in the rhythm of its development, which ended in a rapid evolution of events during the past few years. Today (1993) the Skyrians are preparing for the arrival of mass tourism: in 1994 the first charter flights were expected to arrive.

There is no single attitude, no single set of reactions, not even one constant strategy. The numbers of visitors have grown each year, tourists are there as they are everywhere, and the inhabitants have received them without being able to predict or to control their effects. In general they see tourism as 'manna from heaven': it came by itself, it grows and develops, setting its own rules. There are people who have invested all their aspirations in it; there are others who are reserved; yet others who have seen their status increase thanks to it.

The object of my first visits to Skyros, nine years ago, was an ethnography of the place and a contribution to the anthropology of the Agean Sea. It was already impossible then to overlook the factor of tourism, which made its dynamic presence felt in every aspect of social and economic life. My interest in tourism, although not 'per se' at the beginning (Nunez 1989: 265), was imposed on me by the evidence in the field itself. As the research on the island advanced, so I was persuaded that there was practically no aspect of social life untouched by the tourist influence. As the years passed I realised, together with the Skyrians, that the evolution of the facts was rapid, unpredictable, and therefore unexpected.

This chapter aims simply to report the way locals deal with the presence of tourists. It is based on first-hand case material, collected mainly by interviews and observation and by examination of documents where possible. Very little statistical data exist and are used only as an indication. Unfortunately the numbers concerning agriculture and herding are not reliable and they refer to dispersed dates, so we cannot have a continuous image of their evolution. Changes in land use, such as the conversion of fields to built-up areas, occur unofficially, so in spite of their impressive extent, they do not appear in official registers by their new use.

Skyros: The Past and the Present

Skyros is an island of the Northern Sporades situated in the middle of the Aegean Sea. The surface is 209 km^2 and the population is 2,750 inhabitants, the majority living at the village of the same name and a few in the only port of Linaria. The village of Skyros is built on the top of a hill on the Northeastern coast.

The long history of the island is known to us through many documents. For the last four centuries in particular, an important record of more than 350 notarial acts[1] gives us details of the main features of the life, the economy, and the social structure of this social group. It is a structure that seems to have continued more or less intact up to the middle of the twentieth century, that is, until the dawn of the great changes in the Greek countryside: the urbanisation and the rural depopulation. The term urbanisation is used to describe two simultaneous phenomena:

Figure 5.1 Skyros. View from the monastery of St George.

the growth of the urban population with the parallel decrease of rural inhabitants and the diffusion of models of urban life in the remaining rural population. This period also marked the development of spatial structure and architecture of the village: Skyros acquired two access roads for automobiles, buildings for public services, a new town hall and a central square. The next stage was marked by the monetarisation of the economy and the mechanisation of agriculture. The social and economic organisation that began to evolve rapidly after the war experienced the catalytic influence of tourism and the orientation of the economy towards it during the last two decades.

Skyros was a pastoral island for all its known history. Herding (sheep and goats) and agriculture were the main occupations that ruled the whole social organisation and structure. The almost sterile island lands were more suitable for pasture than for agriculture, so the latter was limited to a secondary, auxiliary role in the local economy. In the past, and until the first changes, there were three main social strata in Skyros. First of all, the *archontes,* the 'noblesse', a small group of families (eighteen family names among 150 in total, in 1850; Perdika 1940: 59). The 'noblesse' were the political, spiritual, and economic power of the island. They possessed almost all the pasture lands, which they leased to the shepherds. These lands were transmitted by inheritance to the sons or by dowry to the daughters. Endogamy rules forbade marriage outside one's class in order to prevent the leakage of the patrimonies to the other classes. The strict application of endogamy rules in a restricted marital market led to a high percentage of celibacy, a typical adverse effect of the system. In addition to this, during the early twentieth century the surplus of females in many of their families obliged the men to choose either celibacy or marriage with a person coming from a lower class. Faced with this dilemma and having a wish for social mobility – the city offered more opportunity – many left for Athens, selling part of their patrimony to the shepherds .

The shepherds, called *tsopanides*, who were the most numerous stratum of the island society, possessed flocks of sheep and goats and rented the pastures from the archontes. Some of them owned a little land. They also followed endogamy rules, trying to protect their capital, but always aiming towards a – mixed – marriage with an archontas. Indeed, when the conditions were favourable a number of wealthy shepherds succeeded in marrying into noble families, thus acquiring pasture land for their animals.

Figure 5.2 The Shepherd's Neighbourhood

During the wars, the economic and political power of the shepherds increased impressively. This was the result of a combination of factors, but primarily of the development of the rural economy. The domestic farms began to be converted into enterprises exporting their products, though they continued working in the old-fashioned way. Then the urban development of Greece attracted an important number of people to the cities. In the case of Skyros, and in most islands, the people who left were either those who had the money to start a new life in the city, or those who had nothing at all except the hope and the promise of the urban attraction. Consequently the rural depopulation severely affected the two most sensitive classes: the landowners and the labourers.

The agricultural labourers, the *kochyliani* (the name comes from their neighbourhood), had been the poorest social stratum during the previous social organisation. In addition to agriculture they had a variety of occupations, labourers, servants, artisans, and more recently merchants and builders and occasionally possessed land of poor quality. The kochyliani were also forced to intermarry, without the hope of a mixed marriage. Such a 'mistake' would be punished by disinheritance of the guilty noble person.

If education was reserved for the wealthy landowners, who had the money and the leisure to devote themselves to and exercise professions of prestige – such as the law and priesthood – craftwork was the occupation of the kochyliani. They were excellent wood carvers and potters, and their craft is preserved up to the present and sold to tourists, together with the embroideries made by the women. We should also note the paradox that as in many other cases, cultural identity is represented today by the work of the ex-marginal groups. In Skyros tourism played a clear and specific role in the promotion of their craftwork, also raising their social status, as we will see later on.

The ancient Skyrian classes, the landowners, the shepherds, and the labourers, were clearly distinguished from each other by a system of signs. The structure and the elements of this system have remained and still function in the collective memory, even after the transformation of the social organisation. The first sign of one's social origin was, of course, the family name. Origin was also indicated by different costumes, strictly reserved for each class. The next important sign of one's social belonging was neighbourhood. Each class used to live in a different neighbourhood with its own church. The houses in each neighbourhood, though with similar exteriors, were quite different inside. The wealthier the family was, the richer the collection of decorative objects it would exhibit. In addition to all of these signs, the relationships between them were also dictated by a complex and strict code. Besides endogamy rules, there were rules for nominating someone as godfather, for participating in religious ceremonies, for the composition of herding groups, and so on.

The institution of dowry existed in parallel with endogamy rules closely related to them. The first-born daughter ought to be endowed with the greatest and best – in material and symbolic terms – part of the patrimony. She would take land, animals, trees, and the house. Goods of symbolic value are movable goods transmitted from mother to daughter: costumes, jewels, objects of value and, of course, the name of the grand-mother, which is transmitted to the daughter's daughter. The maternal house, the house of the family, belonging to the mother through the dowry, was transmitted only to the eldest daughter, or in absence of daughters, to the first-born girl of the first son. This house has great sym-bolic value. The other daughters would take other houses as dowry. If the financial situation of the family permitted, they would also receive some land, animals, or money.

The dowry house could be a separate construction, or an addition to the main house, or in some cases a part of it. The dowry house is considered to be the woman's contribution to the marriage; it is identified with her fam-ily name and legally belongs to her until her death, and to her matriline afterwards. According to custom the husband can administer the dowry only with the agreement and the signature of his wife. The custom that des-ignates the dowry as property of the woman and her matriline was always respected and applied as an unwritten moral law. Until 1983, state law, as opposed to custom, considered the dowry as the property of the husband and transmittable as a part of his patrimony. In Skyros the custom, being stronger than the law, always identified the dowry goods with the matriline: it was a scandal for a widower to claim the dowry of his late wife.

The sons of the landowners, and especially the eldest, received and transmitted the pasture lands and the name of the family. In the other classes the boys would receive what was left after the distribution of the patrimony to the girls. In wealthy families and in those with a small number of daughters, there were usually some land and animals desig-nated for the sons and especially for the eldest. Often though, the sons were excluded, especially when the dowry played an important part in the girls' marriages. During the period of urbanisation, this was a com-mon cause of the emigration of young men to the cities. It should be noted that the dowry system mainly concerns the classes of the landown-ers and the shepherds. Poor labourers did not dispose of important pat-rimonies. Their marriages often took place by abduction, a situation in which no dowry is claimed.

This type of dowry system markedly influences the status of women in Skyros and other Aegean islands. The woman keeps her family name, even after her marriage, and in some cases she transmits it to her children – for social use, unofficially. In rural areas patrimonies are recognised by signs and names, and the family name is a very obvious landmark, so it must be maintained as long as possible in the collective memory. As the woman transmits patrimony, she also transmits the landmark, her family name, to future heirs for as long as possible, usually for two or three generations. She can administer her own property and make decisions about her house, which is, besides, the sign of the continuity of the matriline; a continuity for which she is solely responsible. In fact the great majority of the shops in the centre of the village are listed under women's names. It should be clear, though, that the exceptional status of women in the Aegean Sea does not also mean that they have many privileges in domestic and social life. Women in Skyros are consigned the traditional role of housekeeping and childcare, and power is in the hands of the father, as in all patriarchal systems. The difference is that women have a say in the decisions about patrimony and houses; but not about production: agriculture or herding.

The endowment of the women with a more or less important patrimony that belongs to them and not to the husband, results in a number of facts that are interesting to observe and explore. The upset provoked by urbanisation and the great influence of the 'agent of change' (Greenwood 1972), that is, tourism, have firstly reorganised the use of land and consequently it value. One or the consequences of great importance is the new status of land and houses and thus the new status of their owners, both men and women.

The previous social organisation, as described, and the characteristics of the Skyrian social group, are now quite transformed. Changes have occurred and continue to take place due to the changes in the economy, the new role that Skyros is called to play as a tourist island and, of course, the growing contact with new or foreign cultures. The most stable class (in terms of social movement), is that of the shepherds, which had risen at the beginning of the century by acquiring pastures from departing archontes. The archontes and their families have practically disappeared from the Skyrian society. Their descendants, though, have formed a colony in Athens, and are powerful enough to influence and to intervene in the life of the island.

The dislocation of social strata provoked by rural depopulation, urbanisation, and the dissolution of the landowning families, was also influenced by tourism. Tourism has changed land use and consequently caused changes in land values. In the former economy mountain pasture land was the most valuable property and played the most important role in the herding economy. It belonged, as already mentioned, to an elite. The fields near the coast were of secondary importance as they yielded little for agriculture. They were largely the property of the poor. These fields by the beaches have now been converted into the tourist zone, and exploited for touristic purposes. They have become 'golden land' – meaning that their value can be compared to gold that never falls in value. Thus, the poorest stratum of the island now controls the better lands, a capital with the best future in the new economy.

Hermans (1981: 468) described a similar situation in Cambrils, commenting that it was usually the black sheep of the family or daughters who inherited the agriculturally worthless land near the sea. The great difference with Skyros is that these lands do not belong to the 'black sheep of the family', but to the 'black sheep' of the society; a fact that generates serious social conflicts and not simply 'some ugly inheritance problems'.

Therefore, the social status of the ancient poorest stratum, the kochyliani, has changed. Their role in the new circumstances has also altered because of another development. As we said, some of these families became shop-owners, builders, and artisans. They were the first to receive the tourists, the first who had to cope with them, the first who realised that things were changing. They were the first who benefited directly from the tourist income. As their situation was favourable, they were the first to invest in 'rooms to let', bars, and restaurants, sometimes simply by converting their shop to a 'supermarket' or their workplace into a 'souvenir shop'. Having long been 'somehow culturally marginal', they became the 'innovators' in their society, as Nuñez calls them (1989: 268), commenting that many anthropologists have observed the same categories in other tourist places. Their capital was small, as was their investment. But in fact their decisions were advanced and innovating. 'It is duty that wakes up the driver', they say, meaning that it was mainly new demands that drove them to these innovating decisions. Their new status was due not to the advent of tourism alone, but also the predicaments of the recent past. Tourism was a catalytic agent of change in an already troubled social organisation.

The institution of the dowry was also affected indirectly by the new situation. Houses and plots of land set aside to build houses for daughters, although of great symbolic value, were in fact of secondary importance in the rural economy, in comparison with pastures and agricultural land. The house in the village had value only as habitation, since the material was free and it was built by its owners. This is the reason that it was given to daughters. Today such a property can be exploited converted to 'rooms to let' or to pensions; it can also be sold at a high price. Today such a house is not just a simple habitation. It is a 'traditional' house in a tourist island and its value and importance has increased.

Thus, daughters have rights to the most strategic (in development terms) part of the patrimony, and their status in the domestic group is threatening that of the sons. The ancient system of the transmission of goods is being questioned. Heirs claim an equal portion of the patrimony, using arguments about modernity and the emancipation of women. The paradox is that a son may argue about 'the unjust system of the dowry', but as a future husband he claims a good dowry in order to get married. It is obvious that the dowry house is now more important than ever in marriage strategies. For the women this effect of tourism has not been favourable. Though the value of their property has risen, it has not meant a similar increase in their power. The growth of the value of the houses has meant a growth of the importance of the dowry for the marriage. Daughters are often found at the centre of land claims, in inheritance conflicts.

The Tourist Profile of the Island

During the 1950s, which was a period of innovation in the restoration of the Greek economy, the first attempts at organised tourism were made. Certain places of interest, especially those of historical value (Crete, Rhodes, Delphi, etc.), had been already visited by travellers interested in Greek antiquities. Later on, with the development of travel and tourism, Europeans and Americans who visited the historical and archaeological sites 'discovered' the possibilities of the Greek islands for recreational tourism. Gradually, these places of historical tourism welcomed tourists who were solely interested in the sea and sun. The rising popularity of these places and the change in the type of tourism contributed to the 'discovery' or other islands and coasts that offered more or less similar attractions: sea, sun, relaxation, and cheap services. One of the advantages of the 'new' places was the image of the 'undiscovered' and 'wild'. As tourists were now not interested solely in historical sites, all places could offer similar assets to compete in the market. It was just a matter of circumstances that led to the development of certain places, such as the initiatives of the inhabitants, the interests of some , powerful personalities, and so on.

Skyros was 'discovered' in such a way. Known to Greek intellectuals for its rich tradition, architecture, crafts, costumes and songs, it also offers natural attractions similar to the other islands.

Those who played an important role in the first attempts at touristic development and were the first to introduce the island to particular social circles were the Skyrians from Athens. Mostly composed of members of the 'noble' families, they are a group that appears to have a considerable power on the island. Some of the group belong to the intellectual elite, others are professionals, and are considered successful and wealthy. They vote in Skyros; hence they can influence the local authorities. They also publish a newspaper in Athens, and in general they are respected and can affect local opinion.

They were the first, with their friends and social circles, to regard the island as a summer residence, and were interested in seeing Skyros acquire the basic infrastructure necessary to attract visitors. They used their influence to build the first hotel (1956); they created, together with local people, a cooperative shipping company; they founded a folklore museum. Nevertheless, they have always claimed that mass tourism is undesired and they themselves did not invest in it, at least the first. Today some of them severely criticise the negative aspects of touristic development, while others have invested in it and exploit the possibilities that the island offers.

Skyros had no source of important capital derived for instance from emigration or shipping, as was the case of other Aegean islands that developed rapidly. Therefore investments were limited, and it was only during the 1970s and especially after the construction of the airport and the creation of the cooperative shipping company, that tourism started to develop.

At first tourists found accommodation with families. Later on the first 'rooms to rent' appeared. Until the 1980s the tourist infrastructure was limited to one hotel, two pensions, and one tourist agency. Deficient transport, the militarisation of the island and the strong herding tradition that prevented the main social group, the shepherds, from following new ideas, were the most important factors that delayed touristic development.

The presence of a considerable military force on the island strongly influenced its economic life. Shops, restaurants and bars provided employment throughout the year. The economy of Skyros was healthy and only marginally depended on tourism. Thus developing the latter did not seem to be an urgent necessity. On the other hand, the improvement of the infrastructure (roads, electricity in some areas, telephones) whilst fulfilling military requirements, also inadvertently benefitted touristic development.

The construction of the airport in 1973 greatly influenced the local economy. A large expanse of fertile land (2.7 hectares, for an airport suitable only for light aircraft) was expropriated for this purpose. Owners were generously compensated and a number of people suddenly acquired great wealth. Despite the fact that the first signs of touristic development had already appeared, the majority of locals preferred to buy apartments for their daughters in Athens rather than invest in local business. Only one family took advantage of this compensation and invested in a hotel.

In the early 1980s visitors multiplied mainly because of external factors: the saturation of neighbouring islands, combined with the search by European tour operators for 'wild' and 'undiscovered' places. It was only after 1983 that development surged dramatically. If in the past there was an apparent delay in the tourist development of Skyros in comparison with the nearby islands, today little seems able to brake its rapid progress.

To give an indication of the numbers of visitors each summer I have listed the numbers of ferry-boat return tickets between Kymi and Skyros, which is the main route to Skyros (accounting for more than 90 percent of all traffic).

Table 5.1 Numbers and Return Ferry Tickets Bought Between Kymi and Skyros

Year	Return tickets in June	Return tickets in July	Return tickets in August	TOTAL	Approximate no. of visitors
1981	4,794	9,265	11,538	25,597	12,500
1985	9,995	20,110	25,020	55,125	27,500
1991	10,035	22,242	32,968	65,245	32,500

Source: 'Skyros' Shipping Company

The numbers indicate the tickets, but not the number of tourists, as local people travel by the same boat. I estimate (comparing the numbers of the previous years) that local travellers account for no more than 2,500 every month The figures show that arrivals during the last decade have increased by 155.6 percent, with the largest concentration in August.

Most visitors in Skyros are Greeks, according to the local tourist agent. In July and August, the British, Scandinavians, Germans, and Italians are also regular clients and stay for fifteen to twenty days. There are about 1,500 beds (according to the tourist agent's list), of which no more than fifty are not declared to the licensing authorities. There are seven third-class hotels, and the rest are rooms and houses to rent. The largest and most luxurious hotel, built during the past three years, belongs to an Athenian; the second largest, built in 1956, belongs to the National Organisation of Tourism; and the third also belongs to an outsider. The rest belong to Skyrians and are open all through the year.

Of the fifty-six people who run houses, pensions, and rooms for rent, only twelve are Skyrians from Athens; the rest are Skyrians who live on the island all year. Thee business are open only during the summer. Of the total, thirty are registered under women's names and twenty-six under men's names (according to the police list). This indicates the double activity of the husband, who maintains his rural profession and registers the new business in his wife's name. In some cases the property is a woman's dowry, but the business is usually created by both after marriage, so it could belong to either or to both. Some of the older business (shops, restaurants) are transmitted to women as dowry. There are thirteen pubs, discos, and cafeterias, of which three belong to non-Skyrians, two to Skyrians from Athens and the rest to inhabitants. Four are closed in winter, the rest are open all year long.

It was only after 1985, after the consolidation of touristic developments, that some Skyrians from Athens first began to invest in tourism. The two pubs that belong to Skyrian descendants are viewed negatively by the locals: 'They came to make large and rapid profits, and they do not offer anything to the island. They close and leave early in September and they are not interested in staying a little longer to serve the locals', a bartender said. Some young Skyrians told me that locals boycott these bars.

The accommodation is fully occupied from 25 July to 25 August, up to 75 percent full from to 25 July and from the end of August to the first five days of September, and up to 30 or 40 percent full from the end of June to July and the second week of September. (These figures, the only ones available, are provided by the tourist agencies.)

The 'Association of Tourist Professions' has 120 members – 95 percent of the people working in the existing enterprises connected to tourism (bars, restaurants, souvenir shops, room, etc.). Sixty percent of these professionals are Skyrians; the others come from Athens. By way of comparison, the Shepherds' Cooperative has 200 members.

Until the 1970s, there were plenty of empty houses in the village; some were closed but waiting to be opened in summer by their owners, some were ruined, and others were perfectly ready but waiting for the marriage of a daughter. These dowry houses were usually used as the 'good houses', houses for receptions. Most of the time they are closed, decorated with the best objects, embroideries, etc. They were the first houses rented to tourists. Some of the new houses were arranged in such a way that part of the house could be rented out. As these dowry houses are property transmitted in the matriline, it was normal for their administration to pass to the women of the household. It is they who have actually undertaken this kind of business, keeping the accounts and finding the customers. Some rent the house to the tourist agent for the season. Others find the customers themselves, going to the bus-stop or to the port shouting the only English word that they have learned: 'rooms, rooms!' They are very cunning, guiding the tourists through narrow streets, thus avoiding the main street where the hotels and the tourist agencies are. Some years ago, when the number of visitors exceeded the capacity of the island's registered beds, the local authorities overlooked these illegal rentals. But when hotels and pensions were built, most families legalised their 'rooms', and built extra bathrooms and separate entrances. Others, in fact very few, still rent illegally.

An average traditional house (4 to 5 beds) is rented for 10,000 dr a day (in 1993); the amount of an average daily wage. A double room in a hotel is rented for 5,000 to 6,000 dr. This income is considered to supplementary to the general budget. Usually the women control the distribution of this money, applying it towards the children's studies or putting it away for the daughters. The more organised pensions are run by the whole family. Women usually have a voice in the investment of the income, especially when their dowry is part of the business. Their usual role is to select the customers, when it is possible, and to supervise the rooms.

Those who rent part of their own house do not seem to mind this invasion or their privacy. It does not bother them to live together in one room in order to be able to rent the other to a stranger. They quite easily give up their refrigerator and their bathroom to the guest: 'It is only for two months. We don't mind being jammed for a little to earn some money for our daughter', they say. For the time being, income is more important than tranquillity and privacy.

The Skyrians observe that the room rental situation has at least one positive consequence: a larger distribution of the tourist income. In addition, the money remains and circulates within the island community; an outside businessman would take away this profit. Most Skyrians, on the other hand, either do not have enough capital to built a hotel or they prefer to invest their money in Athens by buying an apartment, a piece of land, or a shop. They do not wish to risk investing in the island. The ideal of the urban life still exists.

Those who did have enough money for investments were the shepherds, but they were not really interested in this new profession. Those who are really interested, the ex-labourers, the 'innovators', usually do not have the capital for great investments. Thus renting rooms is a cheap and easy solution. The professionals realise that they only attract a cheap class of tourists, unless the rooms are pleasant and highly priced. So their efforts are devoted to improving the existing rooms and houses and selling or renting them at higher prices.

A great number of Skyrians have a double occupation, since the profit from tourism is still low.[2] They work in the fields and the farms during winter, supplementing their income in summer by renting rooms or by keeping a tavern. Since agriculture and herding work ceases before summer, they have plenty of time to do both. The characteristic of Skyrian businesses, whether pension house, rental, restaurant, or shop, is that they are family businesses. They are run only by the members of the family, without outside employees. They do not hire anyone even in high season, when they obviously need to. The timetable they follow is one that suits their normal family life. They close for three hours during the afternoon siesta and shut down early at night: an inconvenient timetable for visitors, who are forced to follow the Skyrian way of life. It is apparent that Skyrians do not care if their services are satisfactory. N.X., a restaurant owner described his attitude this way to me:

> Look here, we have this restaurant open all year. The profit is not enough to pay a boy. So we do all the work – me, my wife and my daughter. Our son is doing his service in the army and he helps when he is here. We stay open as much we can. Of course we are closed for the siesta, to have some rest and to prepare for the night. No, I will not take a boy for August. There are twenty tables, and we can manage even if it is full. I don't see why I should stay open all day long. They can wait until after siesta!

An example can illustrate this. Some years ago (in 1988) a woman from a large, prestigious family died in August. During her funeral, in the morning, all the shops were closed. In an interview some days after, the tourist agent, a Skyrian, described this as 'A very positive attitude. It is a way to show that our life is not only money, not only business. And the tourists must understand that they come to a village, not to a factory.' In our most recent interview (1993), the same person seems to have become more worried about the mentality and the rhythms of the village. 'I believe that we do not have the education needed to receive foreigners. We need to travel, to be informed of the proper way to offer services. We have not realised the benefit of tourism and we are not ready to make any sacrifice if needed.' In the same interview he referred to matter such as the dirtiness of the houses, the poor organisation of house rentals, contradictory behaviour to foreigners, and the selection of the customers by the women, a practice that he criticised as unprofessional. He himself works abroad during winter, in related occupations' and considers this experience as useful. He has a lot of exchanges and connections with foreign agencies and tour operators.

G.F., the president of the Association, who recently returned to Skyros and runs a restaurant, is also not satisfied with the situation in the village:

> It is not right to have all shops closed during the afternoon, when the tourist returns hungry and thirsty from the beach. It might be cute to be served by a ten-year-old girl, but it is not serious, it is not professional. We will never have tourism of high quality if the situation continues like this. Yes, I understand the arguments about how good is that the life in the village has not changed much. But Skyrians want everything: their wallets full and their lite as it was. They don't realise that tourism is the only business that will save the island, but it requires sacrifices and of course planning.

The attitude of Skyrians to tourism and tourists depends on the degree of their involvement in it; that is, their temporary or permanent involvement with it, their aspirations, their financial or other investments in it. Persons who have an indirect relation to it think and react immediately without viewing it as a special kind of business. The more a person is involved in the business, the more his opinion is influenced by the nature of this kind of development. Those who work full time in the tourist business were the only ones who underlined the change in their lives. B, a Skyrian boy who works in a bar that remains open all year long, put it this way:

> We have to work full time in summer. When our friends and relatives come we don't have the time to have a drink with them, to go to the local fiestas, to go to the beach. This happens because it lasts for two months and it is not well-organised; we have to do the work for two or three, we run for the money.

In every family there are at least one or two people, especially of the younger generation, who work in the tourist business or plan to do so in the future. Most of the adolescents work in summer. When they finish high school the majority wish to follow applied studies (computing, engineering, accountancy, etc.) with a view to returning and working in the village.[3] Those who decide to pursue studies in a university usually choose the traditional professions: law, medicine, etc. The tourist professions are followed only as a second choice, as an alternative if they have not succeeded in the traditional ones. This happens for two parallel reasons: first, tourism is not yet treated professionally or scientifically, and second the professions mentioned still function as a symbol of upward mobility for the shepherd families.[4]

The ideal of shepherds for their children's future is: (a) to study, (b) to work in the public sector with a regular salary, (c) to buy an apartment in Athens, (d) for the girls to marry an educated man or a clerk .[5] The youths themselves say: 'I don't want to go to the mountains. They call you *vlacho*' (a pejorative term for a shepherd). 'In the *agora* [the market square, the symbol of the village's urbanisation] you get in touch with people, you have friends, you open your eyes. In the mountains you become wild, nobody likes you, you lose your friends'. Tourist development helps realise these goals, offering a good alternative solution. In the non-touristic rural communities young people just leave to go to a city; in tourist places, they can stay, changing profession and status.

The fact that a lot of young people desire to return and work in the village is directly connected to touristic development. No more than ten years ago, studies were mainly an excuse to leave the island and live in a city, where they usually stayed and worked after finishing their studies. Today the image of the city has been revised (pollution, unemployment, high cost of living) and life in the village seems more attractive: there are jobs, and in summer a lot of people come.

The greatest anxiety of the Skyrians who are involved in tourism is the short tourist season, which lasts for only two months. The reason for the short period is inadequate transport. Transportation was and is the field of political protest and manipulation in the island. As the shipping and air companies are private, they need a strong profit motive to become interested in Skyros. The extent of tourist traffic is apparently not sufficient for these companies.

Urbanisation and Tourism

Discussions of tourism usually focus on sociocultural changes that it causes in local societies. The arguments often present tourism as a 'conspicuous scapegoat' (Crick 1989: 335) for all the changes and transformations that have spoiled 'idyllic' places. These arguments would not survive a more sensitive analysis of the facts. Urban attraction and models of the 'Western' life had spread – at least in Greece – well before tourism. Their cultural effects had already appeared before the arrival of the first tourists. Certainly, in many cases urban attraction combined with the influence of tourism, as the example below shows.

One expression of Skyros' local cultural identity is architecture and domestic furnishings. At the time of urban attraction, city life and the new cultural elements that characterised it – and, of course the 'urban aesthetic' – were identified as the house highest value. They symbolised high status, that of the urbanite, as opposed to that of the peasant. During this first period, wealthy Skyrians tended to renovate their houses according to urban stereotypes. They exchanged the old wooden furniture for plastics and aluminium and they threw out their traditional costumes. During this period the village of Skyros experienced its greatest transformations. The extent of the changes was most obvious in the architecture and style of dress, the two immediate symbols of one's status. It was then thought necessary for people to show that they were no longer peasants but had become 'modernised'; that their status had changed to something else. The first things that were changed were the symbols of the peasant life.

Then the 'outsiders' came and the 'things' became 'objects'. The Skyrians 'discovered', first of all, that their cultural elements were objects of interest and they learned to look at them differently, to evaluate the traditional aesthetics. The 'objects' could be sold; they now had a price. They drew the interest of those who 'know', and attracted visitors who paid for rooms and food. Skyrians now speak of these objects with pride; they show them, they promote them, they sell them.

There used to be a small coffee house in the central street where the old shepherds in their traditional costumes used to go after work. The younger generation avoided this coffee house and preferred a modern 'cafeteria'. The tourists preferred to have a drink in the traditional one, because it was more picturesque and the person who ran it was a nice old man, who used to joke and receive his clients kindly. The Skyrians called him 'Ambassador', because all the foreigners went there. Then the young Skyrians from Athens began to go there too and little by little many young people changed coffee house and joined the 'Ambassador's' clientele.[6] This change points out clearly the change in mentality: during the first period, young Skyrians despised the shepherds' coffee as a sign of

Figure 5.3 The Ambassador's coffee-house in the marketplace.

undesirable social belonging. During the second period, they imitated the urbanites and the Europeans, a sign of their desire to be like them. Today young Skyrians proudly exhibit their traditional coffee houses.

Tourist interest in the traditional, superficial as it is, can be easily exploited. As usually happens, imitation of the traditional in architecture and handicrafts was rapid. Since tourists are not really interested in authenticity, and the hosts are aware of this, a game is played by both parties, thereby creating a new kind of 'tourist traditional' that has little in common with the authentic one. This phenomenon does not stop here. Elements, styles, and forms from other islands, which were successful in the tourist industry, appeared in Skyros. One of the most striking examples is the importation of 'Myconian style' in architecture, characterised by arches and vaults. The white arches of the Cyclades islands have been successful symbols of holidays in Greece for more than thirty years. They have 'sold well', and are internationally known. The Skyrian house has nothing in common with this style. The arches invaded the newly built 'rooms to rent' and new beach houses, without being really a conscious and deliberate act of cheating: 'It is cute and it reminds you of vacations, doesn't it?' a carpenter who had recently built such a house asked me. Arches and vaults, dry-stone constructions and peculiar interior decorations symbolise the tourist trade.

The tourist does not really care about the authenticity of the scenery around him, and the inhabitant knows that (Cohen 1979: 184). The tourist seeks the 'other', the 'curious', despite its lack of authenticity. The inhabitants play their role in the game, consciously selling fake authenticity. In Skyros they have given names from Greek mythology to their shops (for instance *Pegasus*, *Kalypso* etc.), or even forgotten words of the local dialect (such as *Melikari*, the name of a flower, *Korfari*, ' rafter'). They also give foreign names such as 'Renaissance', 'Pub house', or 'Food market'(!). From a sample of twenty-two names of enterprises (pubs, hotels, and restaurants) seven come from the Greek mythology, four belong to the local dialect and eight are foreign. The remaining three are simply Greek names.

Locals even exaggerate or falsify history or a local tale in order to sell a bizarre product, or to attract the interest of the visitor. I will never forget the answer of a Skyrian to my question about a place where hot water appeared in the sea. 'For the tourists here they are warm springs. Among us it is water that cools the motor-generator of the electric company!' The same happens with the name of a beach *(Achilli),* that in dialect means simply 'mouth'; but Skyrians say that it comes from the name of Achilles, a Greek mythological hero, who had supposedly lived in Skyros. The whole exchange is based on a lie that satisfies

Figure 5.4 Imitation arches in newly built rooms to rent.

everybody. The alienation of Skyrian culture and aesthetics is based upon both parties playing their roles as if they were 'on stage' (Nuñez 1989: 271).

The Skyrian house is a cubic construction with small windows and a flat roof. The impressively simple exterior is in contrast to the rich interior decoration. A wooden carved construction, called *sfas*, separates the only room into three parts. The walls are covered by all kinds of plates, dishes, and kitchen utensils, embroideries and decorative objects. Small pieces of furniture of carved wood solves the problem of limited space. Today there two points of view concerning the interior decorations. The normal house of a local young couple is built and decorated according to urban models: central heating, sofa, electric appliances, and furniture that resembles that in a normal city apartment. The house for rent, on the other hand, follows traditional decoration and furnishing, but is fashioned with new materials: the *sfas* is made of cement with some wooden parts stuck on it and it is often useless, as its dimensions are wrong. The same sometimes happens with the fireplace: it is only decorative, since it will never be used in summer. Pottery from all over Greece, and peculiar objects such as clocks, dolls, maps, hour-glasses and whatever else one can imagine, are placed on the fireplace, on the walls and on special shelves. Big windows, entrances with arches, ugly cement balconies and bizarre staircases complete the hybrid image created by the marriage of the urban models with the tourist influence, to the detriment of the local architecture.

What has remained intact is the passion of the Skyrian woman to exhibit her household. Women, when asked, actually open their houses to strangers with pride and exhibit their treasures. They usually like to be photographed, asking for the picture to be sent afterwards. They insist on arranging the house before the picture is taken and they like to be in the photograph. They are disappointed when the stranger does not pay attention to their endless explanations about the origins of the objects. Even if they have never travelled, they are sure that their houses are something special, 'perhaps the reason for tourists' interest in our island'. Sometimes, though, they realise that they can profit from the tourist interest: there is a sweet old lady who sits proudly every afternoon outside her door, knitting and chatting with the neighbours. Tourists passing by are attracted by the scene and want to photograph her. She does not object, on condition she is tipped! An informant told me that the same lady some years ago used to shut the door, cursing the would-be photographers.

The Tourists are not Guests

In ancient – and modern – Greek the stranger is designated by the word xenos and the word *philoxeno* (*philos:* friend) means to offer hospitality. According to Benveniste (1969: 361), in Homeric society *xenos* is the stranger, the guest or even the enemy. He notes also that the concepts of 'enemy', 'stranger', and 'guest' which form for us three distinct entities, are very closely connected in the Indo-European languages. (1969, tI: 361).

The relationship between host and guest is ruled by a code of behaviour, by a number of mutual obligations, in the sense that the host is in a superior situation, so he is in a position to offer. According to Benveniste, the guest is in inferior situation. He is deprived of any rights, any protection and any means of existence. Shelter and hospitality are offered to him only by those with whom he is linked by bonds of *philotes* (friendship) (Ibid., 341). Benveniste points out the close relation between the notions of *philos* (friend) and *xeno* (stranger) and the identification of the word *xenos* with 'guest'.

If we leave the Greek world and mythology to examine traditional tales, the stranger, *o xenos,* is always honoured as a special guest. He is either an angel of the Gods that comes to earth to test us, or the God himself, or a ghost of a beloved person bringing a message from the Other World. Thus, taking care of a stranger, offering him hospitality and friendship, is a moral duty, rewarded generously in heaven.

If I discuss the notions of *xenos* (guest), *philos* (friend) and *philoxeno* (to offer friendship, hospitality) it is not because I propose any comparison between the institutions of the ancient and the modern world, but because it is very interesting to note a remarkable inversion. The first reaction of local people towards the tourists (a new, unknown situation) is to see them as xenoi-guests and to behave correspondingly. The lady of the house considers it her highest duty to serve, take care of, and relax the traveller or the stranger and ask him about his family, his home. Of course not for money! But for the sake of X (a son travelling at sea), or for the soul of Z (a late relative). For the stranger is surely tired, he is away from home, he misses his wife and his mother. The lady would replace his mother, she would make him feel 'at home', since the Gods have sent him to her.

Today, the guest-xenos is a tourist, who is a client. The host offer 'services' and not 'friendship', and the xenos-tourist pays for it. Their relationship is ruled by the laws of commerce and now the *xeno* is in superior position, since he has the money. An episode that took place in the late 1960s, reported to me by an informant, will help us to follow these transformations and inversions in people's minds .

His aunt lived alone in a small house near the beach.

One summer day a tourist passed by and stopped to drink water from a fountain. She smiled and she offered him a glass, and then coffee and fruits and later on she invited him to stay at her house. He accepted the invitation and stayed there for a couple of days. When he was about to leave, he offered her money for the 'accommodation'. She protested. She refused firmly. She discussed the matter with the neighbours and her relatives. Somebody explained that 'he is a tourist, coming here for vacations and these persons are just travelling for pleasure !' Yes, she was confused but she understood. But she still refused money. Next morning the 'tourist' left. And she found a thousand drachmas (the price of a room) under the pillow. She was surprised and looked for him at the port, everywhere, but he had already gone. She kept the money a long time, hoping that her guest would return. Next summer some other strangers came, carrying her photo and looking for her. She received them smiling, hoping that they would finally understand the mistake and take the money back. But, surprise! They insisted not only that she keep the money but that they would only stay in her house on condition that she charged them. 'But here it is not a hotel!' she protested. Finally she accepted a symbolic price. She was poor and she had many needs. She accepted with her head hanging, her eyes cast down. With this money her smiles and her care increased: tomatoes, fruit, wine, and chatter.

By the end of the summer she had received a lot of people in the same way and in September she had a small amount of savings. The following summers more and more strangers came. The island is now well known and the women in the yards discus the 'tourists'. There are new hotels and restaurants, new shops. If the hotels are full the women still invite strangers to their houses. Some, in fact, have transformed the 'duty' into a business. Now they know that to receive a 'tourist' means work and money. It is not hospitality any more. Hot water is needed and clean sheets and towels. But the benefits are important. With this money they can finish the dowry house for their daughters, or they can pay for the children to study.

The story of this woman gives the main features of the first reactions and attitudes towards the tourists. Various informants told me that at the beginning they were confused about how to cope with them: to take or not to take money for the services, and for which services, how much, etc. It is an attitude well-known among the travellers of the islands in the 1950s and 1960s. But little by little, as people realised that tourism was an interesting market, their attitudes changed, together with their views about hospitality. Thirty years later, the village has changed a lot, the morals have changed. Now free hospitality is out of the question – even for the ethnographer! The tourists are not guests any more,[7] the old woman has gone and the others still stare at the tourists and cry from time to time: 'Oh, These are not *xenoi* any more [angels, guests], they are demons!'.

Greeks and Foreigners: Us and the Others

There is certainly a difference between the way that a Skyrian receives a Greek and the way she receives a foreigner. The Greeks were and still are the regular customers who come to the island every year. The distinction between the two categories of the guests can be noticed at different level, and first of all in stereotypes.

Greeks from the cities, and specially the Skyrians from Athens, represent a very familiar image. Their code – dress, language, behaviour, and manners – are easily recognised; the host can speak and communicate with them. The stereotypes are far more favourable for a Greek tourist than for a foreigner. A Greek is 'a better client, spends more money, knows better what he wants, he is polite'; in brief, he is 'one of us' .

Despite their origin all foreign tourists represent to the eyes of a Skyrian one culture: the Western one. Skyrians do not distinguish, in general, among nationalities, as people do in more touristic places. Since one 'speaks foreign, he is a foreigner' they say. For Skyrians the foreigners represent the unknown, strange, the 'Other', even a hostile being.

Foreigners represent the model of western life portrayed in the (largely American) soap-operas. The stereotype of the 'luxurious western life' is reinforced by the habits of the tourists, who generally spend more money in holidays than in their normal life. Besides, in a society where the notion of 'leisure' is practically absent, where people do not live in the rhythm of the cities, in which holidays, travel, and leisure are planned, the custom of saving money for leisure is not familiar.

A common attitude towards Europeans is more or less of the type: 'a German [for instance] has the time and money to go on holidays', so 'he must pay'. Consequently, an unwritten law develops: the prices increase for Europeans and decrease for Greeks. Quite strangely, all tourism professionals declare that they 'prefer Greek tourists, because Greeks spend a lot in holidays, especially when they are with their family. The Greek goes to the restaurant twice a day, buys souvenirs, wants the best room, leaves big tips. He is a good customer'. In spite of these declarations they still believe that Europeans are wealthier. But they prefer Greeks because of the possibility of their coming again next year and also because they do not cause trouble, since they know the moral code and how to behave. Those who rent rooms, informally, prefer Greeks because 'we can talk, we cope with them better. A foreigner may be more discrete and correct sometimes, but he will not come back. We prefer to have someone we know in our house.' The professionals prefer them because 'they are better clients, they tip a lot, they do not ask for extravagant things and services', a tourist agent commented. In Greece, service is included in the bill, but the tip is considered a gesture of good will to the servant. As foreigners do not know this code, misunderstandings often happen. The professionals comment that a good tourist is one who leaves money on the island. The non-professionals prefer those who are friendly, who speak with them, who are interested in traditions. The criterion of a 'good' or a 'bad' tourist thus varies. The woman who rents a room in her own house is more friendly with her guests than those who run pensions.

Contact with tourists creates complicated behaviour. Skyrian girls told me that the reaction of some boys was to develop a double personality, one for winter and one for the summer. During the summer they forget festivities and traditional feasts, they do not speak Skyrian, they do not participate in religious festivities, pretending that they have no time. They even avoid the company of their compatriots. In winter, the young Skyrians return to the rhythm of peasant life, sometimes in a very active way.

Confrontations between Skyrians and foreigners occurred during the first years of tourism, some ten years ago. These situations concerned mainly moral matters. Various incidents that I was told about concerned provocative dressing, nudism, and lack of respect towards the local moral code and the churches. Nudism shocked Skyrian society. The beaches near the village are full of local families, as well as foreigners. The appearance of the first topless women in the 1980s offended their sense of morality. The reactions were wild. In some cases the police was called but did not interfere, being afraid of the number of the foreigners, as they reported. After these incidents some restaurants refused to serve the offending persons. As nothing could be controlled by the application of the law, Skyrians followed a defensive strategy to cope with such matters. They began, little by little, to suggest a nearby beach for those who wanted to bathe nude. A few years ago this beach was officially described in tourist guide books as a nudist beach. It is difficult to reach and is avoided by Skyrians. Thus, now such incidents no longer occur. Besides, today topless women no longer shock. A woman walking around the village in a bathing suit shocked Skyrians in the past. 'They don't walk in bathing suits in their countries, so why do they do that here? Don't they realise that there is a village here that they must respect?' an old man remarked to me few years ago. During the first years the reactions were intense. Now they have become used to such sights and are no longer shocked. However, an inhabitant can be offended and act violently if the behaviour of a stranger is provocative, especially if it involves flirting.

Tourists' behaviour in the churches was the second big problem. 'They went there with their sleeping bags, they used this holy place for camping. Now we keep all the churches locked during the summer and the keys are kept by a neighbour.' The custom is that the church should be open at all times, day and night, for those who need to pray. Now this strategy of defence keeps the churches locked during the presence of strangers. It is evident that this mechanism of defence is quite effective in the case of pilfering. A woodcarver told me:

> There were cases in which icons were stolen from chapels outside the village. but the women wake up early in the morning to go to the fields. I remember a case in which a passing woman entered a chapel to light a candle and saw the icon missing. She hurried to the police, and they alerted the authorities, who blocked exit at the port, and so the thief was caught immediately. This has happened a few times. It is a small village and all incidents are immediately noticed.

The moral shocks provoked by the presence of foreigners during the first years affected the attitude towards girls. Girls were always strictly kept in the houses and were not allowed to walk alone in the main street of the village. It was cause for comment when a girl was seen with a stranger. The presence of tourists resulted in a stricter attitude. In the first years the girls' position got worse. Slowly, however, the presence of tourists was accepted and things changed for the better for the girls, who now go out freely. For the older women, alternatively, the presence of tourists was an occasion to go out to the centre of the village, a place almost forbidden to them. 'Oh yes, tourism is a good thing. We mingle with the tourists in the streets and we pass unnoticed', a woman told me.

If hosts and their lives are objects of the tourist gaze, tourists are also objects of curiosity for the hosts. As the inhabitants represent the local culture, so the tourists represent their own. The tourists in the village are the favourite subject for chatter, comments, and satire. Everything bizarre or simply different about them is satirised, sometimes laughed at and in all cases commented upon. As locals do not travel much, the summer is an occasion to observe the different cultures and habits of people and to comment on them, in the spirit of 'we are the best'. C., an Australian girl married in Skyros, underlined this attitude towards foreign cultures: 'They often say "he/she is a stranger, he does not know" or "Europeans can not appreciate good taste, they do not know". My own family here does not expect me to be a good mother and housekeeper, as I am a foreigner and "I do not know"! Also, they are not really interested to learn about my country and our life there'.

To Feast with Foreigners: An Example

There are some local religious feasts celebrated during the year in small circles, on the feast days of the saints. (In Greek culture it is one's name-day, the day of one's saint, that is celebrated, not one's birthday). The days of the great saints, St. Georges, St. Dimitri, St. Mamas, etc., in particular, are all celebrated in a typical way. The Skyrian landscape is full of little private chapels, belonging either to the owner of the land or to a group called a 'confraternity'. Some of the confraternities are very old; their records often date back to the sixteenth and seventeenth century.[8]

The duties of the 'brothers' are to take care of the chapel and its property and, most of all, to organise the annual feast on the Saint's day. On this particular day the chapel is prepared to receive all brothers and their friends. One of the brothers – or a small group of them if the confraternity is large – keeps the icon of the saint in his house during the year. This brother is called the 'administrator' of the year and he is charged with organising the feast with the assistance of all the brothers. On the day of the feast, they go to the chapel early in the morning to prepare the premises. They also prepare the slaughtered animals for the dinner. Food and drinks are free for all the pilgrims and it must be well-prepared and in abundance for everybody; this hospitality is the only rivalry between the confraternities.

As most of these chapels are away from the village, the visit takes the form of a pilgrimage. Small groups gather outside the village and travel on foot or by car. After the liturgy, dinner is served. During the dinner, which lasts all night, they sing and talk in groups. In the past, and occasionally nowadays, the feast was an occasion for boys and girls to meet and flirt discreetly. Some of the visitors stay until morning to assist in the morning liturgy. In the past, when there were no cars, all pilgrims stayed and slept next to the chapel, waiting for daylight before going back to the village. As many of these feasts take place during the summer, the presence of tourists at these intimate ceremonies was inevitable. The greatest feast and the largest confraternity is that of St. Mamas, celebrated on 2 September. The number of visitors was usually no more than fifty or sixty people. Five years ago, the tourist agent decided to exploit this feast by hiring buses for tourists. At this time the number of visitors doubled to between 100 and 150. After the liturgy, the little yard of the chapel was crowded with people who wanted to record, to take photographs and, of course, partake of the free food and wine. The brothers of the confraternity felt obliged to serve all the people, and first of all the strangers. However, during the dinner, the usual intimate atmosphere was spoiled by the flashes of the cameras, the comings and goings of those who wanted to see the chapel and even of a tape-player playing some rock music. Others sat by the tables waiting, without being able to participate or to communicate. A brother of the St. Mamas confraternity related:

> They sat there gazing, doing nothing. They did not participate, they did not understand the jokes. We tried to make them feel comfortable, but in vain. They didn't know the orthodox ceremonies, they didn't understand what was happening and why. We were anxious to serve them, to look after the chapel, to explain this and that and our entertainment was spoiled.

Fortunately the buses left at 10:30-11:00 pm. Then the real feast began. The brothers and their friends, tired and relieved, sat down to enjoy the food, the drink and the songs until the morning. This happened for three years running.

> I stopped this business by myself, the tourist agent told me. I didn't need someone to tell me. I understood it by myself. The quantity of the food and wine is enough for only fifty to sixty people. If strangers come, they are served first and there is less left for the locals. Besides, I don't think that they understand anything, that they feel the atmosphere. Tourists are like sheep. They go wherever they are told to go, wherever we guide them. Now it is not possible to learn about these feasts in the mountains, except if they are invited from a Skyrian. Well, this is different. If someone has some stranger in a room and he wants to show to him this custom, in that case there is no problem.

The agent is a young Skyrian man from a middle to lower class family. He was the only agent for ten years and undertook, all alone, a great number of businesses (tickets, excursions, rooms, a restaurant, real estate business, etc.) with success. He is liked in the village as he is considered to be an active and clever person. This feast was organised by a higher class group. Among the organisers were some Skyrians from Athens. This may have functioned as moral pressure. Perhaps the agent realised that his audacious idea spoiled the feast but yielded little profit for himself. As these feasts are an important tradition, spoiling them creates conflict. As he needs to be trusted to work peacefully with the locals' rooms and houses and to gain acceptance for his innovating ideas, he did not risk continuing the excursions to the feast.

Greek tourists are more accepted at these ceremonies and they are often invited there. They are considered to 'know and understand' the orthodox ritual and customs. They participate, speak with the hosts and even learn the songs. The only factor that can spoil the enjoyment is excessive numbers, and hosts try to control it. Today (in 1993), the strangers are totally ignored at this particular feast. Nobody any longer pays attention to their presence and they are treated as everybody else. But their number is still great, so the brothers still wait until most people have gone before starting the real enjoyment.

Conclusions

Skyros entered the tourist market as a place for seaside tourism. Today the inhabitants make every effort to combine this image with as many elements as they can to attract tourists of high quality. Thus they promote their tradition, craftwork, mythology, and history. For the time being the greater part of the tourist business is in Skyrian hands and consists of family enterprises. The income from tourism is still low and there is no major source of capital on island for big investment, hence the tourist development advances only step by step. As tourism offers jobs and opportunities to the young people, it has practically reversed the phenomenon of depopulation, attracting the youth back to the village.

From the first attempts of tourism to the present the island has passed through different stages in the developmental rhythm, and various transformations in its socio-cultural profile. In general, the inhabitants have welcomed tourism as the best remedy for the stagnant local economy. Tourism has been maintained mainly by private initiative. It is clear that the attitude of the inhabitants to the new phenomenon has depended on their professional and social position. The class that was in the most favourable position to accept and to exploit the new possibilities was that of the labourers, who were economically and culturally marginal.[9] These 'black sheep' of the community saw the value of their infertile lands near the beaches increase impressively. They were also the first who had to deal with tourists, as their occupations evolved into tourist services (handicraft, merchants, etc).

The transformations that have occurred over the past twenty years were transformations in the social structure and in the cultural profile; transformations that took place not only due to tourism, but also because of urbanisation, the other major factor of change for the Greek rural communities. In the domain of aesthetics the contribution and the interactive relation of the two factors is obvious.

Evolution in the attitude towards foreigners – as one cultural element or expression – is interesting. Tourism converts the host-guest relationship into a commercial one and hence reverses the roles. The first reactions are confused but after a short period, people adapt to the new situation. The attitude towards hospitality changes: the foreigner is no longer a guest but a tourist, which means a person who pays for services. So, at first, hosts produce (and sometimes invent) services: accommodation, catering, guided tours, etc., and later accommodation in 'traditional' houses, excursions to 'mythological' places, visits to folklore fiestas. Locals learn to sell 'tradition' and fake authenticity, to invent curious products to attract the interest of the tourists, and to exploit in every way their 'unique' characteristics.

On the other hand, the relationship between locals and tourists has to be managed, and it is up to the Skyrians to set the limits. The attitude of the Skyrians from Athens is very helpful in setting these limits. They, being both hosts and guests when they come to the island, do not wish their tranquillity to be disturbed. Their dependence on tourism, even when involved in the industry, is less than that of the permanent residents, who have fewer or no alternatives. They have a more critical eye towards what is happening on the island and can more easily protect their rights to privacy.

In general, all Skyrians wish to maintain and increase the profits from tourism. Consequently, they follow a smooth, defensive, long-term strategy to avoid confrontation with foreigners that could lead to immediate, violent conflict. For instance, to avoid daily clashes, they have gradually developed a 'nudist beach'. To prevent stealing they lock the churches, even though this is contrary to their custom. Finally, they impose limits on the host-guest relationship by celebrating their own leisure in an intimate atmosphere, away from curiosity and cameras. Nobody likes to be 'on stage' when they wants to drink, sing, and enjoy himself. Thus, in their smooth and pacific way, they wait until the tourists, especially foreigners, have gone so they can celebrate in private. Yet, the difference of behaviour towards Greeks and foreigners remains in the spirit of the 'us and the others'. Even if Greeks are tourists, they are 'familiar', less strangers than the foreigners. Typically Greeks are favoured over foreigner. They are more easily accepted in celebrations, invited into houses, trusted and treated a little bit more as 'guests' and not completely as 'tourists'.

Skyros is one case. The neighbouring islands provide others, which are different although similar. Tourism may be inevitable, unexpected, or unpredictable as an agent of change. The evidence from the Greek islands shows that at first its action was beneficial for the survival of these almost deserted places. For Skyros, especially, the fact that the development depended, until now, not only on tourism but also on other important factors such as farming and the military, protected it partly from the pitfalls of absolute dependence on tourism.

NOTES

1. This record has been partly published by Antoniades in *Skyriana Nea*, 1980-1993.
2. A common feature in rural Mediterranean societies. See Hermans 1981:472.
3. This information is given by the director and the teacher of literature at the high school. Unfortunately there are no statistical data on the choices of young Skyrians, as the registers are kept in Athens and concern total numbers for the whole department. A survey on this subject would reveal the real tendencies and the influence of tourism on the professions.
4. This seems to be a common feature in the rural communities. Herding is less esteemed than agriculture and in general the former sector is not faced as a real professional choice, but as an auxiliary occupation, or as a solution of necessity. Even if the young people had no objection to staying in the village, they would choose professions that furthered social mobility. See Kovani 1988.
5. Information obtained through interviews during the years 1986-1988.
6. To realise fully the meaning of 'changing coffee house' the importance of these places in Greek villages should be borne in mind. Even in smaller villages there is more than one, and each has its own clientele. There is the 'conservatives' coffee house' and the 'progressive's one' that of the fans of football team X or of Z, and so on. To go to a coffee house is a sign of social belonging. See also Papataxiarches, 1992.
7. 'Tourists are not guests at all, but outsiders; a tourist does not become part of any long-term reciprocity structure' (Crick 1989: 331).

8. For the process of the creation of a confraternity, the ceremonies and the rules, see Zarkia, 1988.
9. Nuñez 1989:268; ' Many anthropologists agree that two classes of individuals are likely to be innovators in their own community; those who hold traditional positions of prestige, and those who are somehow culturally marginal.'

REFERENCES

Antoniades, X. 'Archeion Eggralon Skyrou', *Skyriana Nea,* Athens, 1977-1994.

Benveniste, E. *Le vocabulaire des institutions indo-européennes* , tI-II, Paris: Les Editions de Minuit, 1969.

Boissevain, J. (ed.) *Revitalising European Rituals,* London: Routledge, 1992.

Cohen, E. 'A Phenomenology of Tourist Experiences', *Sociology* no. 13 (1979): 179-201.

Crick, M. 'Representations of International Tourism in the Social Sciences', *Annual Review of Anthropology,* vol.18 (1989): 307-43.

Greenwood, D.J. 'Tourism as an Agent of Change: A Spanish Basque Case', *Ethnology,* vol. XI (1972): 80-91.

Hermans, D.'The Encounter of Agriculture and Tourism. A Catalan Case.' *Annals of Tourism Research,* vol.VIII no. 3, (1981): 462-79.

Kovani, H. 'Le secteur primaire et la mobilite sociale des jeunes. Le cas d'une communauté rurale' (in Greek), *Actes du Congrés Franco-Hellenique: Le monde rural dans l'aire Méditerranéenne,* EKKE-KNE/EIE, avec la participation de CNRS et FNRS, (1988): 270-83.

Nuñez, Th. 'Touristic Studies in Anthropological Perspective' in Valene L. Smith, ed. *Hosts and Guests. The Anthropology of Tourism,* 2nd edn, Philadelphia: University of Pennsylvania Press, 1989: 265-74.

Papataxiarches, E. 'The World of the Coffee-House: Identity and Exchange in Male's Gathering' in Papataxiarches, E., Paradelles, Th., eds, *Identities and Gender in Modern Greece* (in Greek), Athens: University of Aegean, ed. Kastanioti, 1992: 209-50.

Perdika, N. *Skyros,* Athens, 1940.

Tsartas, P. *Social and Economical Repercussions of Tourist Development in the Department of Cyclades and Especially in the Islands Ios and Senfos, During the Period 1950-1980,* (in Greek), Athens: EKKE, 1989.

Urry, J. *The Tourist Gaze,* London: Sage, 1990.

Zarkia, C. 'La fraternité ecclésiastique dans l' île de Skiros (Grèce)',*Etudes et Documents Balkaniques et Méditerranéens,* vol. 13 (1988): 77-80.

_____, 'Société et espace dans l' île de Skyros', Thèse de Doctorat EHESS, Paris, 1991.

6. REACTIONS TO TOURISM
A View from the Deep Green Heart of France[1]

Simone A. Abram

When we consider the 'tourist gaze' we may be tempted to think immediately of places where tourists are constantly and unavoidably present. As this paper will show, the presence of tourists need not be overwhelming to have effects and stimulate reactions. It may be profitable to think of 'tourist gazes' in the plural.[2] as the diversity of this collection suggests. This chapter deals not with the prejudices and dynamics of host-tourist relations, but with a more subtle, possibly more profound development of reflexivity which the changing nature of tourism has encouraged. Thus I have concentrated more on the reactions to, rather than the interactions with, tourists.

Tourism in the Cantal, in the mountains of central France, is not the sort of mass tourism found in the major tourist resorts of France and beyond. Although travellers have passed through the Cantal throughout its known history (notably pilgrims on the route to Santiago de Compostella), the present era of tourism can be seen to have developed from the mass migrations of Auvergnats to Paris since the mid-nineteenth century. Many migrant workers returned to their natal villages for holidays or for seasonal work, retaining family property for the purpose, and this pattern continues into the late twentieth century. Hence the vast majority of tourists to the Cantal are French people with some

Notes for this section begin on page 200.

ancestral link to the region, and this has coloured the way tourism has developed along particular themes. The range of tourist activities and attractions within the rural theme in the Cantal is surprisingly wide, but official co-ordination and organisation of the various tourist developments is limited and their interdependence is not easily defined. However, by looking at some tourist activities and their organisers, some ideas and strategies emerge.

The Cantal

The Cantal is arguably one of France's most picturesquely rural departments, the heart of the Auvergne, a region of wild upland moors and valleys radiating from a central volcanic peak. Only fifty years ago the patois spoken as a first language in neighbouring valleys was distinguishable enough to identify the speaker's home, and varied widely between parts of the Cantal that were associated, particularly by trading links, with the North of France, and those that had closer links with the Occitan South. The vast forests of the Margeride, which extend from the Cantal into the Haute-Loire, housed the headquarters of the Maquis during the Second World War, and until then were home to wolves. The people of the Auvergne have no pretensions to separation from France, unlike the Basques or Bretons, but with encouragement from folklorists and politicians in the nineteenth century, the Auvergne is more often seen as the most French of French regions, the place of origin of the French national identity, an impression furthered in the French educational curriculum. However, economic migration, especially to Paris, since the mid-nineteenth century has depleted the Cantal's population from over 250,000 in 1850 to around 150,000 in 1990 and it is often said, with some justification, that there are more Auvergnats in Paris than there are in the Auvergne.[3]

This prolonged migration was of profound importance to the development this century of the perception of the Auvergne in greater France and has been a defining feature of the way tourism has developed in the region. The migrants who lived and worked in Paris tended to retain a nostalgia for their places of origin, which developed into a distinct Auvergnat society within Paris. Thus, when they returned 'home',[4] they brought with them ideas of how their homeland should be, which inevitably differed from the perceptions of those residents who had remained at home (Girard 1985). Very many of the visitors to the Cantal are still either migrants from the region or their descendants. Thus, while the population of many of the Cantal's villages trebles during the tourist season, many of these visitors are not referred to by the 'hosts' as tourists.

A Village

Let us look more closely at some of the people who visit the Cantal by focusing on a specific site. Much of my fieldwork[5] was carried out in a small village (population approximately 195; my own figure), which we will call St. Mary,[6] in a river valley that descends from the central pass in the Cantal volcano towards the east of the department. The village flourished economically and socially in the late nineteenth century around a station serving the then newly introduced railways and it rapidly grew into a vital artisan and market centre serving the upland farming areas to either side of the valley, gradually replacing an earlier village, le Cros, known to have occupied a site on the side of the valley for many centuries.[7] There was a thriving community in St. Mary until the post-Second World War period, when depopulation edged towards crisis proportions.[8]

The last remaining occupant of le Cros died in the 1970s and by the 1980s depopulation had reduced St. Mary to an ageing remnant of its former self. All that remained in the early 1990s in terms of employment was a former water mill that has been converted to produce animal feed (with two local employees), a part-time mayor's secretary, the commune employee (who does general maintenance on public property), a part-time cleaner, two shops, one café, and two hotel/bars that were run by the owners or franchise owners. There were also a very few self-employed artisans, (joiners, builders, an electrician). The primary school closed in 1992 when the teacher took overdue retirement and the seven remaining pupils began to take a bus to a school fifteen kilometres away. Most of the householders in 1990/91 were retired or semi-retired people, some who had spent the better part of their lives in St. Mary, and just a few who had retired there. Although there were about ten families with children, most of the secondary-school aged children boarded at their schools during the week, and most of the young people over school age had left the village to find work and returned only at weekends if it was possible.

Figure 6.1 A village in the Cantal.

Familiars, Tourists and Foreigners

In St. Mary, as in most of the Cantal, the tourist season is concentrated between the dates of the French national holidays, 14 July and 15 August.[9] 15 August is Saint Mary's day, i.e., the saint's day of the village's patron saint. Like most of the villages and towns in the Cantal, the patron saint's day provides the occasion for a fête. In St. Mary, this means a three-day event called the 'Fête Touristique'. This includes boules tournaments (usually called *pétanque*), a torch light procession, three nights of music, dancing, and drinking, and a day of entertainment including a procession of flowered floats with a marching band, professional entertainers on an outdoor stage, and a few stalls and children's games.

Many of the older villagers have children and/or grandchildren who have moved away from the village and it is rare for them not to return to the village for the fête, even if they only spend three days a year there. There are also a number of people who have inherited houses in the village from parents or grandparents, which, due to French partible inheritance laws, often remain in the joint possession of the inheritors as holiday or secondary homes. These familiar people, who easily double the village population, are not referred to as tourists within the village, however. As many of them have grown up in the village or at least spent all their summer holidays throughout their childhood there,[10] they are referred to by name, not generalised into a group. This situation is

177

almost exactly analogous to that described by Cruces and Díaz de Rada in their description of a Spanish valley, where:

> [f]or these people the village is a necessary point of periodic return, as they are related to a good part of the local population. Many are having their old houses repaired to serve them as secondary residences. There is no formal association for them in the village, though immigrant networks in their cities of destination appear to be of some importance. In many ways they still belong to the community, retaining their little plots of land, belongings, and nicknames. Villagers know who is the son of whom. Neither fully insiders nor outsiders, these people merge with the permanent population once or twice a year (Cruces and Díaz de Rada, 1992: 67).

The term 'tourist' is reserved for unknown people, and the only times I heard it applied to a returning migrant who had not been to the village for a while, it was said in jest, delivered as a feigned insult.

Tourists are not only distinguished by their lack of familiarity with the village population, i.e., their social separation, but by the fact that they are separate spatially as well. Whilst there is a small number of properties in St. Mary that are leased as holiday accommodation, usually to people we might call 'non-relatives', and there are two hotels in the centre of the village with rooms to rent, many of the people who might be described as tourists[11] stay at the campsite that is situated next to the football pitch, not far from the road that runs through the village, about a half a mile beyond the village boundary (marked by a road sign announcing the village's name). This is a fairly new campsite, only a few years old, which replaced a much more informal site on a side road off the village up the side of the valley, opposite a house that was then a café. In those days, I was frequently informed, the campsite was much more a part of the village; the people visiting had the opportunity to get to know each other as well as the villagers and many visitors returned year after year until they were considered firm friends with people in the village. Some still visited the former café owners when they visited the area and stayed elsewhere. Now that the new campsite even has its own public telephone, the campers need not even walk through the village to the phone box near the village square, so that the groups of neighbours, mainly women, who sit out on each other's doorsteps to chat away the balmy summer evenings, regret the fact that they do not even see who is staying so nearby.

Sometimes, however, the youngsters of the village do go to the campsite specifically to see if they can find new friends (or enemies, in some cases) and this has led to several quite lasting friendships and romantic liaisons, to the point where partners are included in village activities such as the football team or the village play. Nor is it impossible for other tourists to cross the imaginary boundary from tourist to friend, to become included in the life of the village. For instance, the daughter of a family who rented a holiday home in the village stayed on after her family had left, to work in one of the hotels as a maid for the rest of the summer vacation. Although she was often criticised by local people for her apparent laziness and sullenness, she was friendly for a while with some of the young people in the village who were on their school holidays. This brief anecdote merely illustrates how, if we are to devise categories of visitors or tourists, we must remember that these are not written in tablets of stone, and should be seen as variable and negotiable.

If our first working category is to be those who are not tourists but visiting, 'known', persons, who we may refer to as 'familiars' or 'returnees', then the opposite category of 'unknown' tourists can be divided also. The simplest way to do this would be to distinguish French tourists from foreign tourists. This should also show that foreigners are not one amorphous bunch, but are also relatively known or unknown. The obvious difference between French and foreign tourists is that French tourists behave in relatively recognisable ways, whereas more foreign tourists behave in more odd ways. Thus, for example, it is striking to a British visitor, in particular, that the French seem to take their lunch between twelve and one or two p.m. almost invariably, so that everything else stops between those hours. French tourists are often to be found lunching in local restaurants or picnicking at the roadsides, picnic table, chairs and all, as soon as midday has arrived. Many British tourists make particular comments about this as it seems to them so unusually invariable. For many British people, lunch is the minor meal of the day and dinner in the evening is more important, especially when they are on holiday. Correspondingly, when British tourists are seen hiking or window shopping at a time when any ordinary 'Cantalou' would expect to be sitting down to a three-course lunch, they appear to be behaving a little extraordinarily. This difference is one of the myriad differences that distinguish local routines from those of the foreign tourists and in turn distinguish them from the French tourists in the eyes of St. Mary's population.

The Business of Tourism

As might be expected in such an economically depressed region, there is a significant economic interest in the reactions of some business people to tourists. Whereas many French tourists would expect to use local shops to buy bread and other staples during their stay, it is becoming increasingly clear to local people that foreign tourists, especially German and Dutch as well as British, bring a lot of their own food with them. To local shop owners this spells disaster as they may well rely on the increased summer sales to keep them afloat during the lean winter months. However, this can be seen as an extension of the general malaise in local trading, which is exacerbated by permanent residents who use the out-of-town hypermarkets that are encroaching on the edges of the Cantal.[12] Some business people are making more concessions to the tourist market, though, and promoting goods with tourists in mind.

One of the Cantal's most attractive features to returnees and French tourists is that it is an area where farming has not been 'modernised' and mechanised as much as in other French regions. This fits in extremely well with urban myths of simple and healthy country living that have abounded from the Vichy regime's propagandising to the 'back to the land' hysteria of the 1960s.[13] In the 1990s this had become a very widespread concern about the use of chemicals such as hormone treatments in the raising of farm animals.[14] Although many Cantal farms were running near to subsistence levels, the laws concerning the treatment of livestock were strictly enforced so that veterinary standards accorded to national regulations. Many farms were also small enough (say, thirty hectares and often only twenty to thirty cattle) for farmers to be able to keep a very close eye on their herds. In addition, although they were seen by, and indeed marketed to, tourists as old-fashioned, this very antiquity had become ultra-modern with a different label: 'organic'. In 1990, a group of cattle farmers and butchers in the West of the department began an advertising campaign that exploited the organic nature of the meat from their farms.

Most of the French tourists I spoke to at the local markets described one of the attractions of a holiday in the Cantal as the availability of locally produced food that satisfied their expectations of rural France; i.e., the availability of these goods symbolised the continuation of a way of life on old-fashioned small-scale farms, where the quality of the produce took precedence over its profitability. This provides an interesting reflection on the expectations of other tourists, notably British, for whom the quality of life of the animals took precedence, as opposed to the actual taste of the food, which was the overriding concern of the French buyers. In either case, the food of the Auvergne satisfied customers on both counts. The act of going to a farm to buy produce, such as cheese, milk, eggs, and poultry raised on grain in the farm yard, became an intrinsic part of the holiday, possibly one of the defining features for many tourists, French and foreign alike.

A Museum

The theme of old-fashioned, hard but wholesome country living occurs often in presentations to tourists in the Cantal. The largest single purveyor of these ideas is the Ecomusée, one of the earliest of the provincial outposts of the Musée des Arts et Traditions Populaires, the national ethnographic museum in Paris. The Ecomusée was founded by a group of young people who were members of the entertainments committee[15] in a commune with a small population in the Margeride forests. Many of their activities involved trying to revive very local forms of entertainment (dances, music, etc.) and when, in the early 1970s, a local farm was put up for sale which had not been significantly modernised this century, they seized on this as the opportunity for them to set up a more permanent centre for public education. The old house was cleaned and arranged, with the help of older friends and neighbours who were able to recall the way the farm had been run at the beginning of this century, and turned into a museum. At first they received no support, financial or moral, from the department or the region, but by 1990 the museum had been affiliated to the Ecomusée movement and had grown to include a school, a châteaux and an old castle where exhibitions were held. The director, one of the original founders, had also educated himself in ethnography and museology, and the museum gained renown in the Ecomusée movement and became one of the prime tourist attractions in the Cantal, welcoming many thousands of visitors annually.

Visitors to the Ecomusée were presented with a very specific impression of the Cantal. Apart from seeing a representation of a day in the life of the farm around 1880, they were asked to imagine that this was typical of the life of farmers in the area. However, most traces of the political and economic climate of the time were excluded. No references to the conditions of the rest of the country were apparent, nor any explicit accounts of the relative wealth, class, or status of the farmer referred to as owner of the farm. Only the relative size of the farm compared to others in the village was noted in a publication on sale at the museum. The emphasis, not surprisingly, was clearly on the material conditions of the daily life of the farm, the tools used in the kitchen, the clothes in the cupboards, various domestic arrangements and the organisation of the farmyard and outbuildings, and on a uniform and unifying impression of the Cantal in the past.

In fact, only three people from St. Mary told me they had visited the Ecomusée (although more people who lived nearer to it had apparently visited[16]), and each of their reactions was very different. The first reactions were from two men in their forties, native to St. Mary, both working in agriculture but not directly as farmers. Jean-Pierre had pipe-dreams of setting up his own museum in his barn, with all his farmer-father's old equipment and his own sculptures, and simply said he had found the Ecomusée rather dull. Jacques was passionate about the farming life of the Cantal, and had delighted in seeing the old-fashioned tools and objects that he remembered from earlier days. The third person who had visited the Ecomusée was the daughter of a woman from a neighbouring commune, who had been brought up in England and had returned to the area to run a hotel. Her reaction was to say that as she enjoys nosing around old houses in the area, looking round the farmhouse of the Ecomusée had been an extension of her favourite activity. However, friends from other parts of the Cantal who I met while working in the capital town of Aurillac did not like the representation of the Cantal found in the Ecomusée. One in particular complained that the museum had no relevance to his own family history, that of the cowherds and cheesemakers who were the poorest of the poor and whose history had not been recorded. Rather, the museum gave a very cosy impression of a bourgeois farm. One young woman who worked in tourist-management also explained that the museum was very badly managed and that this may have accounted for the mixed impressions of the visitors.

One could say that, by concentrating on the daily routine, or technology, of work and thus glossing over the political context of the lives of the people who lived those routines, the Ecomusée mythologises the life of the farm it represents, and also the lives of those not quite represented but alluded to by its assertion of the typicality of its exhibits (in what Susan Wright calls a 'Heritage' representation [1992]). Although it specifies the date it is purporting to recreate, the lack of association with the political, economic, or even social circumstances and events in the rest of France, never mind Europe, place it in an ill-defined era of timeless tradition, just out of our reach. The implication is that the practices employed in the running of the farm and the house were long-standing traditions, only then beginning to change with the revolution in farming technology that led to the situation found there in the present day. The political mayhem that defined the state of the rural economy in the 1990s thus appears as something new and foreign to rural life, a modern rupture to the sequence of traditional time.[17] Perhaps because the local history of the Cantal is not well-documented, and interest in such local history has only recently been gaining academic legitimacy, its turbulent history of invasion and occupation (from Roman to Nazi), defiance and defence, landowners' despotism and social inequalities is suppressed and the ideal of timeless traditions glosses over the wider contexts of previous lives.

The idea that the Cantal was too remote from the French state to be affected by national events can be refuted by evidence of local upheavals during the revolution of 1789 (Dalby 1981); the memorial statues in every village provide evidence enough of the effects of the 1914-1918 war. Perhaps not surprisingly, the remoteness accorded to the Cantal by urban French commentators is largely illusory, as the many migrants and travellers through the Cantal have kept people informed of life outside. That people did not necessarily change their lifestyles according to distant trends and fashions does not indicate that they were not aware of them, but may be a result of the distinction between spatial and social distance. In other words, one may know very well that other people live differently but that does not provide sufficient motivation nor resources for one to change one's own way of life.

The way the Ecomusée represents the Cantal's history, by saying: 'this is how it was', has become very pervasive, too, so that its dissemination to tourists has played no small part in determining their expectations of what they might find in the Cantal. The success of the Ecomusée and the Cantal's official museum, and the rise in popularity of what are more or less equivalent to 'Heritage Centres' (Urry 1990), even if they do not necessarily use this title, have encouraged others in the Cantal to join in this wave of recreations of the past and revivals of traditions.[18] This has coincided with a general growth in tourism in the Cantal, which has been adopted as an economic antidote to the failings of small farms in the face of international pressures.[19] It is pertinent to question the nature of these revivals in the light of various studies of the invention of tradition (Chapman 1986; Hobsbawm and Ranger, 1988; McDonald 1989), as it is plain that these revivals do change the practices represented, if not in technical detail then in meaning and significance via their changed context.[20]

One organisation that was gaining in influence and popularity during the early 1990s, is the Occitan Institute. In contrast to Diwan in Brittany (McDonald 1982), the Occitan Institute formalised an 'indigenous' re-evaluation of local language and customs, but with the backing of the Occitan movement from the south of France its members were able to involve Cantaliens in a network of Occitan performances and give access to Occitan publications, thereby according a status to patois that it had not previously achieved. The activities of the Occitan Institute centred around educational programmes in the schools and music and dance events around the Cantal, focusing primarily on re-educating the Cantal's population. It was not particularly concerned with tourism (and will thus not be considered here in any depth) but the two coincided at fêtes of folkloric performances and, for example, when a group of Occitan Institute musicians performed at the St. Mary summer fête.[21]

'Tradition'

Traditionality can be claimed in various ways, through events or practices. This section begins with a brief introduction to the summer patronal fête at St. Mary, which contrasts to other fêtes described later. The fête at St. Mary is traditional in the sense that it is a long-standing annual event, in contrast to a traditionality that revives practices from the past. There are two particular forms of revival that are remarkable. One is the rise in popularity of fêtes that revolved around recreations of past events, such as threshing with an early-nineteenth-century threshing machine, powered by a steam engine, or baking bread in the communal village oven,[22] the other a revival of certain farming practices, particularly cheesemaking, ostensibly for the tourist market.

St. Mary's Patronal Fête

St. Mary's patronal fête, known now as a tourist fête, is quite an attraction in the area, especially as it falls on a national holiday, as mentioned above. It is open to all comers and many of the people who go to the fête, at least on its main day, may be tourists, or at least visitors. This is the main social event in the village's calendar and many months of preparation precede it, but it is not a fund-raising event. In fact, without the proceeds of a door-to-door collection round the village before the fête, the organising committee would make a loss. The practice of holding saints' day fêtes goes back as far as the memories of the oldest inhabitants of the village, but the presence of so many tourists is a relatively recent change, and one that some of the villagers find a little alienating. Although it is advertised as a tourist fête, the organisers claim that this is

Figure 6.2 A Fête.

only to attract more people to the fête in order to make it more lively, but that it is really a patronal fête. In the past,[23] most of the people at the fête were from the surrounding villages and communes and so were at least familiar, if not well-known. This remains in the memories of the older villagers as a desirable characteristic, or an expectation, of the fête. The actual number of people at the fête may have remained fairly constant, though, as the area has been depopulated.

The entertainment at the fête consists of boules tournaments (usually called *pétanque*), a torch-light procession, three nights of music, dancing, and drinking, and a day of entertainment including a procession of flowered floats with a marching band, professional entertainers on an outdoor stage, and a few stalls and children's games. Although the fête at St. Mary can be considered to be a long-standing tradition, it is traditional in a more implicit way than certain other fêtes in the region. The entertainment at St. Mary's fête is always contemporary; i.e., the entertainers are usually television celebrities or popular musicians, and although the parades and boules games are seen as repetitions of those held for many years, they are seen as contemporary rather than representative of the past. In other fêtes, the entertainment is directly representative of the past, in a way that may claim tradition as an authenticating factor, but which places the practices represented clearly in the past rather than in the present, as will be discussed below.

185

The various fêtes vary dramatically in style and content and it would seem that adaptations are made according to the type of audience. Most obviously, the fêtes put on for tourists by the Folklore Institute in Saint Flour are completely different to those arranged for local people by the inhabitants of a small village on the plateau (Esclade).[24] The *Soirée de Battage* in Saint Flour, held at the gym in August, revolves around the use of a turn-of-the-century threshing machine. The machine belongs to a farmer from the canton of Saint Flour who has renovated it into working condition. There is no doubt that it is a splendid machine, an enormous wooden trailer with wheels and pulleys and wooden flaps that batter the grain from the straw, driven by a shining brass steam traction engine that has been lovingly restored, and the whole thing made even more impressive by a group of men in working clothes and hats standing on top of and around the machine to operate it. For the evening of the celebration, it is floodlit and operated for a short spell every quarter or half hour; to run it continuously would require a huge amount of wheat, barley, or rye. Monsieur Laval, from St Mary, spent his working life farming in the winters and travelling the country throughout the summers with a threshing machine. When he started threshing in 1938, it was with such a machine, but during the occupation there was no wood to burn so he used an electric motor. After the war he bought a tractor and abandoned the traction engine and in 1952 he bought his first combine harvester. In fact, the large wooden threshing machines superseded flails, which were used up until the beginning of the twentieth century, so that they were in use altogether for about fifty years. At the fête, however, the technique was presented simply as 'the way we used to work', the impression being that the wooden threshing machine was timeless, forming one of the elements of the golden era of farming and rural life.

Apart from the threshing machine, which was roped off from the public, inside the gym was a stage surrounded by tables and chairs, and a cafeteria serving Cantal cheese, sausage, rye bread, tripe, and blackcurrant tarts: Auvergnat foods. As the evening got underway, the performances began on the stage. A group of musicians playing old local instruments gave a short performance of local songs, then played to accompany dancers dressed in folkloric costumes. These costumes roughly corresponded to the Sunday or festivity clothing of local peasants towards the end of the nineteenth century, as attested to by old photographs. The dancers were members of the local folkloric club, and included children, also costumed. A compère introduced the dances, explaining the origin of each and their peculiarities, and suggesting what kind of people may have danced them in the past, and conjuring up images of simple folk spontaneously breaking into dance after a long day's work or an evening socialising. The entertainment was thus highly formalised and laden with symbolism; in other words, it was the most staged of all the fêtes I saw in the Cantal.

Most of the audience could be described as tourists, i.e., visitors on holiday in the region, either from other parts of France or elsewhere. The presentation assumed that the audience had very little knowledge of the Auvergne, and it was thus an exercise not only in entertainment but education. Their presentation incorporated a highly refined image of the Cantal's folkloric history, moulded to distance the folklore from the present circumstances of Cantalians. Like the museum, this presentation removed any economic or political context, neutralising the past into a quaint nostalgia that gave some picturesque difference to the Cantal, rather than attributing any sense of historical depth to the folklore presented.

In contrast, the *fête du four* at Esclade seemed quite unstaged. For the participants, there was work to be done: the village oven, in a small stone building between two farmhouses just hidden from the village square and church, had to be stoked with wood and cleared out when the stones reached white heat. The elderly man who stoked the oven complained that it was very laborious work; in the past, when the oven was lit during the threshing in order to bake bread and cook meals for the workers, there would have been a rota of men to help. In the meantime, a group of older women, mostly grandmothers (and over sixty, if not seventy), had spent the previous evening and all the morning of the fête preparing tarts, to be baked in the oven. I was told by people in St. Mary that they had previously prepared rye bread, but that now it was too hard work for them. Most of the tarts had been ordered in advance by people from the area who knew how good they would be, as many people have very fond memories of the taste of food cooked in wood-stoked ovens. Indeed, when one compares wood-baked bread to ordinary bread, the former's flavour is richer and fuller.

The more public part of the fête was the evening meal, where people were served pigs' trotters and peas cooked in the oven, once again reminding people of the days when casseroles could be left to cook in the oven overnight whilst it was still hot. There was little obvious staging of this event; most of the people at the meal were local or familiar to the area, and none of the participants dressed up. If there were men wearing 'peasants' blues' working clothes, this was because they usually wore them, although some wearing of Auvergnat hats may have seemed appropriate as confirming markers of the Cantal-ness of the occasion. Music of the type played at the Saint Flour performance was also used as background music, in a similar way. According to people at the fête, they played the local music because that was the music that they liked. Without any marked outside gaze, they were able to enjoy the music for its own sake, not for its symbolism, although the local feeling it enhanced was generally found gratifying. It is notable that in contrast to the very marked division between performers and audience at the threshing fête, (divided with a rope barrier around the threshing machine, and by the stage for the dance performance), those at the fête at Esclade were all participants. The latter fête was thus much more informal and inclusive as well as implicit in its significance for the participants. Rather than being a staged entertainment to be watched, it was a social event that formed part of the social calendar of the commune.

It becomes quite obvious from these and other fêtes in the region that the representation of Cantal-ness or Auvergnat-ness depends on to whom it is addressed, and this should not be a surprise. However, it is impossible to know quite how much people's reinterpretation of the past, or their construction of a history, has depended on the presentation of accounts of it for tourists. The question of Auvergnat identity is as old as any of the French regional characterisations, but having tourists who actually come to look at them at home, as opposed to being stereotyped in Paris or in Spain, may have encouraged a local reformulation of Auvergnat-ness.

There is another interesting similarity between these fêtes and those described by Cruces and Díaz de Rada (1992). Although the fêtes described here could not easily be divided into those that are 'declining' or 'persisting', as Cruces and Díaz de Rada divide religious, patronal, and other festivities, there is a similar distinction between those that are performances for tourists and those that emphasise local identity. Many other fêtes are held at other times of the year, but the patronal fêtes that are held in the summer are the best-attended and thus the largest. They become the focus of the village calendar, because in villages that are described as dying for lack of people, the influx of visitors to the fête is seen as a bringing back to life. This is closely tied in to a sense of return to the past, when the villages were much more crowded, with much higher populations.

It is almost the opposite, then, to the assertions in the Jerte valley that 'Nowadays there aren't feasts any more, because we're "in feast" every day' (Cruces and Díaz de Rada 1992: 67). In St. Mary, the village is 'dead' every day, and the fête is a very special occasion because it is one moment in the year when the old life before the drastic depopulation of the post-war period (especially since the 1960s) reduced the village to a skeleton of its former self. The new festivals of the Jerte valley correspond only in a limited way to the new festivities of St. Mary and surrounding villages. The new festivities are precisely those that recreate the past, such as the *fête du cidre* created in October 1991 in St Mary, which recreates the festivities that formerly accompanied the pressing of apples into cider. People from all around St. Mary used to bring their apples to the presses owned by one or two people in the village, and the presence of these visitors provided the occasion for impromptu parties. Reflecting on this, when trying to devise some new entertainment for St. Mary, the entertainment committee saw it as an ideal opportunity to create a fête, following the example of the chestnut fête staged to revive the exploitation of chestnut forests in the west of the Cantal. The fête was an attempt thus not only to provide entertainment, but also to encourage people to maintain the dwindling orchards in the valley and to remind people of livelier times. This was not expressed as a desire for consolidation of local identity, but rather as a way to revive the village as a social arena; not necessarily to impose a unifying identity, but merely to encourage some activity, rather than the torpor of the everyday village. It is difficult to associate this with the rise of the market economy of industrial capitalism, as Cruce and Díaz de Rada do (1992: 63, 77), but it can be seen as an attempt to rescue some sociability from the ruins brought on by the socio-economic and political difficulties that have stripped the Cantal of much of its population.

The other form of revival could be described as a marketing exercise. Any visitor to a tourist office in the Cantal may find information about *Rallyes Gourmands*. These are groups of farmers[25] (about 18 groups of six to eight farmers, in 1990) who have formed associations with the advice of the farmers' union[26] to market their produce specifically to tourists. This is done on the basis that it has some local significance and can be described as traditional. However, produce such as cheese and charcuterie that may be sold to the public must fulfil the requirements of the hygiene and public health regulations.[27] Those who wish to produce and sell foods that they can claim to have produced in a traditional way must, to be in accordance with the law, drastically change the very processes they are purporting to represent. This is a rather different scenario from the subtle decontextualising of the museum projects, as the context of being a small landowning farmer is essential to the exercise, but the methods they adopt consciously update and develop traditions.

This extension of traditional practice was the very aim of one farming family in a Rallye Gourmand, the Severacs, who set up their dairy as a way to avoid the restrictions of milk quotas, introduced in the late 1980s. Their dairy was rebuilt from a semi-derelict farmhouse in a way that 'recreated history' by using 'traditional' cheese-making techniques in a modern way, in their own words. They did not want to create a dull, lifeless museum, but a place that was very much alive. Thus they lived and breathed, and especially, ate their history, whilst running a solvent business despite a heavy burden of debt. The general idea was that passing tourists should see the sign at the roadside by the turning to the farm, or see some of their publicity at the tourist office, and stop at the farm out of curiosity, have a look round, see the cheese being made, taste it and be so impressed that they would buy a large portion to take home with them. By and large, this is how it worked, as well as coach tours from Saint Flour stopping at the farm for a quick tour and providing a captive market for cheese sales. The quality of the cheese was much better than that available in supermarkets or in many other regions of France so that many people were keen to buy enough for their holidays if not some to take home as well. This was not limited to French tourists: on one occasion in 1993, a Polish couple on holiday in the region bought twenty kilos of cheese to take home with them.

The Severacs' enterprise had been developed with tourists in mind as the potential market for their cheeses, but, although during the summer their sales increased as tourists bought from them, it was the regular, local customers who bought from them every week at markets all year round who formed the basis of their custom. Without this clientele, the business would not have been sustainable. This sums up the economic situation of tourism in the Cantal, where tourism could not sustain the economy alone. However, as a source of extra income, it enables other businesses to survive the financial year by boosting sales, apparently making the difference for many businesses between profit and loss. It is not clear, however, what the exact economic contribution of tourism is to small businesses, although a survey in 1990 showed that half of sales at the country markets (see below) were to local customers, and half to tourists, although 63 percent of customers were local and 37 percent tourists. These markets only contribute a fraction of the annual sales of the producers, however, so that the proportion of sales to tourists could be estimated at under a third of total sales for members of the Rallyes Gourmands.

The Severacs were under no illusions that their enterprise differed from the cheese-producers of earlier generations. Although their cheeses have been awarded licences (under the *Appellation Contrôlée* system) and are thus certified as genuine Cantal and Salers[28] cheeses, they are not produced from the milk of Salers cows, the breed peculiar to the Cantal, nor is the milk curdled in wooden vats, but in stainless steel. What is more, the milk of two milkings is used so that the first batch is refrigerated and reheated when required, so that only one curdling a day is required, leaving the afternoons free for other farm work. Even the conditions of sale at market were highly regulated, and veterinary inspectors frequently visited the markets to ensure they were complied with.

During the summer, the Rallye Gourmand to which the Severacs belonged organised joint *marchés de pays*, country markets, in order to sell produce to tourists. At these markets, set up in old market halls or town squares, foods were sold from trestle tables with colourful cloths on them, and Auvergnat music was played, either from recordings or by local musicians. At the time, the advisor at the Chambre d'Agriculture was a very resentful person whose attitude to farmers was ambivalent, to say the least. Whilst ostensibly helping them to organise their *relais* and markets, in fact he was advising many people not to think about developing their businesses, holding up loan applications and the like, and sending veterinary inspectors to the markets to enforce practices not bothered with at everyday markets. As a result, stallholders selling food were obliged to use refrigerated display cabinets, an expensive and inconvenient obligation at a market purporting to be 'olde worlde'. The laudable rationalisation of this vigorous enforcement of E.U. directives at the Chambre d'Agriculture was that it was essential that tourists should see that Cantaliens were absolutely up to the minute in their hygiene and methods. This brings us to another issue central to the development of tourism in the Cantal. The paradox between representing themselves as old-fashioned in a wholesome way, yet not appearing to be backwards and ignorant was unresolved. In fact, it was a constant difficulty for the tourist committee of the departmental government. Their job was to promote the Cantal as a tourist venue within France[29] and there was an apparent dichotomy between their desires to portray the Cantal as a modern, well-resourced place to holiday, where many fashionable sports were catered for, but also as a place that was unspoilt, whilst dispelling the idea that it was backwards. It was sometimes said, and not only by emigrants or outsiders to the area, that after all the depopulation over the century, the ones who were left behind were those who had no get-up-and-go, but it was always acknowledged that some had had the foresight to realise the Cantal was a beautiful place to live and were determined to stay there. The idea of the dull relations who stayed behind was certainly part of the repertoire of images of the Cantal in usage at the time of my fieldwork.

The Buron

Given the necessity for farmers to comply with stringent modern working regulations, in what ways could they claim to be recreating the past, or producing goods '*à l'ancienne*'? Which were the features that could be sacrificed and which were necessary? In other words, what were the signifiers and markers of 'authentic Cantalness' (see Culler 1988)? It was possible to compare fairly directly the methods used in dairies, as in 1990 there was one remaining mountain dairy, known as a *buron*, still in operation. This was owned by an elderly farmer who employed three men to work for the summer season in the way they had worked since the Second World War, if not before. This particular buron was the subject of an ethnographic study, which was readily available as a picture book in many local bookshops (Roc 1989). This dairy had not been renovated during the owner's lifetime and no modern mechanised equipment had been brought in. There was no electricity nor gas; in fact the only concession to modern comfort were a couple of battery torches. All the other equipment was hand operated. Machinery such as the creamer (or separator) and the presses were manufactured around the turn of the nineteenth century; other equipment such as the wooden barrels for collecting and curdling the milk were made by the Cantal's last remaining barrel-maker to the specifications he had always used.

This buron was a working dairy with two milkings per day outdoors in the milking pen where the Salers cows were milked with their calves tied to their legs in order for the cows to give the milk, the distinctive feature of dairy farming in the region.[30] However, as it was definitely the last of its kind in the Cantal (although there were reputedly others in the neighbouring department of Aveyron), the tourist office at Saint Flour arranged coach tours to the buron to see the afternoon curdling. The morning session took place soon after dawn, and was evidently unpopular with tourists. In fact, the 'tour' as such consisted only of a minibus with a driver that took people from Saint Flour the forty miles or so to the buron in the mountains. Once there, the visitors were free to go into the fields to watch the milking in the fenced milking-park where the

Figure 6.3 Inside the buron.

burronniers milked the cows, putting the milk carefully into a barrel on
a wooden cart, and once the milking was over, harnessing up a pair of
cows to pull the cart back to the buron. At the buron, the tourists could
enter the dairy room to see the process of cheesemaking, and ask questions of the workers or chat with them. The three workers, two of whom
had featured in the ethnography, found it amusing and mildly flattering
to be visited by the tourists, but they were not permitted to sell any
cheese to them. Quite apart from the fact that the cheese must be
matured for at least three months before being eaten, it was clearly out
of their remit to be involved in selling the produce. The owner had an
agreement with a local cheese-seller, who purchased and sold on all of his
production, despite the fact that he could have made greater profits by
selling it directly to tourists from the buron. The owner of the dairy,
however, for whom it was simply an outpost for the herd during the
summer months following a practice of transhumance whose recorded
history goes back at least a thousand years, made no concessions to the
tourists. It was precisely because the owner was not interested in modernising that the buron continued to be used in the way it was and thus
why opportunistic commercialisation was not a priority.

The only cost to the tourists was the coach fare, as the buronniers
made no charge to visitors. As Jacques, from St. Mary, explained:

[The buronniers] are so isolated for the four months they are up in the
mountains that they are glad to see people. They don't do it for money: you

193

can explain to people that Auvergnats are friendly, they like to see people and chat with them. If you take a good bottle of wine with you, that always goes down well and there's a little box by the door too, marked 'tips' and they use that money to buy a bottle or tobacco; you don't have to leave a tip, but most people do. They let you taste the cheese, but they're not allowed to sell it. You know, last time I went up there, they sold me some of the butter they make for themselves up there. It was delicious.

According to Jaques, too, most of the tourists at the buron were French people with 'farming roots', people who made comments such as, 'I remember my grandfather doing that'. Indeed, one of the reasons many visitors came to the Cantal was to 'rediscover their country roots', as has been mentioned, so that the trip to a buron, apparently working as it may have done fifty years ago, played directly, if unwittingly, into the nostalgic memory of such tourists. If they viewed the buronniers as local yokels, they could not fail to recognise the quiet confidence and a certain pride with which they carried out their work, and most visitors seemed to respect the skill involved in the work. It seems, also, that many visitors went to the buron because they knew the Cantal cheese and liked it, and held it in some respect as a symbol of local identity as is the case for many cheeses in France. Any real economic dependence between the workers and the tourists could only be said to occur if the tourists went down to the town to buy the finished cheeses from the retailer.

The apparent authenticity of life at the buron was not consciously staged for the tourists, although the box for tips and the willingness of the workers to talk to visitors shows that they were willing to present themselves to the outside world. They did speak patois among themselves, but this was more likely to be because patois was their first and common language rather than a ruse to impress tourists, as they spoke French whenever they thought anyone was listening.[31] The work was primarily functional and only marginally a performance, so that as far as the workers were concerned, they were going about their ordinary work, with an occasional audience to appreciate them, in contrast to the many months of being isolated.

When the farmer retired in 1991 and his son took over, it was expected that the buron would close,[32] rather than be modernised according to the E.C. directives, not only because that would require a huge capital investment not available to the farmer, but also because the workers were also ageing and no young apprentices were to be found. Considering the complete lack of modern facilities in the buron and the measly sum the workers were paid, it was not surprising the trade had died out. Up until the Second World War the workers in the burons were predominantly teenage boys, who were without home commitments and thus able to work through the summer months away in the hills. According to several men at St Mary, who had worked in burons during their youth, the highlands were crowded (there was apparently an estival highland population of several thousand) and it was not always easy sharing everything in close quarters among three or four youths. They did have wistful reminiscences, though, as there were dances to go to in the nearest villages, and at the end of the season, leftover food from the buron gardens (rabbits and pigs were brought up too, and were certainly not taken down again) provided a feast for neighbouring workers.

The spectre of older men working in the buron in relative isolation, then, gave quite a false impression of what may have been considered normal practice for earlier generations of Cantal farm workers. The techniques used, however, were true to those of the 1930s certainly, and probably very similar indeed to those used long before then. So, even of these techniques, what comparison was there between the buron and the Severacs' dairy? By the end of 1991, when the Severacs' dairy was tiled, the only similar pieces of equipment to those at the buron were the implement for breaking up the curds, the curd press, the cheese presses, and the butter barrel. The creamer and the curd grater used the same basic technology but were powered by electric motors in the newer dairy, as opposed to hand cranks in the buron. The Severacs did not have Salers cows, nor wooden barrels, nor was the milk used immediately, as mentioned earlier. However, these differences in method were considered to affect the quality but not the identity of the cheese. The taste would not be comparable between the two dairies' cheeses, but the cheeses were still recognisably of the same type. Somehow, though, the Severacs' cheese was more 'authentically' Cantal than the factory Cantals made in large mechanised dairies, but not quite as authentic as the cheese from the buron.

The significant features of the Severacs' farm, in their own terms, was that it was *'artisanale'* (i.e., not a factory or a co-operative dairy, but an independent concern), and that they were recreating a previous lifestyle, but using modern conveniences. Their motivation was ostensibly purely economic, but the necessity to make a living was tempered by the desire to do so within dairy farming and in M. Severac's place of birth. They had, in fact, bought the dairy and their farmhouse specifically to set up on their own after a spate of redundancies in the dairies where they had previously worked. The knowledge of this former lifestyle that they were trying to recreate came from Mme. Severac's upbringing on such a dairy farm run by her parents.

There was no doubt that the Severacs' dairy was created to serve a growing tourist market. Other members of the Rallye Gourmand sold produce that was not central to the function of the farms. For instance, one woman sold poultry that she had raised in her farmyard (of a dairy farm), that she had previously only raised for domestic consumption. The extra production was undertaken specifically to sell to a tourist market to which the Rallye gave them access. The farmers had expectations, then, about the tourists, and about the tourists' expectations of them, but it was clear that not all tourists were included in their version. Their presentations of old-fashioned genuineness with modern production standards, which could then be interpreted as 'organic', tended to appeal to both nostalgic returnees and some French tourists. Most other foreign tourists would actually find it hard to differentiate between the rather reflexive *marchés de pays* and ordinary town markets, except that the latter where much busier and livelier, and less pretentious. Members of the Rallyes gourmands, those who sold produce as their mainstay (i.e., not a supplementary seasonal activity), also took their goods for sale to regular town markets, where they worked alongside people for whom this was the only outlet for their goods. The Severacs, for example, had regular clients at several town markets who bought their cheese rather than co-operative dairy cheese because it was made the way they considered it correct, and they preferred the taste. To these people the old way was simply the right way and the best way to make cheese, and the Severacs produced the kind of cheese they preferred to buy. The living-museum, tourist attraction aspect of the Severacs' farm was irrelevant to them. That the Severacs entertained tour groups from the nearby town's tourist hotels was not a concern, although they may have been more interested in the school groups who visited the farm as part of the farmers' union publicity efforts. If tradition is interpreted as actively developing, rather than as a static form, then the town markets could be considered to be a much more convincing tradition than the marchés de pays, with their musicians in Auvergnat hats (one of the most common markers).

McDonald's assertion that for Bretons 'local dirt and poverty are too close to be revalued as the wonders of nature and ecology' (McDonald 1982: 377) does not completely describe the situation in the Cantal. For some people, local dirt, if not poverty, is being revalued as authenticity and tradition. At the same time, the farmers' lobbies are fighting very hard to allow farmers the chance to escape the miserable cycle of loss and bankruptcy that is reducing their numbers so drastically. In 1990 they were campaigning vigorously against imports of cheap, poor-quality meats from Eastern European countries and for a rationalisation of milk quotas to redress the bias of subsidies towards large lowland farms in an effort to repeal the relative economic disadvantage that was their most significant problem.[33]

From one farm to the next the situation can seem to vary dramatically. For instance, only a few fields away from the Severacs' farm lived farmers who were surviving on the minimal pensions of their retired parents, who were still having to do farm work to keep them. Farmers are classed as self-employed in the eyes of the welfare system, so while they have to pay significant local and national taxes, they cannot claim unemployment benefits, and few can afford private pension schemes to supplement their meagre state pensions. Those farmers who have not been able either to diversify their farms nor to develop some kind of tourism, from direct-selling to renting out holiday accommodation such as *gîtes*, are in very serious financial difficulties indeed. It is not imagined that tourism is a miracle solution, but a possible supplement, and it is not suitable nor sufficient for everybody.

Conclusions

We have seen that the Cantal receives a range of visitors who are attracted by diverse activities. We have also seen that the impact of the various visitors, tourists or relations, unknown and familiar, and thus the reactions of local Cantal residents is correspondingly diverse. Within this diversity, however, there is no doubt that Cantaliens are asking: 'who are we?' and 'what do we look like to other people?' Without any formal body dictating the answers to such questions, people are beginning to find their own versions of their past, of history, using their own recollections, supplemented by whatever local information is published and available.

Whilst many Cantaliens are motivated by the potential economic rewards of exploiting a new market as the older ones dwindle, their choice of theme to sell their products as old-fashioned, local, and thus intrinsically better than other, mass-produced or somehow foreign produce bears no causal relation to the economic circumstances, but to the ideological climate. Selling goods by selling an idea of themselves as quintessentially the definition of their homeland has much to do with French ideas of 'paysannerie' and anti-French ideas about regionality, particularly an Occitan identity which is growing in popularity. The purchase of goods at the marchés de pays can be thus thought of as the purchase of a set of ideas, that of '*la vie en arrière temps*' and of Cantalness. Is this not another way of describing the commoditisation of culture? However, this commoditisation is part of a very positive process by which people are beginning to re-evaluate their history and shake off the shame of peasantry that has been pressed on them in their education through the generations, specifically in the denigration of the use of patois earlier this century. Commoditisation can then be seen as influential in the recreations of the past by people like the Severacs and in the general discussion and re-evaluation of the Cantal's place within France and the new Europe.

However, to suggest a link between the economic importance of tourism and the development of reflexivity would err towards economic tyranny, in which causal links impose an ordering rationality on situations that are not so organised. It may be possible to suggest that economic circumstances have provided scope for the development of some types of reflexivity, but this development seems to have happened by hearsay. Someone in the entertainments committee of Esclade went to a fête du four in another village and thought it would be a good idea to renovate the *four* in Esclade. The Severacs' Rallye Gourmand was created on the basis of one that had been devised by a particularly imaginative and perceptive woman farmer[34] at the other side of the Cantal, a much more touristic area near the Lot valley, in response to visitors' comments about the quaintness of her farm. It seems that she seized upon the marketing potential of this aspect of her business, but that the idea caught on so rapidly owes to the attractiveness of the idea as a reassurance of the value of localness and Cantalness as a means to improve business.

The senior management of the tourist facilities in the Cantal rationalise their encouragement of this kind of development by stating that the Cantal must find some unique qualities that it can sell to tourists to entice them to the area rather than going elsewhere. Thus, while they promote the modernity of the Cantal in terms of the sports available, they also promote its ancient rusticity modernised into 'quality' of the ecological and alimentary environment. The economic benefits arise from the popularity of the ideology; in other words their marketing tactics are successful, as they have understood what their customers want. The commoditisation of cultural attributes is thus interactive: without the participation of both locals and tourists it would not be possible. However, it does not require the approval of all of them, and the diversity of reactions stems from this division. If a shopkeeper in Saint Flour regrets the fall in the number of tourists during the summer period, explaining that 'There are fewer this year: sales are down', visiting relatives may chide that: 'It's terrible at the Puy Mary: the place is packed with tourists'.

Not all locals are farmers, of course. A young professional woman who works in Aurillac, who administrates the organisation of holiday homes (*gîtes*), and thus deals with tourists as well as residents, commented:

> I see people walking round the old streets of Aurillac, and I overhear them saying how quaint and old-fashioned it all is, and how backward it all seems, like stepping back fifty years, and I feel like saying: hey, hang on a minute, I live here too and I'm not backwards! It's so strange to hear them talking like that about *my* home and *my* friends. That isn't how I see it.

So how does she see the Cantal and why did she move back there after working in Paris and why is she keen to remain there when so many of her contemporaries have moved away? Why is the Cantal better than anywhere else?

> It isn't in comparison to the way things might have been in the past, even though people do relate things to the past pretty often, but relative to a particular lifestyle which I see my friends living. You know, when I lived in Paris, I had a tiny bedsit which cost the earth, and I felt like I couldn't breath. And when we visit our friends in the suburbs and see them trying to cope with commuting for an hour at least, to get to work and back, we say to ourselves, well, we get fed up sometimes and complain about the Cantal, saying we want to go somewhere more exciting or radical, but compared with what other people put up with, our lives are so pleasant, we come back here and realise how lucky we are.

The local as tourist, then, brings yet another perspective on tourism, allowing us to glimpse the paradox between the tourists as leisured and wealthy possessor of economic power, for whom culture is commoditised, and the tourist as unfortunate, misguided runner in the rat race who needs to be educated into an understanding of life in the Cantal and into a different way of thinking that prioritises space and time over convenience and speed.

NOTES

1. 'Auvergne: Deep Green Heart of France' was the title of the introduction to FRANCE magazine's supplement to their Summer issue 1991.
2. As Urry suggests (1990: 1).
3. An account of the Auvergnats of Paris can be found in Girard 1985. For an account of migrations to and from Spain, see Poitrineau 1985.
4. Auvergnats in Paris, known as 'Bougnats', visited the Auvergne more frequently after 1904, when a special vacation train service was commissioned for them by the creator of the newspaper 'l'Auvergnat de Paris'.
5. This fieldwork in 1990/1991 was funded by the Economic and Social Research Council of Great Britain.
6. All place names and personal names are pseudonyms.
7. One of the earliest detailed maps of the region, produced in 1642, shows the village in roughly the same early site. Its church is known to date back at least to the eleventh century and is believed to be the site of the evangelist Mary's dwellings in the first century A.D.
8. The official census shows the population of the Cantal falling from over 260,000 in the middle of the nineteenth century to around 200,000 in 1920 (after a fall of over 20,000 during the First World War) to under 160,000 in 1990, and the population of St Mary followed this trend.
9. All descriptions refer to the years 1990 and 1991, although further communication suggests it would equally well apply to the following year as well.
10. It is common practice in many parts of France for parents who live in cities to send their children to grandparents who live in the country during the school vacations in the summer when the parents may well still be at work.
11. Numbers of tourists at the campsite vary from year to year, but from June to August 1993 there were 294 parties of campers (i.e., people occupying one campsite-space), of whom nearly two thirds were French, nearly one fifth Dutch, a tenth German, a twentieth British. The remaining 23 parties were: Swiss, Belgian, Spanish, Scottish, Danish, American, Czech, Australian, and Finnish.
12. In 1993 the building of out-of-town hypermarkets in the Cantal was banned.
13. For an account of this see M.E. McDonald 1982.
14. Demonstrated most dramatically by the farmers' actions of the summer of 1990.
15. It is standard practice for communes to elect committees to organise local activities. These committees are effectively part of the most local government structure in France's highly decentralised government and they are usually awarded a budget by the communal council (from local taxes) and sometimes supplemented by grants from the departmental council (roughly equivalent to a county council).
16. As the Ecomusée was quite far from my fieldwork site, especially conceptually as it was over the plateau, the reactions of people local to the museum who had visited it only reached me through hearsay from the museum, and, not surprisingly, they were said to have enjoyed their visits.
17. See Zonabend's consideration of disruptions and ways of thinking about time (1984).
18. See Boissevain 1992.
19. The disastrous machinations of the E.U.'s Common Agricultural Policy and the G.A.T.T. negotiations are infamous.

20. The way in which revived traditions are inevitably changed is also considered in Borofsky 1987.
21. Their performance was very well received, but they were not invited back the following year as their fees were too high for the St. Mary fête's budget.
22. A fuller account of these fêtes can be found in my doctoral thesis (1994).
23. In fact, this trend is returning: in 1993 there were many more local people at the fête than tourists.
24. Both fêtes described were those held in the summer of 1991.
25. This term is used to refer to female farmers, more often called farmers' wives, who may not be title holders of the farm but have an essential role in the running of the farm.
26. A Chambre d'Agriculture, an advisory and welfare organisation, independent of the state and funded by farmers' contributions, thus it is effectively a trade union for farmers.
27. These regulations have been substantially revised during the 1980s and early 1990s as part of the infamous European Community directives to standardise production methods and supposedly improve hygiene in food manufacturing. Unfortunately these new standards have been devised with only large manufacturers in mind and without any consideration of the circumstances of smaller producers. As a consequence, production of cheeses that are known from historical records to have employed certain methods for centuries are being prohibited on what are largely seen by small farmers as spurious if not conspiratorial reasons. Cantal cheese, for example, is curdled at the temperature at which it is milked, i.e., it is used straight from the cow, and derives flavour from the wooden barrels it is collected and processed in (as opposed to Swiss cheese, for example, which is heated in copper vats). The European directives require dairies to be completely tiled according to precise guidelines, and forbid the contact of foodstuffs with wood of any kind, specifying that all machinery must be made from stainless steel. The investment necessary for an individual farmer with a turnover of one or two cheeses a day (one Cantal cheese of about thirty kilos requires the milk of a herd of twenty to thirty cows) to rebuild the dairy and replace all equipment is prohibitive. Many such farmers have had to admit defeat and stop farming, when they can say that in all these centuries, nobody ever died from eating a piece of our cheese, so why should we suffer from the incompetence of a few careless mass-manufacturers? However, until the regulations are strictly and effectively enforced, farmers continue to make and sell cheese the best way they can. It may be noted that recent EU directives propose to allow the production of certain specifically regional products, but it is not yet clear exactly what the effects of this will be.
28. Salers is a form of Cantal cheese produced from the milk of cows grazing on Summer pastures called *estives*.
29. The national Maison Francaise promotes French tourism internationally and the local Tourist Offices provide information for tourists once they have arrived in a particular place.
30. Incidentally, the reason given for milking being 'men's work', was that women were supposed not to have the strength required to manhandle the hefty calves. Single women farmers (of whom there were always a few) tend to keep other breeds which are easier to manage.
31. The mixture of shame and pride in which patois is held is too complex to be dis-

cussed here, but see, for example, C.N.R.S. 1970-79, Besson 1914, Raison-Jourde 1976, Roc 1989, Sylvere 1980, and Weber 1976.

32. In a later visit to St. Mary, in 1993, I was told that the buron had not closed down after all, but that the old farmer was still going strong, despite being about 83 years old. It was assumed that the buron and farm would close down when he eventually retired, or more likely died, and that until then the E.C. directives would probably not be enforced.

33. By 1995 the rate of *installations* (new farmers setting up in business) in the Cantal had become the second highest of any French department, suggesting that the actions of the young farmers, in particular, had paid off.

34. I mention the gender of the farmer in order to suggest that the opening up of the farmyard to visitors and the re-evaluation of farmyard produce such as poultry and prepared foods necessitates a renegotiation of the gender politics of farming, where men's work producing meat, milk, and cheese has been thrown into crisis by national economic circumstances, whilst women's produce, as sold at the country markets or from the farm itself, has become the mainstay of some agricultural groups. This is an issue that obviously needs to be developed elsewhere.

REFERENCES

Abram, S. A. 'Recollections and Recreations: Tourism, Heritage and History in the French Auvergne', Unpublished D.Phil. thesis, University of Oxford, 1994.

Besson, P. *Un Patre du Cantal,* Aurillac, 1914.

Boissevain, J., ed. *Revitalising European Rituals,* London, 1992.

Borofsky, R. *Making History: Pukapukan and Anthropological Constructions of Knowledge,* Cambridge, 1987.

C.N.R.S. *L'Aubrac,* Paris, 1970-79.

Chapman, M. K. 'A Social Anthropological Study of a Breton Village with Celtic Comparisons', Unpublished D.Phil. thesis, University of Oxford, 1986.

Cruces, F. and Díaz de Rada, A. 'Public Celebrations in a Spanish valley' in Boissevain J., ed., *Revitalising European Rituals,*London, 1992

Culler, J. *Framing the Sign: Criticism and its Institutions.* Oxford, 1988.

Dalby, J. R. 'The French Revolution in a Rural Environment: The Example of the Department of Cantal 1789-1794,' Unpublished Ph.D. thesis, University of Manchester, 1981.

Girard, R. *Quand les Auvergnats partaient conquerir Paris.* Paris, 1985.

Hobsbawm, E. and Ranger, T. *The Invention of Tradition.* Cambridge, 1988.

McDonald, M. E. 'Social Aspects of Language and Education in Brittany, France,' Unpublished D.Phil. thesis, University of Oxford, 1982.

_____, *We are NOT French: Language, culture and identity in Brittany.* London, 1989.

Poitrineau, A. *Les Espagnols de l'Auvergne et du Limousin du XVIIeme au XIXeme siecle,* Aurillac, 1985.

Raison-Jourde, F. *La Colonie Auvergnat de Paris au XIXeme siecle,* Paris, 1976.

Roc, J.-C. *Le Buron de la Croix Blanche,* Brioude, 1989.

Sylvere, A. *Toinou, Le cri d'un enfant auvergnat,* Paris, 1980.

Urry, J. *The Tourist Gaze: Leisure and Travel in Contemporary Societies,* London, 1990.

Weber, E. *Peasants into Frenchmen: The Modernisation of Rural France, 1870-1914.* London, 1976.

Wright, S. 'Heritage and critical history in the reinvention of mining festivals in North-East England' in Boissevain J., ed., *Revitalising European Rituals,* London, 1992.

Zonabend, F. *The Enduring Memory. Time and History in a French village,* Manchester, 1984.

7. Dealing with Fish and Tourists
A Case Study from Northern Norway

Roel Puijk

Introduction

*O*ne day in March 1992 the flag of one of the largest Norwegian enterprises (Hydro) waved on top of a traditional wooden fishing-boat at the entrance of Henningsvær, a small fishing village on the coast of the Lofoten islands in northern Norway.[1] It was meant as a welcoming sign for the top managers who were spending some days in the village. Several local inhabitants, especially women, were upset and asked whether the company had bought the village.

I will start with this incident because it symbolises different attitudes towards tourism among the local population. To the local population the fishing-boat – the first object to be seen as one crosses the bridge from the main island to the small village – symbolises the village. Of course it is not difficult to understand the anger of those who saw the raising of a foreign flag on their boat as a sign of capitulation. However, on the other hand, the same fishing boat is also a result of tourism. A local group, mainly representing the tourism sector, arranged to get the old vessel mounted as a statue on top of the rocks. This example shows that the local population may identify with some symbols generated

Notes for this section begin on page 225.

principally for tourists, while they reject others, representing other forms of tourism.

The old vessel was originally mounted beside a fish factory – it is supposed to be the first fishing boat that unloaded there. The vessel on display may be called an authenticity sign. The support that this sign has among the local population indicates that it functions not only for tourists, but also as a symbol for the local people. For the local population the wooden boat indicates the past, the time when people rowed to the fishing grounds in open vessels and spent the nights in the fishermen's cabins. It was a time when the village was crowded during the fishing season. Times have changed though, the fishing fleet is modernised, fishermen sleep aboard and no longer in the cabins. The fish factories too are modernised even though much of the fish is still hung on the racks to dry. When the local population identifies with a kind of staged authenticity objects such as a wooden vessel, this indicates that they have the same kind of 'modern' attitude, the same nostalgic longing for the authentic, as the tourists. As MacCannell (1989b) notes, the division between the traditional host and modern tourist does not hold in the current situation. Host populations are modern in many aspects, in some ways maybe even more than their guests.

The study of tourism in Europe accentuates that tourism often is just one of several modernisation processes. The 'traditional' sector may be modernised and dependent on international markets, and the population may, through their integration in national systems (e.g., laws regulating working conditions, education, and communication), share national standards of taste and consumption. These changes again will be incorporated into the way tourism is perceived and reacted upon by the local population. One obvious example is that the local hosts may also become tourists elsewhere, projecting their experiences abroad back to their situation at home. This implies that tourism cannot be treated as *the* main modernising force; maybe quite the contrary.

Even though tourism as such is narrowly connected to modern conditions, tourists cannot be seen as simply modern. Some analyses consider the tourists as being in a liminal or liminoid period (Graburn 1977; Wagner 1977), breaking, as it were, out of ordinary life, maybe gaining new insights into their ordinary conditions. In the same vein, MacCannell (1989a) argues that tourists search for authenticity – they look for original, less complex ways of life where they 'may grasp the division of labour as a phenomenon *sui generis* and become a moral witness of its masterpieces of virtue and viciousness' (1989a: 7). One may doubt the universality of MacCannell's point (many tourists seem rather to live simply themselves, taking it easy on the beaches of the Mediterranean or relaxing in a mountain cabin as many Norwegians do; see Urry 1990: 11), but he draws attention to an important point. When tourists are interested in foreign cultures, their preference for authenticity is marked. This demand not only often leads to a rearranging of traditional cultural elements in new combinations (c.f. 'staged authenticity'), it also leads to new constellations between 'modern' and 'traditional'. Among the host population the most 'modernised' may ally with the 'traditional', while those striving to modernise in other sectors may become 'traditional' as regards tourism.

At the same time the elements that are supposed to give the tourist an authentic experience become something the local population has to relate to. As in the Hydro example, the image that is created may offend, or it may give the host population a sense of identification – a kind of 'root' feeling.

Like many of the other fishing villages in the Lofoten Islands, Henningsvær is not unfamiliar with a periodical influx of foreigners. During the winter fishing season many non-local fishermen arrive. To a certain degree both groups are strangers, though tourists may be considered a more modern form of stranger, with other interests and different behaviour. The two sectors, fishing and tourism, are interrelated in several ways – not only is fishing used as a central element in tourism, but fish merchants were the first to use the opportunities, housing tourists in fishermen's cabins. As the main fishing season is from January until April the non-local fishermen are not in the village during the main tourist season. However, the tourist sector tries to extend the tourist season to include these winter months as well. As a consequence both tourists and non-local fishermen are confronted with each other directly – a situation that easily leads to conflicts.

The two kinds of strangers that arrive in Henningsvær enable us to compare the differences between tourism and 'occupational travelling', the relations between these strangers and the host population, and to analyse the interrelations between the main local economic sectors – fishing and tourism. In this chapter I will try to analyse how the developments in both sectors are interrelated and how the local population reacts to these developments. A main point will be that one cannot understand the local attitudes toward tourism if one does not take into account both the total local context (including fishing) and the local population's integration into national systems. As the tourist sector is dependent on fishing, the activities directed towards the tourists, including the urge to show local authenticity, also concern the local population and their self-conceptions. Before focusing on the village, let me give a short overview of tourism in the area.

Figure 7.1 Rorbus in a neighbouring village.

Tourism in the Lofoten Islands

Tourism is not new in the Lofoten islands. Already at the end of the nineteenth century several famous painters and writers from the 'national romantic' school, which was very much the leading one in Norway at the time, had made the area known. They had been staying in the area for a period of time to find inspiration for their art. From 1930 to 1960 the fishing activities in the winter season generated some traffic, mainly elites from the southern part of Norway, Sweden, Denmark, Germany, and the United States. These tourists usually travelled on a round-trip tour, staying in the area only for a short time. According to the local population the differences in class were very obvious – well-dressed tourists looked on the fishermen, dressed in bloodcovered oilskins, as exotic animals. The locals still remember the denigrating remarks that these elites made.

During the 1960s the fishing industries were declining and, as an extension of the fishing season, a regional effort was made to capture part of the rising mass-tourism market in compensation. Partly funded by the national government, a tourist office was opened in the municipal centre (Svolvær) that propagated the possibilities for cheap summer holidays in the region. The traditional fishermen's lodges – *rorbus* – were offered to tourists in addition to more traditional accommodation in hotels and guest-houses.

The rorbus were quite simple – normally consisting of two rooms (one combined living/sleeping room, and a simple room where the fishermen kept their nets and outfit), without running water. The rooms were offered to the tourists cheaply – the only difference being that tourists were often provided with mattresses. There was an explicit reference to camping as the tourist office used the term 'rorbu camping' in its propaganda. The tourists were supposed to supply the owner only with a little compensation – according to a note by the tourist manager at the time, tourists' spending would be mainly in the shops, restaurants, etc. The Royal Norwegian Automobile Society was involved both with organising the rorbu camping and with their promotion, not least among 'ordinary' Norwegians. Also through reports in magazines and radio the term 'rorbu-vacation' became well-known in Norway, representing a low-cost, romantic alternative to vacations in mountain cabins and travels abroad.

In the 1960s the tourist sector was rather small – in 1964 there were 200 beds available in hotels and guest-houses and approximately 150 in rorbus. In 1990 the total number of beds available in the region was estimated to be 4,250. The total number of overnight stays on the Lofoten islands has also increased significantly the last twenty-five years: from 25,000 overnight stays in 1965 to 300,000 in 1991.[2] The main expansion has been in the rorbu and camping sector, accommodating some 71 percent of the tourists in 1991. Not only did the rorbu sector grow, but the standard of these cabins also rose in general. Even though some of the oldest rorbu camps still have a very modest standard (and price), the newer camps especially are neither very simple nor very cheap.

Almost half of the overnight stays (45 percent) in 1991 were foreigners, mostly from Germany, but also a substantial part from other European countries and the United States. The traffic is mostly concentrated in the months of June, July, and August, but in some places there is activity outside the main season when (Norwegian) groups come to combine professional activity (e.g., seminars) with a trip to an unfamiliar environment. This off-season activity accounts for approximately 15 percent of the overnight stays.

Summer tourists are in general highly educated. In a survey amongst summer tourists in private cars, it was found that 62 percent had more than twelve years of education – the percentage amongst foreign tourists was as high as 70 percent. Almost one-third of the tourists travelled with their spouse only, one-third travelled with spouse and children, while the rest were either alone (4 percent), or were accompanied by persons outside the nuclear family (26 percent). In addition many foreign tourists travel by group in buses.

The main attraction of the Lofoten islands for tourists is, as in the rest of Norway, nature – the dramatic scenery where sea and mountains meet. Apart from the natural environment, the small fishing hamlets *('vær')* that lie spread along the coast constitute a main attraction. Most of the tourists stay only a few days in the region – they travel through by bus or private car, visit some of the hamlets and, to a lesser degree, the museums, and spend much of their time taking pictures and being in the company of their family.[3] Those who spend more time often walk in the surroundings and/or hire a boat to go fishing.

Figure 7.2 Hanging codfish to dry on the racks.

A Fishing Village

Henningsvær is a well-known and oft-depicted fishing village in the Lofoten islands. It consists of several small islands, nowadays connected as more and more passages are filled. A small passage between the two main islands provides a natural harbour for fishing boats, especially after a dam was built on one side in the 1930s. During the winter season, from February until April, the cod shoals come to the west-fjord to spawn. During this season several hundred fishing boats from all over Norway come to the Lofoten islands, many of them to Henningsvær.[4] Apart from the fishermen, the central economic actors in the village are the fish-merchants. The quay consists of an almost uninterrupted row of fish factories where fish is salted or prepared for drying on the numerous fish racks, on the rocks just outside the village.

The fishermen used to be housed in rorbus – which literally means 'dwellings for those who row'. These dwellings were normally owned by the fish merchants, though sometimes by fishermen themselves. As those living in a merchant's rorbu were obliged to deliver him their fish, the provision of dwellings was a means to guarantee the owner of the rorbu a supply of fish. There used to be competition between the merchants, but there were also rivalries between the different types of fishing boats. These rivalries led to official regulation and control of the fishing grounds as early as 1786.

The yearly Lofoten fishing season, attracting thousands of fishermen from many parts of Norway, can be considered a liminal period for the fishermen involved – especially for young boys. Among the coastal population a Lofoten fishing expedition was considered a proof of manhood. The work and living conditions used to be rough, but there were chances to make good money if there was enough fish.

After the Second World War the coast fishing fleet was modernised and the fishermen normally sleep aboard their vessels now. Only a few fishermen, using a special fishing technique, and labourers in the fish factories, use the rorbus nowadays.

The cod fishing season has traditionally been the main season, around which nearly all activity in the village turned. During a short period the village was crowded. The shops and cafés had their main season in wintertime; several were closed for the remainder of the year, when the village seemed deserted. The local fishermen used to have two additional fishing seasons – cod fishing further north in summer and herring fishing in autumn – but most income was generated during the winter season.

During the last decades there have been problems with fishing: herring has declined dramatically, and codfish has also fluctuated. Some fish merchants have started fish farms (salmon, trout) but in terms of employment these farms are rather marginal. As the fish has declined, so has the village. The population has fallen from 1,036 (1950) to 500 (1990), most shops are closed, the number of fishermen and fish merchants has decreased, etc. However, a bridge to the main island was constructed in 1983, facilitating the contacts between Henningsvær and the main commercial and administrative centre (Svolvær). At the end of the 1980s the tourist sector was reactivated by the establishment of several enterprises.

Local Tourist Sector

In Henningsvær two rorbu camps were in action from the beginning of the 1970s, both owned by local fish merchants. (Later another, owned by a fish merchant living in Svolvær, followed.) The style of these two camps is different. One of the owners has good foreign relations through his fish business, speaks English, German, and French, and has 'updated' his camp through the years using 'normal' (though modest) home-standards (running water, showers, electric stoves, coffee-machine, insulation, fridge, and freezer). His camp is open only during the summer season, when the rooms often are rented to foreigners (mostly Germans) who come year after year. The other camp is less modernised – showers and running warm water were installed only few years ago.

At maximum the two camps can accommodate approximately eighty visitors. The daily affairs of both these camps are mainly run by the wives, although the men are responsible for maintenance. Today the owners are retired from their fish factories, but they continue the camps. The camps have always been an additional income. They will probably be closed down, or sold, in the near future as none of the children are interested in taking over.

By the end of the 1980s several new enterprises had started in the village with a total capacity of twenty-seven accommodation units and eight rooms (approximately 140 people). A couple in their thirties came back to the village, where the man had grown up, to start a rorbu-camp in a fish-factory. They rebuilt the factory to contain a café, sauna, jacuzzi, and solarium. His wife is in charge of the camp, but he also helps out in addition to his regular job as an insurance salesman in Svolvær. They restored the old cabins that are situated just next to the factory and built some new cabins in traditional style. The complex is run on a more professional, all-year-round basis. Compared to the other camps, both the level of comfort and investments are higher, as are the prices per rorbu (NOK 600 per night – approximately $100, almost double the price in the 'traditional' camps).

A fish restaurant was also started in a former fish factory and included several rooms for rent. In 1991 another fish factory was restored and now contains both an art gallery and multimedia show. At this 'Adventure centre' safari tours in rubber dinghies are also offered. The centre alone had about 20,000 paying visitors during its first year. These three businesses are all family enterprises and have a local connection as one of the spouses is native to the village. The camp and the restaurant are run by man and wife, using seasonal help during the summer season. The owner of the adventure centre lives in Svolvær. He is active as a journalist, photographer, and film-producer and also owns the regional newspaper. He created the multimedia show and often guides the sea-safari. His brother-in-law, living in the village, takes care of the daily activities in the centre and does other odd jobs.

These three enterprises today form what may be called the professional triangle within the tourism sector. Sometimes they operate in common, especially when groups come to the village outside the summer season. In 1992 all three received money from the Ministry of Home Affairs to improve their products.

In addition to this triangle, several other activities were established in recent years. The local guest house, that directs itself mainly to the local and regional market, was taken over and restored. Again it is a couple originating from the village that has returned. He is a helicopter pilot who will retire in the near future. One fishing factory was modernised and the rooms used by the fish labourers during wintertime are let out to tourists during the summer season. The rooms are restored in a simple modern style first of all with an eye for the labourers. The owner lives elsewhere but the factory is managed by a local couple who also manage the rooms for rent during the summer. Another fish merchant has plans to do the same.

In 1991 a young couple running a mountain-climbing centre in the nearby town of Narvik bought a fish factory and use it as a centre for their climbing courses. The same facilities are also used to accommodate tourists. They have, amongst other things, installed a little café that is redecorated in a simple but tasteful style.

Some other local actors are trying or planning to exploit the possibilities offered by the influx of tourists. The so-called fisherman's home, run by a religious organisation, provides the fishermen with a homely, non-alcoholic, relaxing place. Up to now they have only been open during the winter season. This once very traditional institution is now adapting to the situation and plans to extend its services also to tourists, and is rebuilding so as to be able to offer lodging during summertime.

The local taxi driver, who lives beside the harbour, had plans to build a rorbu camp next to his house. Having problems realising this project, he reduced his plans to a site for campers, but it is doubtful whether these plans will be realised.

Apart from this some women have put up small enterprises (café, shop) directed both towards the local and the tourist market.

Figure 7.3 The harbour of Henningsvær during the fishing season. Note the polluted water in foreground.

An Authentic Fishing Village

For tourist purposes the village is advertised as an authentic fishing village. To quote the opening statement from the brochure that was issued in 1991:

> Welcome to Henningsvær, a fishing village built without the help of engineers or planners. Welcome to Heimsundet, the harbour basin referred to as the fishermen's 'Piccadilly Circus'. Welcome to Norway's most distinctive fishing village, to the place where no house is alike; where all the buildings have their own faces, all the corners their own particular angle of inclination. Henningsvær is a relatively new fishing village, its development not showing any signs of rapid growth until the middle of the last century. Until then, it consisted merely of a few islets and a handful of inhabitants. But when things

eventually started happening, they happened rapidly. From being an outlying district, it grew into one of the country's most important fishing villages. The significance the village gradually attained is illustrated by the fact that in 1862 Henningsvær was the first place in North Norway with its own telegraph station. Today, there are 600 inhabitants in the village. Ever increasing activity in conjunction with the Lofoten Winter Fishing Season brought considerable prosperity to the village. At its busiest, the tiny village would be invaded by 6,000 fishermen from all over the country. A new Klondike. An air of gambling, profit, ruin and hard work. During the best seasons, as much as a quarter of the total Lofoten cod quantum might be landed in Henningsvær, and a normal Lofoten Season provides with a total catch of approximately 50 million kilos of Norwegian Arctic cod.

Of course the rhetoric in the text is accompanied by evocative colour pictures of the harbour, fish factories, and fishing boats. Three tourist accommodations – the restaurant, the Adventure Centre, and a fish factory producing tinned caviar and smoked cooley (those who contributed to the financing of the brochure) – are exposed with both pictures and text. These texts do not fail to mention the authenticity claims, connecting the lodgings both with history and fishing ('lodgings available in authentic Lofoten surroundings'; 'authentic setting for preparing fish'; 'restored in accordance with original Lofoten traditions'; 'the oldest rorbus were built towards the end of the 1800s'; 'established in 1828 and one of the oldest in North Norway').

Rorbu-holiday became a well-known concept in Norway during the 1960s and 1970s. The concept was connected not only with cheap accommodation but also with 'the real fisherman conditions', and pictures of romantic little red cabins on poles along the quays, as well as more general features from northern Norway (midnight sun, scenery). Locally the rorbu concept has a more extended meaning – here it refers to all housing used for the fishermen and labourers in the fish factories, including the lodgings on the second floor in the fish factories. Here many rooms lay side by side, sharing kitchen and toilets. Tourists usually prefer the cabins and several were disappointed when their rorbus turned out to be in a fish factory. The tourist office decided to use a different name for this accommodation, calling it 'quay lodging' (sjøhus).[5]

However, simple conditions do not seem to be the right kind of asset these days. Most tourists not only want traditional housing, they also want the idealised red cabin and comfort. Even so, comfort being equal, the oldest cabins are often preferred. The oldest local camp in particular, notes these changing preferences among the tourists. The owners advertise: 'This one-time fish company, now rorbu camp, started renting out cabins to tourists twenty years ago. These rorbus are just as they were when the fishermen stayed in them a generation ago. Even so, most of them are equipped with shower, toilet and cooking facilities.' (Henningsvær brochure, 1991). Even though the rorbus are cheap, this camp has some problems attracting costumers – the authenticity argument does not seem to convince every tourist today when it is accompanied by signs of decline and disrepair. Locally this camp is not very popular either. Several people I interviewed considered the camp a disgrace to the village, the main arguments being: the cabins have a poor standard, they are right next to a fish factory that is not in use and falling down, and there is rubbish outside (rusting barrels, etc.). In this context the authenticity argument is also doubted – as one local critic noted: 'why say that this is the original condition of the fishermen? In the 1960s most of the fishermen lived in rorbu covered with formica – that is authentic too!' It must be added that these local critics often do not seem aware that showers and running water have been installed.

As for the local population, there seems to be a limit as to what can be properly defined rorbu in a tourist context. In a nearby village a tourist complex was raised some years ago, using only some stylistic rorbu elements. When asked about this complex most people reacted negatively – maybe not so much because these cabins had not been used by fishermen (the newest cabins in the local camp are also constructed for tourists only), but mainly because the complex lies on its own, outside the village. 'There is no maritime milieu' several informants told me. It would seem that the context – the Lofoten-fishing, the fishing boats, the local harbour – is considered as important as the cabins itself. The complex is considered deceiving, because this local context is absent.

When this context is present, as it is in Henningsvær, the locals too may appreciate the romantic red cabins. When talking about these different types of rorbu camps, one of the locals, the owner of a fish factory, told me he had come to the rorbu-camp in the village one day and had been moved by the romantic sight: 'It was nice weather and when I saw some people fishing, the gulls flying over the sea, I almost got tears in my eyes!'

Fish Merchants and Tourism

Until some years ago the fish merchants, together with the local fishermen, were the economic centre of the village. Several of them were also

engaged in politics, representing various political parties in the municipal council. In recent years the actors in the tourism sector have become
competitors in the internal politics in the village and vis-à-vis the municipal administration. Fish merchants usually expressed roughly the same
opinions. They told me that the village would benefit from a limited
expansion in the tourist sector. It creates work and offers services that the
local population can also use. Even so, they told me, the actors in the
tourist sector should be aware that fishing is the main activity, and the
future for the village. They illustrated this by saying that the turnover in
a fish factory during only one day in the winter season may be bigger
than the yearly turnover in a tourist camp. The tourist sector, in other
words, should be careful not to try to run the place and dictate to the
fishing industry. The fish merchants are very aware of the fact that the
tourist sector is dependent on the fishing industry, but that the fishing
industry is not dependent on the tourist sector.

Conflicts arise especially on environmental issues. Pollution of the
harbour – especially during the winter season when the cod guts and
sometimes liver and heads are dumped and float around – is a main
issue. Local actors in the tourist sector have been active in trying to stop
this pollution by writing articles in the regional newspaper and by
engaging the County Environmental Department. The fish merchants
argued that they are aware of the pollution question, but that some
organic waste and smell should be tolerated. Severe regulation could
easily cause economic problems for the fish factories.

Fishermen and Tourists

For the last few years in particular, large numbers of tourists have visited
the village. Not only do both Norwegians and foreigners stay in the
rorbu camps, many tourists that visit the Lofoten islands take a day trip
to the famous village. During the months of June/July/August lots of
cars and buses circulate in the narrow streets, sometimes causing small
traffic jams. When asking the local population about their reactions
towards tourism, at first I was surprised to hear that almost everyone was
positive and hardly anybody reacted negatively towards the number of
tourists. People, especially women, might have complaints about specific
conditions and some thought the limit would soon be reached, but the
general impression I got was that no one reacted to the sheer number of
tourists. When asked, people pointed out that the local population was

used to 'invasions' of non-locals during the winter season. The older people, I was told, were reminded about the good old days when the village was crowded during the fishing season. The younger people were also glad that things happened, friends come back from schools and universities, relatives come and there are possibilities to have a beer or soft drink in the open, on a terrace. Summer tourism had changed a rather dull season into a lively one. Even though the summer season had changed character, the basic traditional concept of a year divided into different seasons had not changed.

If we compare the fishing season with the summer season – the relations between the local population and fishermen on the one hand and with tourists on the other – both similarities and differences appear. During the fishing season hundreds of fishermen come to the village. There is a lot of activity – fish are landed, boats fill the harbour, and so on. As for the relations between fishermen and the local population they consist primarily of interaction between fishermen and fish merchants and their employees (many of them are also non-local). Both fishermen and fish merchants interact frequently with the fishing authorities (patrolling the fishing grounds and inspecting the factories).[6] During the daytime the fishermen leave the village quite early and return in the afternoon. In the evenings and on days when the weather prevents the fishing boats from leaving the harbour fishermen regularly turn up in the local pubs.[7] On Saturday evenings local societies (music, sports) organise dances where both locals and fishermen join in. Even though this kind of mingling allows the fishermen (who may come to the village year after year) and locals get to know each other, the relationships do not normally extend beyond this public sphere. A fisherman commenting on the locals said: 'They let you come to the doorstep'. This kind of restricted interaction also applies to tourists, although quite often tourists just come and go, and do not get to know local people, not even in the public sphere. Some tourists may visit several years in a row, and may get to know some locals as well, while others again have relatives in the village and 'know everyone'.

Even though there are similarities between the fishermen and the tourist 'invasions', there are also differences. First of all fishermen come by sea, while most tourists come by car or bus. Traffic problems (the number of circulating and parked cars) are the most frequently mentioned as a drawback caused by tourism. The lack of toilet facilities are also often mentioned. These obvious problems are now dealt with by the authorities; in summer 1992 public toilets were put up near the harbour, and there are plans to construct a parking lot at the entrance to the village.

A second difference between fishermen and tourists consists of different use of public and private space. While fishermen stay mostly in the harbour and the pubs (situated near the harbour) tourists wander around the village – in between the houses, under the fish racks, around the fire-tower (which is privately owned nowadays), etc. Of course there is a seasonal difference – during winter time temperatures are low and it hardly gets light even during the day, while it is warmer during summer when the (midnight) sun shines. But there is another difference. Being a tourist implies being away from the routine of everyday life. As Urry (1990: 12) notes, tourists also pay special attention to the familiar; the tourist gaze implies that the ordinary gets a special meaning.[8] Combined with the notion of a liminoid period where other rules of conduct apply, tourists often act in ways they would not do at home. Several women complained that tourists do not respect the local definition of differences between public and private space. In this part of Norway the houses are traditionally not surrounded by gardens and this leaves a rather undefined space in between the houses and the roads. Children can play freely around, and adults also walk through these areas. Normally adults have some aim when trespassing on the area between houses. Tourists, though, often just wander around with no other purpose than looking around, looking at how people live. Problems primarily arise outside the houses – the space that can be called 'private places in public view'. The conflicts arise not only because more and more tourists come; it also has to do with changing local ways of living. Little by little people have become more occupied with private space around houses. Some people have followed the conventions normal in the southern parts of the country – fencing off parts of their property to be used as a garden. Also terraces, where the women may be sunbathing or the family taking its meal, have become popular during summertime. In particular women told me they felt annoyed by the tourist gaze. This will probably speed up the process of fencing, implying that the free areas between the houses will disappear, and that the typical character of the built environment ('a fishing village built without the help of engineers or planners') may change.

Activities

The developments around tourism are not only confined to the tourist enterprises as such. A local committee *(interessegruppa)* has been set up, consisting of five members (four women and one man) with the aim of

Figure 7.4 Codfish drying on racks near the houses.

ameliorating local conditions. One of the main achievements of this committee is the organisation of a Stockfish Festival during the summer season for the last three years. One of the committee's members, a local school teacher, staged a revue in 1991 that held its performance one evening during the festival. An Italian cook was also invited to prepare Italian food using stockfish.[9] This festival not only attracted tourists, including people from the surrounding villages, but also the local population. As a local woman told me: 'We – my husband and I – took the day off and went to taste the Italian food. He had prepared stockfish on a barbecue. Later on we went to the restaurant. I liked it very much, it was as if we were tourists in our own village.'

This remark not only indicates that local people appreciated the festival, it also shows the reflexive stand the woman took. Of course the members of the local population are citizens of the Norwegian welfare state. This means, amongst other things, that most of them also have holidays and are regularly tourists in other places.[10] This implies that the locals also can imagine what it is to be a tourist, and that they also are flattered by the marketing of the authenticity of the village. As we have seen, the local population identify with fishing and they are impressed with the scenery around them.[11] They do not have a problem with seeing why tourists are interested in the village. Still, this does not imply that there are no critical comments. Most of them are concerned with the possibility that tourism or tourists will change the character of the village. Several also mentioned that 'we should be more clever getting money out of the tourists who come here', but all agreed that mass-tourism, as in the Alps/Mediterranean, would be a disaster. Plans of an investor in Bergen to construct a holiday-camp on the island at the entrance to the village were not welcomed, even though this might have created more work.

Winter Tourism

As the tourist sector becomes more professional, the need to attract tourists for more than three months in summer grows. The oldest rorbu camps were based on a combination – fish merchant and camp-owner – and were a means to extend the winter season. Although some of the owners of the new enterprises have additional income, these enterprises are more capital intensive. Their goal is to extend the summer season by also attracting tourists during the fishing season. The problem of a seasonal industry has been recognised by the regional tourist office ever since it started; in a note written in 1964 the tourist officer already mentions that attracting tourists during the Lofoten-season is one of the main tasks. Until a few years ago little had been achieved, partly due to problems in organising the regional tourist office. In the 1990s the activity during winter time has augmented somewhat.

The main attraction during the winter season is the Lofoten fishing – the activity on sea, in the harbour, on the quays, etc. Of course it is a special experience: hundreds of fishing boats leaving the village when it is still dark at 6 o'clock, returning in the afternoon unloading and cleaning tons of cod-fish, the hanging of the fish, the general level of activity in the cafés, and so on. Still, this kind of tourism is quite different from summer tourism. It attracts another kind of tourist and generates a different situation as regards the relationships between hosts and guests. Not only do the relations between the tourist and local population change, tourism during the fishing season entails that the two categories of strangers also come together.

During the fishing season it is impossible to attract families who are limited by school holidays. Furthermore there are no snow and ice activities in the region. The main market for winter tourism is the so called 'incentive/executive' market – mainly people travelling in connection with their work, either as a reward or to combine travelling with a seminar. These kinds of trips are provided by specialised travel agents with strong quality requirements – service and exotic experiences are two catchwords here. These kind of tourists do not ask for prices, but they want a tip-top arrangement.

The Hydro group, mentioned in the introduction, may serve as an example of the kind of tourism that may be expected during the winter season. Not only the flag incident, but also several other small episodes show the kind of problems that may arise. The local committee had asked the people in the main street to clean the newly fallen snow from their doorsteps. Some people commented on this request, arguing that every house owner is responsible by law and custom; it should not be done especially for some foreign tourists. The question is not whether such small actions are right or wrong; the feeling that things that everyone agrees upon are done just because of tourists is hard to support. The equality principle was also broken when one of the members of the group got sick. They had asked whether there was a doctor in the village. There is one doctor living in Henningsvær, but he works at the municipal health centre in a nearby village. His wife was contacted but, even though 'money was no problem' she referred them to the health centre. Her reaction was that these tourists do not respect people's leisure time and expect us to run, just because they have money.

These kind of attitudes have clear connections with egalitarian traditions in Norway – that everyone should be treated equally. One notes this on a national level as well. Just to mention some examples: Norwegians are very proud of their (former) king paying his fare when he uses the tramway (a famous picture is circulated in the media); Norway has a national health system without class; everyone has the same rights. Of course there are differences within Norway (even though less pronounced than in some other countries), but one should not show it. Since the 1980s the egalitarian system has been under attack, but still the underlying ideology is forceful in many fields of activity. In northern Norway, having been submitted to foreign (Hansa) and southern dominance for centuries, this question plays a special role; the asymmetrical attitudes that are involved remind the people of the bad sides of the past.

At present the level of winter tourists is still rather low, but this kind of tourism may cause problems when it expands. It may cause problems both inside the tourist sector and in the sector's relations with the local inhabitants. The kind of service and luxury that is demanded by the executive tourists will be materialised in the camps.[12] This implies that summer tourists will have to pay for things they might not be interested in. We have already noted that the cheaper forms of rorbu are on their way out; more winter tourism may imply that this tendency will be strengthened. Maybe this again will influence the summer markets, attracting a more exclusive public.

The relations between tourists and the local population during the summer season may be characterised as relatively equal. People from different places meet on almost equal footing, even though the contacts may not be very intensive. There may be differences in language – both foreigners and Norwegians speaking other dialects can easily be singled out – but the main contexts for summer tourists are leisure and the nuclear family, implying that they dress informally, have plenty of time, and stroll around the village. As we have seen, tension is usually created when tourists intrude upon the private sphere. However, except for the locals involved in the service sector, the locals are mostly confronted with tourists when they themselves engage in some kind of leisure activity in the public sphere (e.g., in cafés). Because of the informal context these tourists are in, class differences with the local population are under-communicated.

During the winter season the differences are more pronounced. While there is hardly any activity in the harbour and the fish factories during summer and the tourists have to content themselves with observing the picturesque buildings, there is plenty of activity in public view during the fishing season. Winter tourists walk along the quay side and take pictures when the fish is landed and cleaned by fishermen in their colourful oilskins (partly covered with blood). As long as the tourists do not dominate, this is accepted, but when the fishermen are interrupted all the time by picture-taking tourists, they may easily get annoyed. As a fisherman said to me: 'I can't understand why they are that interested to see someone do some honest work'. The feeling of being gazed at, being an exotic animal worth taking pictures of by strangers does not combine very well with the self-conception of the free fisherman.

An additional factor that complicates the situation during winter time is that the tourists mostly come as part of a group, combining profession and leisure. Even though summer and winter tourists may not vary very much as to their class background,[13] it seems that group dynamics (often implying an occupational context) interfere with inter-action with the local population. Unlike summer tourists, winter tourists often have meetings or seminars for which they dress more formally, in suits and ties. As the groups are offered a fully organised tour, they will mostly stay together, using only the best local establishments. This not only implies that only the most professional local enterprises can take advantage of winter tourism, it also means that class differences between tourists and the local population are more marked during the winter season.

The group context also may be relevant when members of the group interact with the fishermen. When one member of the group starts a conversation, he often has to finish talking in a hurry, because the other members of the group continue their walk around the harbour. In other situations the remarks between a fisherman and a member of the group only fuel the ongoing conversation within the group, leaving the fisherman puzzled behind.

As the village and the local population become an explicit part of the 'product', combined with the augmenting demands from the exclusive market, the success of winter tourism potentially depends upon the service level from everyone in the village. The fear of the fishermen and fish merchants that the tourist sector dominates the village will become even more acute. The fact that many of the fishermen who are gazed at are non-locals themselves, makes it difficult to appeal to their local solidarity. If the situation becomes too intolerable for the fishermen it might be that they will avoid Henningsvær and deliver their fish in some other village less dominated by tourists. This, of course, would imply that the basis of the local attraction would disappear.

Conclusion

In this case study of tourism in a marginal region of Norway, I have tried to analyse some of the processes connected to the development of tourism, taking into account the fact that even the population of marginal regions in Europe can no longer be considered traditional. Even though tradition and the traditional setting are some of the main assets in attracting tourists, modernisation processes – of which tourism is just one part – have changed the local situation.

Gender relations is a point at issue. While many women used to work seasonally as manual labourers in fish factories, fewer job opportunities in this sector forced them to look for different kinds of jobs. Nowadays several of them commute to the municipal centre where they work in the health sector. For some it was hard to adjust to the change from seasonal jobs, to working all year round (implying amongst other things sending their children to kindergarten instead of solving temporary child-care needs inside the informal sector).

Both the fishing sector and the tourist sector clearly have one main season, dividing the year into intervals marked by plentiful and scarce work. However there is also a difference as to the number of women in managerial positions. Within the fish sector no women have leading positions,[14] while several enterprises in the tourist sector are either run by women or managed by a couple on equal footing. This difference reflects the changing gender relations in Norway – gender relations that are probably more easy to realise in a less established sector.

Gender differences are also notable in the reactions to tourism. While many of the men in the fish sector talk about the tourist sector in political and economical terms (they often state that the turnover in the tourist sector is marginal to the turn over in the fish factories[15] and some see the tourist sector as a threat to their political dominance in the village), women seem to be more occupied with the social consequences of tourism. Some of the reactions may be seen as a consequence of former division of labour. Many men used to be absent from the village when fishing, while women stayed in the village and took responsibility for general well-being. This probably also resulted in different attachments to the village as a place to live. However, adaption to more modern customs, such as sunbathing, also makes women in particular more vulnerable to the foreign gaze.

The local population's integration in Norwegian society in some ways facilitates tourism – the local population's affinity with modern values and attitudes assures a reflexive modern position towards tourists. Not only does this imply a kind of understanding of what it is to be a tourist, but the symbols and authenticity claims also have an important function vis-à-vis the local population itself: they reinforce their self-conception and sense of being part of a proud fishing tradition. This 'internal' function may even blind the local population to the tourists' needs. While most of the activities in the tourist sector are connected with fish and fishing, most tourists who come to the Lofoten islands state that they come primarily because of the scenery.[16]

During summer time tourists, including natives who have migrated to other parts of Norway, revive the village. Without tourists the village looks quite deserted during summer as there is little activity in the harbour (only a very few vessels are present and the fish factories have closed). Most tourists stay near the marketplace in the 'centre' of the village, and spend only a short time visiting the Adventure Centre, the kiosk, and restaurant. Here there may be problems because of the sheer number of tourists when they pop out of buses, but in general the relations between summer tourists and the local population in the public sector is characterised by equality. The liminoid situation of the tourists implies that they are relatively relaxed and seldom show signs of class differences. Apart from the service relations inside the tourist sector, the interaction between tourists and locals in the public sphere (especially in the restaurants and cafés) is usually restricted to gazing at each other, each of the actors contributing to the other's curiosity. Within the public sector the tourists, despite their differences, can easily be incorporated in the category 'ordinary people'. The main frustrations with summer tourists are connected to logistic problems and the intrusion of foreign gaze into backstage life in and around the houses.

During the winter season, when there is no outside activity around the houses, the gaze is directed to the fisherman's work, an occupational back stage accessible from public space. Here 'authenticity' is not staged for tourists as in the Adventure Centre or rorbu camp, but is part of a regular production process. As the winter tourism attracts different tourists, the differences between the tourists and the natives become more pronounced, making it difficult to include these in the modern reflexive conception of 'we – ordinary people'.

NOTES

1. The research on which this paper is based is part of a larger research programme, 'Tourism and Community Development', a collaboration between Lillehammer College and the Eastern Norway Research Institute, financed by the Norwegian Council for Applied Social Research (NORAS). Fieldwork was carried out during winter and summer 1992. I would like to thank the editor of this volume, Jeremy Boissevain, for helpful comments.

2. These figures from the National Hotel and Camping Statistics do not include 'wild' camping.

3. Field observations on this point were confirmed by a survey conducted by students of Lillehammer College in 1991.

4. Around the turn of the century some 4,000-5,000 fishermen were in the village during the Lofoten fishing season, while the population was 249 in 1900. Even in the 1950s approximately 5,000 foreign fisherman came to the village, but their number has declined steadily since. According to official statistics in 1992 there were 327 boats and 514 fishermen, while the population is about 500 people.

5. In English the term holiday-camp may be used both for housing in fish factories and for a complex consisting of several fishermen's cabins.

6. During the season the fishing authorities run an office in the village.
7. There also are some places for fishermen only – a so called 'fisherman's home', and a welfare station.
8. For foreigners all Norwegian (wooden) houses may look unfamiliar, though the activities that take place within them are probably not very different from the ones they are used to.
9. Stockfish is produced by hanging cod to dry on the racks. Some of the fish is salted and shipped to southern Norway to produce clipfish. These conservation methods ensure that the fish is well suited for warm climates. Though huge quantities of stockfish are produced in the village almost all stockfish is exported to southern Europe and Africa. The local population hardly use stockfish themselves.
10. Some years ago it was popular to spend some time with a caravan in northern Sweden. Many locals have been on charter trips to southern Europe. In fall 1992, twenty-five youngsters travelled to the Mediterranean with the sports club.
11. Without fail, the private houses I visited had pictures of fishing boats and/or the Lofoten scenery on the walls in their living room, often in the most conspicuous places.
12. The newest rorbu camp has invested in, for example, life jackets, an advanced internal telephone/intercom system, a jacuzzi – facilities not typically used by summer tourists.
13. A substantial part of both summer and winter tourists are well-educated (upper) middle class. The class background of the summer tourists varies more than that of the winter tourists.
14. The fish sector has not been closed to women altogether; the founder of the fish factory producing tinned products was a woman.
15. Some fish merchants talk about their factories in terms of 'money machines'.
16. In the above mentioned survey the tourists were asked to characterise Lofoten in three words. The words used most had to do with nature. According to the regional tourist office most requests are for walking routes.

REFERENCES

MacCannell, D. *The Tourist. A New Theory of the Leisure Class*, New York: Schocken Books, 2nd edn, 1989a.

MacCannell, D. 'Introduction' in *Annals of Tourism Research*, 16, 1, 1-6, 1989b.

Graburn, N.H.H. 'Tourism: The Sacred Journey.' In V.L. Smith ed., *Hosts and Guests. The Anthropology of Tourism,* Philadelphia: University of Pennsylvania Press, (2nd edn 1989),1977.

Wagner, U. 'Out of Time and Place: Mass Tourism and Charter Trips.' *Ethnos*, 42, 38-52, 1977.

Urry, J. *The Tourist Gaze. Leisure and Travel in Contemporary Societies,* London: Sage, 1990.

8. The Social Construction of Mokum

Tourism and the Quest for Local Identity in Amsterdam

Heidi Dahles

'The act of walking is to the urban system what the speech act is to language....'
(De Certeau 1984: 97)

Introduction

'*I*n Amsterdam there are holes in the wall for everybody', Ulf Hannerz noted after having lived and worked in the city for about a month (De Waal 1991).[1] Hannerz experienced the overwhelming diversity of the Dutch capital,[2] the conspicuously different lifestyles, the ongoing spectacle of 'fun-city' with its variety of leisure services, shops, theatres, terraces, cafés. Amsterdam is a place to browse in and wander about, watching the flourishing gay community, the bustling red-light district, the hustling around the cannabis-cloaked coffee shops, the industrious ethnic businesses, the transnational corporations, banks, and embassies behind the cool façades of glamorous buildings, the tireless nightlife, the National Monument crowded with young people from all over Europe, the display of World Music on the square at Central Station.

Notes for this section can be found on page 245.

Besides the immigrants, the youth, and the transnational corporations, tourism further enhances the position of Amsterdam as a world city. Amsterdam is among the ten most popular tourist cities of Europe. In 1991 the city was visited by 1.8 million foreign tourists who stayed for at least one night (Amsterdam Tourist Board 1992: 3). It is estimated that, in addition, about 11.5 million visitors – mostly domestic – spent a day in the Dutch capital (ibid.: 6). On average about 38,000 tourists visited the city every day: i.e., one tourist for every 18 inhabitants (Amsterdam Tourist Board 1993, 3: 1). Aside from the mass tourism, which is concentrated within the ring of canals, there are numerous other touristic patterns. One glance at the recent *Rough Guide to Amsterdam* reveals a highly differentiated market, offering tourist experiences geared to the demands of many different social categories, such as youth, gays, women, and senior citizens – to mention but a few. Along with the widely varying touristic patterns go different discourses for establishing the image of Amsterdam as a tourist centre. Particular sets of cultural specialists and intermediaries exploit and develop new markets for touristic goods and experiences. These interpreters and promoters play a decisive role in the thematising and translation of urban space into touristic discourses.

This article explores the way in which cultural interpreters develop discourses on Amsterdam, or 'bodies of expertise' to use a concept coined by Urry (1991: 92). These discourses, emerging in an interaction process between interpreters and tourists, construct (parts of) the inner city as a tourist attraction. This article, however, focusses specifically on the narratives that are developed by tour leaders and guides. The way in which visitors deconstruct and attribute meaning to these narratives and transform them into images of the city will remain unaddressed. I will discuss and compare two discourses: first, the famous canal cruise, a widely used medium for catching a glimpse of the city's attraction; second, the construction of Amsterdam by a voluntary association of senior citizens, which organises walks through the inner city. Both claim to take tourists on a trip to the 'real', the 'authentic' Amsterdam; both, however, differ in the way they move about in the urban space, the routes they choose, the discourses they develop, and the types of tourists they attract. After a short discussion of tourist developments in Amsterdam to establish the social and cultural context of the narratives, I will map the routes and analyse the stories told about attractions along these routes, as space is a 'practiced place', and walking the space is a process of appropriation and at the same time an acting out of the meaning attached to the space

(De Certeau 1984: 98). By walking the city, we will learn about two different ways in which the identity of the inner city is constructed. As identity emerges with reference to a significant other, and as every discourse on identity inclines towards what it is not, towards an implicit negativity (Cohen 1985: 115), we have to investigate to what extent the two discourses are constructed as each other's contrast, what they are actually contrasting, and in which contexts they do so.

Tourism in Amsterdam

There are few other places in the world that have been so involved in international trade and communications for as long as Amsterdam has. In its golden age Amsterdam was the prototypical model of the world city of mercantile capitalism and it has survived various phases of formation and reformation to remain among the higher ranks of contemporary world cities (Soja 1993: 85). Yet, despite the willingness to compete internationally, it is by no means certain that the city will prosper as an international city in the future as it has in the past. There will be more Amsterdam-like cities in the Europe of the future and the competition will intensify, not only among the major cities in Europe but also among the emerging regional centers that prosper within the national economies (O'Loughlin 1993: 25). Although Amsterdam is still perceived as the symbol of national culture – the city is called the cultural capital of the Netherlands – it must compete in the cultural and economic arena with other large cities in the Randstad (Rotterdam, Den Haag, Utrecht), and more recently with Maastricht in the south. Both the national and global competition account for the recent revitalisation of the city.

The strained municipal budgets in the 1990s seem to have shifted the focus of urban development towards transforming Amsterdam into a tourist metropolis. In the tourist policy of the 1990s much stress has been put on historical themes such as the Golden Age (1993/94), Van Gogh (1990), Rembrandt (1992), and Mondriaan (1994), which have been supported by impressive expositions and manifestations. However, there is a widening gap between the institutions responsible for the city's tourism policy (i.e., the local government), on the one hand and the Amsterdam Tourist Board on the other. To enhance the reputation of Amsterdam as a centre of culture, the Tourist Board wished to promote not only the museums, canals, and famous buildings, but most importantly the city's historically close link to the sea and trade (VVV-Amsterdam 1993). Thus, the Tourist Board campaign presents Amsterdam as a *Zuider Zee* fishing village which became the capital of a seafaring nation and trading empire (Amsterdam Tourist Board 1993, 8: 1-2), a history that has generated today's liberal atmosphere, another important asset in the Tourist Board's promotional activities (ibid. 1993, 12: 5), as is the significance of the hippie mecca of the 1960s for modern popular culture (ibid. 1993, 9: 7) and global youth culture (ibid. 1993, 10/11: 1-2). More recently, the Tourist Board started a campaign in the United States highlighting 'Amsterdam, the Gay Capital of the World', a campaign that had to be cancelled after protests from the Amsterdam tourism industry, which feared it would scare off other, more conservative target groups. The local government, however, is not supportive of the idea of promoting the liberal atmosphere, the youth culture, and the 1996s, as these themes attract target groups different from the tourist categories that the city council prefers. The bureaucrats do not want to encourage any further growth in the number of tourists visiting Amsterdam. They do however, want to encourage tourists to spend more money, stay longer, and cause less trouble. The governmental policy is aimed at attracting more middle-aged, well-educated and well-to-do tourists (Amsterdam Toeristenstad 1989, Amsterdam Tourist Board 1993, 12: 5). Young backpackers and touring-car transported mass tourists will have to give way to cruiseship passengers adding allure to a revitalised harbour (*De Volkskrant*, 30-11-93).

Tourists – foreign and domestic alike – are curious to see Amsterdam's picturesque Golden Age setting *and* its present-day residents. The representation of the city of Amsterdam as a tourist attraction is characterised by a mixture of cultural fragments of past and present, the traditional and the modern, the elite and the popular, the local and the global. The tourism industry is capitalising on the city's glorious past, the display of 'high culture', scenes of everyday life, and the 'rough' edges of the downtown area. The image of Amsterdam as a tourist city is based on two major themes. The first is the image of the city being dominated by the urban town design of the early modern period. Visitors have clear expectations of Vermeer townscapes composed of tightly packed canalside buildings. As a tourist site Amsterdam is characterised by a physically compact and thematically cohesive inner city. The touristic resources within this area depend upon an urban ensemble from the seventeenth and eighteenth centuries, and serve a show-case function, which is supported by entertainment facilities of a national and international reputation (Ashworth and Tunbridge 1990: 181-183). The second is the current popular image of Amsterdam, which was formed in the late 1960s and is based upon a youth culture of sexual liberalism and narcotic indulgence. More recently this image has been strongly linked to a 'dirt and disorder reputation'. Amsterdam has been presented by the international media as the city of vandalism, insecurity, and lack of public order (ibid.).

This image of 'history, heretics, and whores' is not detrimental to tourism; it has on the contrary become the major attraction of the city. As recent research on the image of Amsterdam among visitors has shown, 78 percent of the tourists are attracted to the city because of cultural-historical aspects, i.e., museums and exhibitions, and more than 50 percent because of the liberal atmosphere (Amsterdam Tourist Board 1994, 2: 6-7). The tourist industry is aware of this. Almost all city guides to Amsterdam mention the interweaving of different strands of life that constitute the city's attractiveness: the reminders of the wealthy Golden Age trading city dominated by a few Calvinist families, the sleazy port, the remnants of a proud maritime nation and affluent colonial empire, the reputation of tolerance and liberalism, the rich bourgeois culture, the radical hippie mecca of the 1960s grown comfortably liberal, and the red-light district. Some tourist guides (for example, the *Rough Guide*) mention the drug dealing and the gay scene. References to 'national' and 'global' history go hand-in-hand with local images of the past, tales of the vicissitudes of ordinary people and scenes of everyday life. The cultural diversity reflected in the tourist images takes shape in local discourses.

Two Discourses on Amsterdam's Inner City

Taking the Boat

Visitors leaving the Central Station are encouraged to take one of the boat trips that lead tourists through the ring of inner-city canals. And most of them indeed do so. The canal cruise is the most important tourist attraction of Amsterdam, with 2,400,000 visitors in 1992; the second attraction, the Rijksmuseum, only drew half that number (VVV Amsterdam 1993: 6). As figures of the Amsterdam Tourist Board show, the bulk of canal-boat passengers (about 79 percent) are foreign tourists; only 15 percent are Dutch and 6 percent are Amsterdam residents (Attractiepunten in Amsterdam 1992: 17). There are seven local shipping companies involved in canal trips, and they operate a fleet of glass-covered boats, each of which can transport about 150 people. Such a boat trip takes about an hour and costs eleven guilders for adults, and a reduced fare for children. The boat trips usually encompass the inner city with Prinsengracht as the outer boundary. The boat trip usually takes visitors to the harbour beyond the Central Station, entering the canals through one of the locks west of the station, continuing through Prinsen, Keizers, Herengracht or Singel, the Amstel river, Zwanenburg-wal and Oude Schans back to the boarding piers in front of the station. To avoid a traffic jam on the canals, some tour operators take the opposite direction or vary among the four principle canals. There are several other mooring places for pleasure boats in the city's waterways.

Figure 8.1 A staff member of Plas shipping company
inviting tourists to take a canal trip at the boarding pier on Damrak.

The trip I took was with *Rederij Plas*, one of the local shipping companies, based on the Damrak, the street that leads from Central Station to the Dam. It was a rainy Monday afternoon in July, and the streets were less crowded than usual. On the landing, a couple of tourists were queueing to pay the fee for the boat trip. About fifty people boarded: contrary to the statistics, mostly Dutch families with young children, some Americans and Japanese, some French and Italian couples, and some people speaking 'exotic' languages I could not understand. Aside from the captain no employees were on board, except a boy who was selling soft drinks and sweets who left the boat before departure. Setting out to the harbour, a female voice from the loudspeaker welcomed the passengers in Dutch, English, French, and Italian (in this sequence). This taped voice was our guide during the trip, commenting on the attractions witnessed from the boat. Each was indicated by an irritating bleep, admonishing people to listen. As the commentary was spoken in four languages it started long before the attraction was visible, leaving the Dutch passengers to stare to the right or left in vain, and forcing the Italians turn around to catch a last glimpse of the vanishing attraction. To give an idea of the information the tourists received on this trip, I will quote in length the (somewhat telegram-like) transcription of the English text I made during the trip, starting with the first comment after the welcome:

On the right the Central Station, built on an artificial island, brought into use in 1899. – bleep – The harbour, one of the largest in Europe; as the vessels grew bigger, new basins were built along the North Sea Canal connecting Amsterdam with the North Sea. – bleep – The Westerdock, the old port; in the past many ships were built here. – bleep – These locks are called unicornsluice, an old brewery. -bleep – The brewers' canal, which once housed many breweries. – bleep – We are leaving the brewers' canal and entering Keizersgracht, the emperor's canal. On the right, at number 40 to 44 the greenland storehouses, the oldest and most beautiful storehouses of Amsterdam. – bleep – At number 123 the House of the Heads; the legend says these are the heads of six thieves who tried to break into the house but were beheaded by the maid in 1622. – bleep – On the right the Westermarket with the Wester church belltower. – bleep – The low rails along the canals have been put there by the city council at a hundred guilders per meter to prevent cars from driving into the water; still an average of one car per week is dragged out of the canals. – bleep – On the left, no. 321, the seventeenth-century house was the home of the painter Han van Meegeren. – bleep – Watch the gables; there are plenty of different types, such as the neck gable, the bell gable, the spout gable, the cornice with crest, the straight cornice. – bleep – The Herengracht, or gentlemen's canal, dug in the seventeenth century is one of the most beautiful canals of the city. – bleep – We are approaching the golden bend; the richest and most distinguished merchants and their families lived here. Nowadays these houses accommodate banks, embassies and insurance companies. – bleep – Number 502, the house with the balcony and the two pillars is the official residence of the mayor of the city. – bleep – We are now approaching a beautiful spot, watch the six humpbacked bridges of Reguliersgracht on the right. It is interesting to know that Amsterdam has 100 canals with a total length of 1,000 kilometres and 1,000 bridges. At high tide Amsterdam is 1.5 metres below sea level, surpassed only by the national airport which is 5 metres below. – bleep – We are now sailing on the Amstel, the river that gave Amsterdam its name. – bleep – On the right the Meagre Bridge, one of the oldest bridges of the city. – bleep – On the right Waterloo square, now occupied by the new city hall, but once the heart of the Jewish Quarter. – bleep – On the left, the Munt Tower, an old defence tower from the fifteenth century, the upper part was added in the seventeenth century. – bleep – The Zuiderkerk, South Church, the first Protestant church built in Amsterdam, in 1614. – bleep – The Oude Schans, part of the defence works. On the right, storehouses from the seventeenth century which have recently been rebuilt. On the left, the Montelbaanstower, also an old defence tower, like the Munttower built in the fifteenth century, the spire was added in the seventeenth century. In the past it was called 'Silly Jack' by the people of Amsterdam as its clock ran irregularly. – bleep – Watch the houseboats on the right. Amsterdam suffers from housing problems, which explains why people move into the houseboats along the canals. – bleep – On the left the Schreierstower, part of the defensive works of the city. In the past this was the place where sailors bade farewell to their loved ones. Beyond it, the Church of Saint Nicholas, built in 1887; saint Nicholas is the patron saint of the sailors.

After being told that postcards can be purchased on board depicting the most beautiful spots we have seen during the trip – 'ten cards for only six guilders' – and that a small gesture of appreciation would be welcomed by the captain (the word 'tip' being avoided) all passengers leave the boat. Another group of tourists is already waiting on the landing.

Taking a Walk

Those who want to see more of the inner city have to take a walk along its main attractions. The city guides available in Dutch and several foreign languages recommend a variety of city walks the tourists may undertake on their own. The Amsterdam Tourist Board has set out a route through the former working-class neighbourhood, De Jordaan, west of the inner city, which is described in a small brochure. Except for a 'lunch cruise' organised by Holland International, a large commercial tour operator, there are no guided tours within the city (Keet 1994). Yet, there is one initiative to take visitors on a guided walk, which emerged independently of the Amsterdam tourist business. Dutch people reading the national newspapers may be acquainted with a tiny ad announcing a city walk guided by 'proud old citizens'. It is called 'Mee in Mokum', which may be translated as 'join us in Mokum'. 'Mokum' is a synonym for Amsterdam. The term is derived from the Hebrew word 'mahem', meaning 'place' (Koord 1981). Many words from the Hebrew language have entered the vernacular, as Amsterdam possessed a large Jewish community until the Second World War, consisting of both well-to-do as well as working-class citizens, the latter of which lived in the humble dwellings of the Jewish quarter in the inner city. This reference to the past is of importance in understanding the special character of these city walks. This aspect will be dealt with at length in the final section.

Mee in Mokum is an initiative of the Foundation 'The Guild' (Stichting Het Gilde), established and subsidised by the city council. The aim of the foundation is the emancipation of senior citizens, the revitalisation of a social category that is often condemned to an inactive life upon reaching retirement age. The Guild functions as a mediator between senior citizens who offer expert knowledge (for example, language courses, special trades and handicrafts) and people looking for assistance. The services of Guild members are free of charge. Of all activities of the Guild, the city walks have been the most successful, success being measured by the enthusiasm of the senior citizens involved as well as the satisfaction of (growing numbers of) visitors joining them on their walk. Although the guided walk was not established with the purpose of competing in the tourist market, it has developed into a non-commercial 'alternative' tourist product, offering an inside view of Amsterdam. The Amsterdam 'Guild' adheres strictly to a non-competitive and amateuristic image, even denying their participants the title of 'guide' to avoid any association with the professional category. In other Dutch cities, in which this initiative has been copied, the Guild cooperates with the local Tourist Boards catering to an expanding market of domestic tourism.

About five years ago the Amsterdam Guild started the guided walks by Amsterdam senior citizens with only a small number of participants. The number of senior citizens involved, however, grew quickly. In 1992, 110 older people were guiding the walks, with dozens more on a list waiting for a chance to become one of the regular guides. The guides, men and women in their fifties, sixties, and even seventies, the majority being well-educated with a middle-class background, most of them born and raised in Amsterdam and all of them with a special tie to the city, show around small groups of visitors. As these city walks are only advertised in Dutch newspapers, the participants are mostly Dutch visitors on day trips from other provinces, but occasionally foreigners are also shown around. The mastery of foreign languages, especially English and German, and to a lesser degree French, among the guides is sufficient to cater to the few foreigners who find their way to Mee in Mokum. As far as my limited perception stretched, I witnessed mostly middle-aged and senior nationals who displayed an above-average interest in the city's history, but also some concern about the negative developments of metropolitan life, especially the drug dealing, prostitution, and delinquency. Very rarely did groups of young people participate in the walks, as the Guild operates under the rule that at least one adult must accompany three minors.

In the summer of 1992 Mee in Mokum offered three different walks: one centred around the inner city, one through De Jordaan, and one 'surprise-tour'. There were plans to add one or two tours to this programme. From Tuesday to Friday, and occasionally on Saturdays, Mee in Mokum operated with six to ten guides; the number of walks per day depended on the peaks and lows in the tourist season. The groups varied: I took part in groups of three to twelve participants. Except for the starting point (the Amsterdam Historical Museum) and the neighbourhood, it is completely up to the guide to determine the route taken and the attractions visited. It is part of the emancipatory philosophy of the Guild that it is the guide who should have a satisfying day, and in his or her wake, the participants. Thus, each walk through the inner city differs according to the preferences of the man or woman who shows one around. The walks begin at eleven o'clock in the morning. The participants are welcomed in the café that has been established in the museum. Here, the groups are arranged and the guides are introduced, mostly by their first names. Having joined them in Mokum many times this summer, I found that most guides agreed on a basic route leading from the Historical Museum (where all tours start) via the Begijnhof to the old part of Amsterdam: the pawn shop at the Nes, the old hospital on Oudezijds Achterburgwal, Waterloo Square, Rembrandt House, New Market and Waaggebouw, the Old Church, and the red-light district. It was stated that the walks would last about two hours; however, none of the walks I was on took less than four hours, with one or two long breaks at a local café. During the walk, the guide told stories about the buildings, the streets, the churches, the canals, the bridges, the monuments, the works of art, and the people ranging from an almost forgotten past to more recent events, sometimes sprinkled with personal experiences. The participants learned about Amsterdam through the eyes of their guide: the city's vicissitudes from a biographical perspective. As the walks took several hours, it is impossible to give an 'authentic' summary of the route and the stories told; I figure that even the many long pages of my ethnographic notes contain only fragments of the discursive and non-discursive information given during each walk. So I will confine myself to a number of examples that I hope will illustrate my point.

As was mentioned previously, all walks began at the Historical Museum, which can be reached through the Kalverstraat (the main shopping area). Walking there from the Central Station takes approximately ten minutes. Until the 1950s the building was the Amsterdam orphanage, and except for three rooms on the ground floor the whole building was renovated to meet the requirements of a modern museum. Whereas most visitors enter to pay their fee and proceed to the museum, our guides led us to the three rooms that have a permanent exposition of the material culture of the orphanage, showing the daily life of the orphans and their tutors through artifacts and paintings – material on which the guides would elaborate (once, our guide happened to be an 'eyewitness', who had spent his childhood in the orphanage).

Next, we entered the Begijnhof through the Schuttersgalerij. The Begijnhof, a calm square walled by old gables (one of them covering the oldest house of the city), once housed an order of lay nuns, the Begijnen. The order was founded in the fifteenth century and its members, through self-effacement and powerful family connections, remained undisturbed by the religious upheavals of the following centuries. The nuns were devoted to charity and chastity – the last point being elaborated on by our guides. I learned that the nuns were forbidden to receive male visitors, even to house male animals (one of the guides exclaimed: 'no cocks allowed!'). At night, the double gates giving access to the square were closed, and even the (male) porter had to stay outside, in between the inner and the outer gate. Even now the Begijnhof preserved its strictly female character, as only unmarried women were given a residence permit by the city council and the gates were still closed at eleven p.m., male visitors being obliged to leave by then. The guides pointed out a stone in the gutter of the square: the grave of the Begijn Cornelia Arens who is said to have requested burial in the gutter because her family had converted to Protestantism, which she regarded as a disgrace (according to the folk-lore version, however, she ended in the gutter because she broke the rule of chastity). The guides proceeded to the original medieval Begijnchurch, which was offered to the Protestant dissenters fleeing England in the seventeenth century, who later sailed to America and became the Pilgrim Fathers. This church was not visited, as our guides immediately turned to a church-like building facing the English church. This building turned out to be a conventicle, in which the Catholics held secret services during the Reformation. Entering the conventicle the guides dwelled at length on the strategies of camouflage that enabled the Catholics to practice their belief undiscovered for many years.

In this vein the city walks continued, with more conventicles of the once-persecuted Catholics being visited as well as hospitals, prisons, homes for the poor and the leprous, and the pawnshop at the Nes, a narrow street parallel

Figure 8.2 A group of tourists on a guided tour in the Begijnhof.
(Photo by P.J. Margry, May 1993)

to the Rokin. Our guides pointed out the former Guild houses scattered along the route with their gable paintings, and told about the life of the industrious guild members in the past. They lingered a while at the prestigious new City Hall with its adjacent opera house to complain about the modernish style and the costs involved with its completion. They stopped for a cup of coffee at a 'reliable' (i.e., cannabis-free) coffee shop at the corner of Jodenbreestraat and told of the vanished Jewish quarter and of the hardships of the war. They elaborated on the miserable ending of Rembrandt's life while in front of the Rembrandthouse, his dwelling in better times. They visited the Zuiderkerk (South Church), recalling the last winter of the Second World War when ten thousand bodies were kept in this church as they could not be buried because the ground was frozen. They summoned up long lost times when describing the trade on the New Market: ships unloading, exotic goods being bought and sold, and people being tortured and executed in public. They commented on the drug addicts, beggars, and homeless and what should be done to keep them from roaming the streets. They visited the red-light district, to show the prostitutes and drug addicts, but most of all to tell about their misery from the point of view of Major Bosshardt, the famous woman officer of the Amsterdam Salvation Army who still patrolled the pubs and coffee shops of the inner city.

Constructing the Tourist Gaze of Amsterdam

There is no single tourist gaze as such. One local setting is the object of many different tourist gazes. As Urry has argued (1990: 2), such gazes are constructed through differences, in relationship to opposites, to non-tourist forms of social experience. What makes a particular tourist gaze depends upon what it is contrasted with. To consider how social groups construct their tourist gaze is a good way of getting at just what is happening in 'normal society': by considering the typical objects of the tourist gaze one can use these to make sense of elements of the wider society with which they are contrasted. This approach to the tourist gaze, however, raises the question of what 'normal' life is. Applying Urry's approach implies the construction of an alleged 'normality' of 'everyday life', which adds another interpretation of 'authenticity' to the already existing ones.

To understand the similarities and differences of the two local narratives about Amsterdam, one has to take into account the 'significant other' towards whom the narratives are addressed. Basically, the canal cruise is a medium for establishing the image of Amsterdam in front of a 'global audience', visitors from all over the globe expecting to find the world-famous Vermeer townscape. The taped voice on the boat is catering to the expectations of a mass of rather superficially informed and moderately interested international tourists. The 'international' tourist gaze is constructed of tokens of the 'remembered empire': the famous canals, the numerous large and small museums, merchant mansions, warehouses, churches and other buildings, dating back to the sixteenth, seventeenth, and eighteenth centuries.

First and foremost the route is constructed using absolutely distinct objects that evoke a sense of Amsterdam: the canals, the merchant houses and their gables, the Wester Church belltower, etc. Second, there are particular signs evoking the 'typically' Dutch: the waterways and bridges, the houseboats, the storehouses, the port, the docks, and the painters. A prominent role is played by objects that evoke the glorious past of Amsterdam as the capital of a world empire. The 'remembered empire' is visualised ('on the left the storehouses', 'on the right the docks', etc.) and at the same time verbalised ('one of the oldest', 'one of the most beautiful'). The boat trip is an example of the established routine of the tourist business operating within mass tourism. The approach to tourists is 'authoritative': people are told what to gaze at and when and where to look. Heads move to the right and to the left depending on where the taped voice identifies another attraction 'one has to see'. In the mass tourism business 'authority' is claimed by a sudden and startling precision of facts contrasted with the general vagueness of the discourse. Most of the time tourists receive a body of pseudo-information; and very often the dating of buildings and events is wrong. The taped voice on the boat keeps it casual: almost everything seemed to have happened 'once upon a time in the old times', except for the killing of the six burglars by the courageous merchant's maid, which took place in 1622! There are a lot of churches, mansions, and bridges, but – mind you! – there are neck gables, bell gables, spout gables, the cornice with crest, and the straight cornice. There were a lot of breweries on the brewers' canal, but the city council of Amsterdam has spent a hundred guilders per metre of running rail along the hundred kilometre-long canals, which are crossed by a thousand bridges and from which one car per week is dragged out of the water.

As the city of Amsterdam perceives itself as a world-city, as a centre of commerce and culture, the narrative alludes to the leading cultural and economic position of the city. That this position has been lost is hidden behind the famous facades and gables, remnants of past glory that symbolically confirm the city's self-perception. The 'significant other' then is defined by other world-cities Amsterdam is competing with in a global tourist market. The boat takes visitors on a trip through ever-changing times and places, and the city becomes a jigsaw puzzle that has fallen apart to be re-arranged using pieces taken from other puzzles. It consists of fragments of cultural heritage from different centuries. Like the tourist menu, it is an easily digestible, though tasteless mixture of ingredients. The cultural capital of the city is moulded in such a way that the urban space becomes consumable for a wide range of social and cultural categories. The mass tourist discourse presents a body of global knowledge that is the commonly-held idea that people have of Amsterdam. These bodies of global knowledge – spread by the media – make it possible for people who have never been to Amsterdam to know what it is like. In the mass tourist discourse this body of global knowledge meets its local context, and in order to prevent the local context from interfering with the image and expectations that tourists hold, it is cut down to global size. The view from the boat is the city's 'public' face, to use Cohen's theory of the symbolic construction of community (1985); it is symbolically simple and adorned with gross stereotypical features. This 'public' face is performed on the 'front stage' of canalside buildings and scenes, reducing the cultural variety of Amsterdam to a number of simple selected statements.

The discourse of Mokum starts from a different body of 'cultural capital' than that of the mass tourist discourse. It presents a different narrative style, which meets the expectations of a different public. The Guild presents a perspective of Amsterdam that reflects a middle-class preoccupation with folklore, oral tradition, local history, but also with welfare and resettlement programmes. Guild members derive their historical knowledge, their discursive authority, so to speak, from the works of local historians; among our guides was the owner of the largest private library of books in Amsterdam, numbering 1,500 volumes. They do not confine themselves to quoting these works; they appropriate this knowledge and make it part of their own biography. Owing to the wide range of sources from which their knowledge is derived, the Guild guides master different stories about one and the same attraction, distinguishing, for example, written history from the folk version: the nun in the gutter. They lead visitors through the red-light district so that they can witness the trade of the dealers and prostitutes; they may even tease the participants by making them enter the condom shop in Warmoestraat and buy a little 'souvenir', which some people greet with disgust. All the while, they are speaking from their own experience on what it takes to keep a heroin prostitute from taking her last shot, and how frustrating it is to find that only ten percent of the addicts in the resettlement program will kick the habit. The mastery of different discourses establishes the guides' authority, as they are able to convince people that it is worthwhile to take a closer look. They encourage visitors to look with interest at an enormous diversity of artefacts, cultures, and systems of meaning. None are presumed to be superior and the main role of the guides is to interpret them for the visitor. Although their dating of events is just as vague as it is in mass tourism, the tales are of a fundamentally local character and can only be understood in the specific context of the Amsterdam inner city. After walking the streets of Amsterdam with the Guild, people affirm that they had not had the faintest idea of what Amsterdam was really like – although they initially had thought that they did. They find their preconstructed image shattered, only to be replaced by a presumed 'back-stage view'.

However, they do not realise that what they got was not a back-stage view. What they got was a 'staged' back-stage (MacCannell 1973), shaped by a narrative style that mingles pieces of the glorious past with the history of ordinary people, the exotic and extraordinary with everyday life, using oral history, and mixing historiography with biography. In the meantime, 'real life' is enacted in the streets of the city: the people of Amsterdam are going on errands, walking the dog, riding their bikes, chatting on street corners, having a beer in the pub or buying some cannabis. In the eyes of the interpreters, this everyday life is regarded as too 'common' or familiar to be made into a tourist attraction. The guides of *Mokum* prefer to construct a more imaginative picture of the city. The route they follow almost avoids the points of attraction that are visited by mass tourism – in fact it never crosses the busy canals – but grants a glance into the backyards of the inner city. For that reason, it is not possible to compare the guided city-walk directly to the boat trip, nor can we contrast the taped discourse to the oral tradition of the 'proud old citizens'. The city-walk is a construction of *Mokum*: it is a tale of the city from the perspective of the everyday life of ordinary people, mixing past and present, the beautiful and the ugly. While the official route does not refer to the humble quarters and the deprived categories of the Amsterdam population, the Guild does not take us along the main canals, but along the back streets of Amsterdam. They do not visit the churches, but the conventicles of the once persecuted Catholics. They do not stop at the merchant houses, but at the former orphanages, hospitals, prisons, homes for the poor and the leprous, and the pawnshops. They do not visit the Anne Frank house, but tell a tale of the vanished Jewish quarter while standing on the corner of the Jodenbreestraat. They do not linger at one of the trendy outdoor cafés, but have a cup of coffee in one of the brown pubs in the back streets of the cities. They visit the red-light district, to watch the prostitutes, their clients, and their pimps. They pity the young females who sell their bodies for a shot of heroin.

The narrative of *Mokum* is constructed 'from within' and 'from below' by mixing fragments of popular culture with fragments of high culture, telling about the world of ordinary people, the poor, the marginal, the lost, as they lived and still live in the shadow of the rich. In Cohen's terms (1985: 74) it can be interpreted as the 'private' face of the city. As object of 'internal' (i.e., national) discourse, the conceptualisation and symbolisation of the city is complex. The stereotypes that are so prominent in the discourse about the international tourist city are felt to have no validity as accounts of how Amsterdam people see themselves and their city's history.

Conclusion

As the analysis of the 'two tales of one city' shows, the discourses incline towards what they are not: towards an implicit negativity. Paramount to the narrative style during the boat trip is the 'remembered empire': the Amsterdam of the harbour, the vessels, the storehouses, the merchants, the painters, the churches. The discourse of the Amsterdam senior citizens is a negation of this narrative style: the 'remembered empire' is reinterpreted by a construction of 'the extraordinary life of common Amsterdam people'. As the decline of Amsterdam in the world economy and the homogenising effect of mass tourism is experienced as threatening to local identity (Dahles 1994), this identity has to be reasserted in symbolic terms. Since identity implies the reference to a 'significant other', almost any matter of perceived difference can be rendered symbolically as a boundary of one's own identity. This identity is formed by contriving distinctive meanings within the local discourse.

The social construction of Amsterdam involves complex processes of production in order that regular, meaningful, and profitable tourist gazes can be generated and sustained. Such gazes are not left to chance. Both the commercial tour operators *and* the Guild construct a local tourist gaze of the townscape in their narrative style. It is a *local* narrative focussing on distinct objects and typical signs functioning as clear markers for Amsterdam as a tourist attraction. It is obvious that the identity of Amsterdam has been tarnished by its 'dirt and disorder reputation'. Both discourses are directed at countering that reputation: by showing, to foreign tourists, the city's history and monuments; and to domestic tourists, its caring, even heroic nature. Yet, the mass tourist narrative is directed at a different public than the Mokum narrative. It takes a route through Amsterdam that is taken for granted in the 'Venice of the North': i.e., the boat through the canals, which provides the visitors with information of what is being seen from the boat. The speed of the boat does not allow for more than concise and simple statements, which integrate objects and signs of high, popular and mass culture into one discourse that may be understood almost universally and matches the images international tourists have when arriving in the city. The Guild, although it does not explicitly contrast its route to the ones taken by mass tourism, constructs its narrative in opposition to this discourse. The Guild's narrative is a different genre directed at different categories of visitors. Their gaze is of a complex nature; it reproduces the past and present of the common people, which is closely intertwined with their own experience of being a citizen of Amsterdam. It is not the detached narrative of the tourist industry, but one linked to the popular culture of the city. Both discourses, although contructed to render an appealing image of the city, differ in their symbolical complexity. The image of the city's public face that is shown to foreigners is symbolically simple; but, as the object of an internal discourse – a discourse with domestic, 'understanding' visitors – it is symbolically complex. In the public discourse stereotypical features are attributed to Amsterdam; but by Dutch people such stereotypes would be regarded as superficial, perhaps even as caricatures. As Cohen (1985: 74) put it: in the public face, internal variety disappears or coalesces into a simple statement; in its private mode, differentiation, variety, and complexity proliferate.

Considering the ambivalent Amsterdam tourism policy, one may note that the 'Mokum narrative' would mesh nicely with the gentrification strategy of the local government as well with the thematic approach of the Amsterdam Tourist Board. There could be more *Mokum*-like discourses catering to the needs of a differentiated tourist market, appealing to different categories of tourists, who are visiting Amsterdam for various reasons, but are all looking to find their image of the 'authentic' Amsterdam.

NOTES

1. I am indebted to Jeremy Boissevain, Mary Bouquet, Ton Dekker and René van der Duim for their inspiring criticism on an earlier draft; to Wout van Doornik, director of the Amsterdam 'Guild'; and to the P.J. Meertens Instituut for generously providing literature on the city's folklore and history. An earlier version of this article has appeared in Dutch in *Volkskundig Bulletin* (1993, vol. 19, no. 2). Further I want to thank Peter Jan Margry for giving his permission to use the two photographs that go with this article.
2. Whereas The Hague is the political centre of the Netherlands and seat of the national government, Amsterdam holds the status of cultural capital.

REFERENCES

This paper is partly based on material taken from two Dutch newspapers, *De Volkskrant* and *NRC Handelsblad*, and from the monthly periodical, *Toerisme en Amsterdam*, which is published by the Amsterdam Tourist Board.

Amsterdam Toeristenstad, *Amsterdam toeristenstad, kijk op de jaren negentig*, Gemeente Amsterdam, Afdeling Economische Zaken, 1989.

Amsterdam Tourist Board, *Toerisme en Amsterdam,* published monthly, Amsterdam.

Ashworth, G.J. and J.E. Tunbridge, *The Tourist-Historic City*, London/ New York: Belhaven Press, 1990.

Attractiepunten in Amsterdam, *Attractiepunten in Amsterdam. Een analyse van het bezoek aan attractiepunten in Amsterdam 1992*, VVV-Amsterdam Tourist Office, 1992.

Britton, S., 'Tourism, capital, and place: towards a critical geography of tourism', *Environment and Planning D: Society and Space*, vol. 9, (1991): 451-78.

Certeau, M. de, *The Practice of Everyday Life*, Translated by Steven F. Rendall. Berkeley/Los Angeles/London: University of California Press, 1984.

Cohen, A.P., *The Symbolic Construction of Community*, London/New York: Tavistock Publications, 1985.

Crick, M., 'Representations of international tourism in the social sciences: sun, sex, sights, savings and servility', *Annual Review of Anthropology*, vol. 18, (1989): 307-44.

Dahles, H., '*Mahem* is gone. An analysis of tourism policy in "globalising" Amsterdam'. Paper presented at the LSA Annual Conference, Glasgow, April 5-8, 1994.

Keet, E., 'Bij ons in de Jordaan. Het dagelijkse leven als bezienswaardigheid'. M.A. Thesis, Tilburg University. Unpublished manuscript, 1994.

Koord, Ch., *Oude Amsterdamse Volksverhalen*, Maasbree: Uitgeverij De Lijster, 1981.

MacCannell, D., 'Staged authenticity: arrangements of social space in tourist settings', *American Sociological Review*, vol. 79, (1973): 589-603.

O'Loughlin, J., 'Between Sheffield and Stuttgart. Amsterdam in an integrated Europe and a competitive world-economy', in Léon Deben, Willem Heinemeijer, Dick van der Vaart eds, *Understanding Amsterdam. Essays on economic vitality, city life and urban form*, Amsterdam: Het Spinhuis, 1993: 25-68.

Soja, E., 'The stimulus of a little confusion. A contemporary comparison of Amsterdam and Los Angeles', in Léon Deben, Willem Heinemeijer, Dick van der Vaart, eds, *Understanding Amsterdam. Essays on economic vitality, city life and urban form*, Amsterdam: Het Spinhuis, 1993: 69-92.

Urry, J., *The Tourist Gaze. Leisure and Travel in Contemporary Societies*, London: Sage, 1990.

———, 'Tourism, travel and the modern subject', *Vrijetijd en Samenleving*, jrg. 9, no. 3/4, (1991): 87-98.

VVV-Amsterdam, 'Strategisch Marketing & Communicatieplan 1991-1993. Amsterdam', VVV-Amsterdam, 1993.

Waal, M. de, 'Zweedse stadsantropoloog Ulf Hannerz op sight seeing in Amsterdam. "Wat er in Amsterdam gebeurt, zie je in een stad als New York in het kwadraat"', *NRC Handelsblad*, donderdag, 19 December (1991): 3.

POSTLUDE

Tom Selwyn

*I*n this postlude I will argue that there are eight principal themes which, to a greater or lesser extent, appear in each of the previous chapters and which underlie the book as a whole.

The first concerns the sort of world from which tourists come and which shapes their interests and motives. Taking a lead from MacCannell (1976) and others, there are underlying assumptions and implications throughout that tourists are seeking temporarily to retreat from a world that for many is, in some fundamental sense, not only economically and politically fragmenting but also socially alienating. Thus the tranquillity of Nogués Pedregal's Andalusian village of Zahara de los Atunes and the romantic little red cabins in Puijk's Henningsvær, which help conjure up senses of the fishing village community as it was in the mid- nineteenth century, provide near-mythical settings in which senses of the authentically social may be recovered. Such tourist landscapes have the capacity to provide tourists with views of imagined communities of people with specially appealing, and in some cases almost heroic, characteristics. Henningsvær, for example, is presented as a place that in the mid-nineteenth century was a 'new Klondike' to which adventurers came to seek their fortune. Glimpses are thus caught of ideas and values to which tourists themselves (hot showers being provided, of course) would subscribe. In the sense that the tourist also catches reflections of a self that he or she would like to be, tourist resorts appear as sorts of 'magic mirrors'.

A slightly different but directly comparable case is provided by the tours in Amsterdam described by Dahles. Guides who work for the city council's 'The Guild' conduct middle-class Dutch tourists around parts of the city that appeal directly to the desire by the tourists who take them to rediscover a sense of place. *Mee in Mokum* ('Join us in Mokum') tours take inspiration from the Hebrew *makom* (place) and visit inner-city neighbourhoods associated not only with inner-city 'problems' but also with the close-knittedness of working-class communities as these are imagined by middle-class tourists. Once again we have an example of a site being imaginatively used to recreate a sense of the social.

However, it is not only international leisure tourists who construct myths and images of a socially reassuring, comforting, or even stimulating kind. The Parisian returnee to the Cantal observes that, as she walks around Aurillac, she feels how lucky she is to have escaped a bedsit in the capital where she was 'unable to breath'. Furthermore, in Aurillac there are some festivals, such as St. Mary's patronal fête, in which long-standing residents attempt, in Abram's words, 'to rescue some sociability from the ruins brought on by the socio-economic and political difficulties that have stripped the Cantal of much of its population'. In other words, the production of nostalgic myths and memories often needs active collusion and participation by local people who themselves feel the ravages of an economic and political system that has left families and settlements uprooted and dispersed.

It seems clear, then, that one of the motives of tourists is, so to speak, to find a 'culture' in which nostalgically to become immersed in order to fill an emotional and intellectual void left by the glacial processes of modernity.

The second theme concerns the term 'culture' itself. Each chapter demonstrates the importance in any ethnography of a tourist destination of asking in a detailed way who is involved -and why they are involved – in the definition, production, and consumption of 'culture' there. Odermatt and Crain, for example, both bring out the tension between 'culture' as organised and managed by the government and/or private sector for the promotion of the tourism industry and the popular, quotidian culture of the locations discussed. The distinction between these two ('mark 1' and 'mark 2' culture, we might term them in shorthand) is similar to the 'high culture'/'folk culture' distinction, but it is not identical, since both 'mark 1' and 'mark 2' cultures in the present context share the same raw material. Thus, for example, Odermatt's Nuraghe Losa of Abbasanta is, at the same time, a monument of national/international archaeological significance and (during some periods of it history at any rate) a meeting place for Abbasanta's villagers. In the same way, the Doñana Natural Park described by Crain is both a destination for international tourists to Andalusia interested in nature conservation, and also a popular site for local poachers and hunters.

That said, however, each of the contributions draws our attention to the fact that what is at issue is not simply the distinction between 'mark 1' and 'mark 2' cultures, but rather the relationship between them. Nogués Pedregal, for example, draws attention to the differences in Zahara between, on the one hand, Carnival and the Chestnut Festival and, on the other, the *Feria*. The latter is promoted extensively by the local municipality and is popular with tourists. The two former, on the other hand, are events from which tourists are customarily excluded and which, for Nogués Pedregal, constitute examples of what Boissevain and others have termed 'revitalising rituals' (1992). The argument here is thus that these latter rituals (examples of 'mark 2' culture) are partly constructed in a spirit of dynamic opposition to rituals like the *Feria* (an example of 'mark 1' culture) and that they give local participants opportunities for cultural, psychological and emotional 'renewal'.

Apart from anything else, such arguments as these challenge the 'host and guest' paradigm by showing up the analytical frailty of treating 'host culture' as some sort of homogeneous entity standing in opposition to 'tourist culture'. On the contrary, what these chapters demonstrate is that it is precisely the ability of 'hosts' to provide some cultural space for tourists while simultaneously preserving other, more private, spaces for themselves that gives them the capacity to 'cope with tourists'. It is a theme which Boissevain has articulated for Malta elsewhere (1996).

This brings us to the third theme. This is concerned with the *limits* of the commoditisable, 'mark 1' type of culture associated with the tourism industry. Two events in Zahara-the breaking up by the villagers of the surfers' shed and the forced removal by them of gates to *El Palacio*, which the legal, but absentee, owner had erected, but which were seen by villages to be an obstruction to local walkers-were both signs of a limit having been reached to encroachment and cultural influence by 'outsiders.' In contemporary Mallorca there are some comparable feelings about 'outsiders' buying up the island's *possessios* and closing off access through their grounds. But such direct action is only one out of the several types of resistance strategies identified by Boissevain in his Introduction, and it is these ways of 'coping' with tourists that are the central concern of the book as a whole.

One of the theoretical consequences of the close attention paid by the authors to these (often seemingly quite successful) strategies of resistance is that, once again, the weakness of simple minded functional analyses of social and cultural processes in tourist destinations is emphasised. For example, high on Black's list of orthodoxies to be demolished is Doxey's oft-quoted 'irritation index' which purports to show how a 'host society' progresses through a series of stages, from euphoria to ultimate rejection of tourists and their culture. However, the sheer variety and ingenuity of the responses of Malta's population to tourists demonstrates the total implausibility of such an index. Once more the danger of regarding a 'host culture' as a homogeneous entity is highlighted.

The fourth theme concerns yet another aspect of the debate about culture and has been of interest to anthropologists of tourism since the early days. It concerns the process of cultural 'commoditisation' associated with tourism. Early on in this debate certain assumptions were made which became commonly accepted. High amongst these was that tourists effectively strip cultural productions of meaning, reducing them to the level of objects to be bought and sold in the same way as other consumer goods. In this light the tourist, in search of souvenirs for example, appears as a sort of modern and/or postmodern hunter roaming the globe combing through cultures in order to identify decorative objects which may then be wrenched out of context and displayed, like trophies, on metropolitan walls and mantlepieces. But the approach to cultural commoditisation and the nature of tourist-related consumerism adopted here is altogether more sophisticated.

So what *is* it that the tourists seek to consume? There are clearly different ways to approach this question and it is likely that a book such as the present one, which mainly concerns 'cultural tourism', suggests types of approach that might not be appropriate in other settings. That said, there does seem to me to be one particularly productive path of enquiry, which the book's authors point towards. One of the signposts to this consists of Abram's description of how visitors to the Cantal are on the look out for symbols of the idea of 'la vie en arriere temps' (such nostalgia for earlier historical periods being a consistent feature of all the essays). The question then becomes: what, sociologically, do the 'old days' actually mean to tourists? Abram's own ethnography suggests several pointers, none of which are either unique to the Cantal or surprising to students of the sociology of tourism. They include notions of 'traditional' chemical-free agricultural methods; local food production; 'wholesomeness'; and regionalism (in the sense of regional integrity in relation to the nation). An attempt to comment sociologically on these might lead to observations about nostalgia for a world that was pre-scientific, in which social relations were anchored in a locality (where, in other words, there was a close fit between kinship and place), in which there was a sense *both* of organic solidarity (the *Ecomusée* displays varieties of old-fashioned tools, farming implements, and methods suggesting the sort of multi-craft economy reminiscent of a contemporary Indian village) *and* mechanical solidarity (in the reconstructed memory of tourists to Aurillac the village and its region appear as sites of harmonious work towards the common good). In short, we have a vision of a pre-capitalist, premodern economy whose rough edges (such as the stark social inequalities and injustices of such economies) have been airbrushed out by a distinctively modern bourgeois imagination. It is a potent idea.

To our question about what it is that tourists seek to consume, then, we arrive at an arresting answer. We may remind ourselves, to start with, that contemporary tourists are children of image- led market economies, who, bludgeoned by Thatcherism and Reaganomics, are rooted in political and social individualism and the commoditisation of everything. However, despite all the apparent investment in the inculcation of such values and aspirations, fit for a postmodern landscape of this kind, what appears to be sought after most in the Cantal is their exact antithesis. In this sense, and in this context, it seems as if we have found in consumerism the seeds of its opposite.

The fifth theme concerns local and regional political engagement with, and institutional reactions to, the entry of tourists into the economies and societies described by the book's contributors. Abram goes so far as to argue that the commoditisation of the Cantal's history for tourists 'is part of a very positive process' (involving amongst other things the putting together of a museum, the running of a traditional dairy, and so forth) 'by which people are beginning to re-evaluate their history and shake off the shame of peasantry that has been pressed on them in their education through the generations'. Furthermore it is also apparent from Abram's ethnography that tourist consumption, based, as some of this is, on the search for authentically traditional products in the village market place, has both directly and (perhaps more importantly) indirectly supported the village economy. Thus, for example, while the impetus for keeping the dairy going came from tourists, the majority of consumers for its products throughout the year are in fact local residents.

In the two Spanish cases presented by Crain and Nogués Pedregal, tourism has led to the formation of new local associations as well as enhanced activity by existing ones. In both cases these have considerable cultural and political significance. Thus Nogués Pedregal describes the setting up of the Zahara Neighbours' Association in 1990, formed with the support of the Catholic Church to fight for better facilities in the village, there being a general consensus there that the profits of tourism were flowing too readily towards the principal town of the Municipality. Crain describes how local hunters and ranchers have been joined by other local people concerned to maintain access to religious sites and to voice concern over the Doñana National Park. She traces the outlines of a developing political struggle that has important economic and ideological dimensions. On the one hand there are the combined forces of international, national, and local planners (who all favour an increased tourism-especially 'eco-tourism'-sector for the region) together with those (by and large more wealthy) locals who stand to benefit from such a tourist economy. On the other hand there are the local groups of hunters, pilgrims and others just referred to. As in other Spanish locations it will be interesting to follow the involvement of a potentially powerful player, the Church.

The sixth theme develops the one above and concerns the sheer complexity of the social and cultural changes that may be induced by a tourist economy. Zarkia, for example, examines in some detail several of the ways in which the social and ideological structures of the Greek island of Skyros have been almost literally stood on their heads by the tourist economy. Her description has many echoes throughout the Mediterranean. In the case of Mallorca, for example, coastal land was traditionally owned by the youngest (and consequently poorest) sibling of the family (Selwyn, 1996). As the development of tourism began to take place on the coast these younger siblings became rich at the expense of their elder siblings, thus challenging traditional familial hierarchies. Zarkia shows how in Skyros the coastal land was traditionally owned by agricultural labourers-who formed the third tier in a fairly rigid class structure. Following coastal development, the wealth of these *kochyliani* grew dramatically just as that of the former upper-class landowners in the island shrunk. No less radical than the social structural *bouleversement* that these changes in land values produced were such ideological transformations as the virtual implosion of the 'hospitality code', under the influence of tourist-induced cash economy. Fundamental changes have also, according to Puijk, taken place in Henningsvær. Here the relationships between the public and the private, which have traditionally been subject to informal understandings between residents, have been placed under such strain by the entry of tourists into the village that villagers have begun fencing off their property to keep people out.

There is a strong sense of an economic and ideological transformation in which the realm of the individual and the private is radically asserted at the expense of the collective and the public.

The seventh theme concerns the role, in each of the local situations examined, of continental government: references to the role of policies of the EU are made in almost every essay. It seems inevitable that the significance of the EU's role in tourism policy will markedly increase in the years to come (see ECOMOST, 1994) and the essays in this volume make it clear that anthropologists could and should take a vigourous part in the debates in the Commission's corridors-not necessarily because they know answers to questions about cultural policy, but (as the evidence from this volume demonstrates) they know several relevant, if sometimes disturbing questions.

This latter leads on to the final theme, which is another of the central themes of the book as a whole. It concerns the nature of the political and economic forces at work shaping the tourism industry, the presence or absence of controls and regulatory frameworks to which these are, or are not, subject, and the capacity of local people to control and 'cope with' these forces. Consider that the old heavy industries of northern Europe have declined with the same speed as the decline in the south of the primary agricultural economies, and that both north and south are rapidly becoming increasingly dependent economically on service industries such as tourism. In such a context of national and international economic pressures it is hard to be confident that tourism at local levels can remain in the hands of the local residents of tourist destinations. Yet all the anthropologists who have contributed to this volume would probably agree with Odermatt's assertion that 'neglecting or even violating the right of the host to be in charge of the (re)presentation can have far-reaching consequences'. Indeed it may reasonably be argued that the importance of tourism studies of Europe's regions (especially along its Eastern and Southern frontiers) is that they illustrate the importance of local people being in charge of economic activities in *general.*

The evidence from the contributors in this book suggests that people in various parts of Europe have developed an extensive range of imaginative responses to tourism. People are, indeed, 'coping'. However, Boissevain's observation that they are 'coping *so far*', suggests that anthropologists and interested others need to consider the conditions that need to be met for local people to continue 'coping' and also those that might prevent them from so doing.

REFERENCES

Boissevain, J., ed., *Revitalising European Rituals*, London: Routledge, 1992.

Boissevain, J., 'Ritual, Tourism and Cultural Commoditisation in Malta: Culture by the pound?', in T. Selwyn, ed., *The Tourist Image: Myths and Myth Making in Tourism*, London: John Wiley, 1996.

ECOMOST, *The ECOMOST Project: Planning for Sustainable Tourism*, Brussels: Commission of the European Union, Lewis: International Federation of Tour Operators, 1994.

MacCannell, D. *The Tourist: A New Theory of the Leisure Class*, New York: Schocken Books, 1976.

Selwyn, T. 'Tourism, Culture and Cultural Conflict: A Case Study from Mallorca', in C. Fsadni and T. Selwyn, eds, *Tourism, Culture and Regional Development in the Mediterranean*, Malta: University of Malta, 1996.

Notes on Contributors

Simone A. Abram is a Research Fellow in the Department of City and Regional Planning, University Wales, Cardiff. She received her D.Phil from Oxford University in 1994, with fieldwork in central France in 1990-1991 (sponsored by the ESRC).

Annabel Black is a Research Associate at Oxford Brookes University and a visiting lecturer at the Université Libre de Bruxelles. She studied anthropology at University College London and carried out ethnographic research on the development of tourism in Malta for her PhD (1986). She is currently carrying out the research for a book on the changing culture of spouses within the Foreign and Commonwealth Office.

Jeremy Boissevain is Emeritus Professor of Social Anthropology, University of Amsterdam. Currently a Fellow of the Amsterdam School of Social Science Research, he also helps coordinate the MED-CAMPUS Programme for Sustainable Tourism, University of Malta. After directing CARE programmes in the Philippines, Japan, and India, he carried out anthropological fieldwork in Malta, Sicily, Montreal and Amsterdam. He has published extensively on local politics, ethnic relations, small entrepreneurs, ritual change and tourism. His most recent publications include *Revitalizing European Rituals* (London: Routledge, 1992). Translations of his work have appeared in Dutch, French, Italian, Spanish, Hungarian, and Japanese.

Mary M. Crain has written extensively on rituals, politics and gender relations both in Spain and Latin America (Ecuador). Most recently she has taught these subjects in the Departments of Anthropology and Latin American History at the University of Barcelona. Her recent publications include 'Celebrating the "Indian" San Juan: Shifting Power Relations and the Performance of Competing Moralities in the Ecuadorean Andes', in Pina Cabral, J. de and Erikson, T.H., eds, *Morals and the Margins*, forthcoming and 'Introduction', *España Oculta: Public Celebrations in Spain*, Washington, DC: Smithsonian Institution Press, 1995.

Heidi Dahles is a cultural anthropologist with fieldwork experience in Austria, the Netherlands, and Indonesia. She received her Ph.D. from Nijmegen University in 1990. At present she is Assistant Professor in the Department of Leisure Studies at Tilburg University. Her current research deals with cultural brokers in the tourism industries of Amsterdam and Yogyakarta (Indonesia). She is presently preparing a monograph on tourist guides.

Peter Odermatt studied cultural anthropology at the University of Amsterdam and at present is a doctoral student at the Amsterdam School of Social Science Research. He received the Andries Sternheim Prize for his M.A. thesis on tourism in Sardinia (Amsterdam, 1991). He subsequently carried out field research in Germany and is now preparing a Ph.D. thesis on (re)presentation in Weimar. He recently published *Een Hard Sardisch Gelag: Toeristische Attracties Systematisch Bekeken* (Amsterdam: Het Spinhuis, 1994).

Antonio Miguel Nogués Pedregal is affiliated to the Amsterdam School for Social Research as a post-doctoral researcher. He has carried out fieldwork in Andalusia and Guatemala and taught anthropology at the Universidad Internacional Menéndez Pelayo, Seville, during 1991-1992. His recent publications discuss the role of tourism in social and cultural constructions.

Roel Puijk is Senior Lecturer in the Department of Media Studies, Lillehammer College. He has done fieldwork in France and Norway on local development, journalism and television. Currently he is involved in an anthropological study of the Lillehammer Winter Olympics.

Tom Selwyn is Professor of the Anthropology of Tourism at the University of North London, and co-ordinator of one of the European Union's MED-CAMPUS projects in the Eastern Mediterranean. His books *The Tourist Image: Myths and Myth Making in Tourism* and *Tourism and Society* are published in 1996 by John Wiley and Prentice Hall respectively.

Cornélia Zarkia is an architect and social anthropologist. She has carried out fieldwork in Greece. Her Ph.D. entitled 'Société et espace dan l'île de Skyros' (Paris, 1991) relates to the correspondence between social and spatial structures. She is now working as a freelance researcher with the National Hellenic Research Foundation and the National Centre of Social Research.

INDEX

Subject Index

Name Index